BURPHAM
A Gateway to Guildford

How a Surrey village grew from a rural hamlet into a busy suburb

By

Moira MacQuaide Hall

Also by Moira MacQuaide Hall

A History of Burpham Primary School 1908 - 2014

[Cover designed by Martin Hall with the OS Map of Burpham 1869, courtesy of Surrey History Centre]

About the Author

Moira MacQuaide Hall was born and went to school in Northampton before moving to college in Oxford, where she then worked in higher education and the health service for sixteen years. She married Martin and moved to Surrey, where she worked in Guildford hospitals for eleven years. While their daughter Sarah was a pupil at Burpham Primary School, Moira became a Parent Governor and then worked as School Bursar from 1997 until her retirement in 2012. She has taken up writing as well as becoming a keen member of the Guildford U3A.

First published in Great Britain 2017

ISBN 978-1-9997146-8-0

To Martin and Sarah;
and everyone who has shared their stories with me.

Contents

PREFACE

I was useless at history when I was at school - I didn't take the subject at O Level because I'd done so poorly in the mock exams. However, I became interested in family history after my father died and have spent a lot of time since then researching my ancestors, with quite a lot of success. So where does one start when writing a history book? The story of Burpham village goes back beyond the Domesday Book, so there was a lot to research.

When I wrote the history of Burpham Primary School it was easy – start when the school opened. Having worked there I had access to a wealth of information kept at the school. When I was a Parent Governor I came across some of the old school documentation and was hooked. By the time of the school's centenary I had talked to many ex-pupils and staff, some of whom were willing to share their memories and stories about the school and the village. I retired from working as the School Bursar in 2012; the following year I found the time to start my research properly and write the book. Memories and photos bring a history book to life and make it much more interesting for the reader. When I started selling the book in late 2014 I found that many people were remembering not only what the school was like but also what life in the village was like when they were young. It was this that started my interest in writing a book about the village and its inhabitants, and the feeling that these memories should be recorded.

My research has taken me to the Surrey History Centre, where I've spent many hours poring over old documents (the oldest piece of paper that I have held was a rent receipt dated 1424, before the Wars of the Roses), also Guildford Museum, Guildford Library, Guildford Institute and around Burpham itself. There were books to read, websites to investigate, census records to analyse and people to talk to - all bringing varying slants on the development of the village. I am enormously grateful to those who have researched the village before me - Norman Hamilton (1977) / updated by Linda Flynn (1984); Roger Marjoribanks (1997); the compilers of the Burpham Neighbourhood Plan (2013); Burpham Community Association; Jim Miller's book 'Jacob's Well - How the Name got its Village' (1994); and Michael Drakeford's book 'The History of Abbotswood' (2008). The West Surrey Family History Society have done some fantastic groundwork in indexing births, marriages, deaths and wills, and these have provided some fascinating information.

Norman Hamilton's History

Roger Marjoribanks' History

Andre Langlois at the Surrey Advertiser and David Rose at Guildford Dragon have kindly provided me with news articles and photos relating to the village. Frank Phillipson, a local historian, has given me access to his research about Burpham, some of which I had not come across before. The Burpham Will Remember Them project team has shared their research about the Burpham War Memorial. Vincent Tickner has shared his research about the Heath family of London Road, which provided much more detail than I had found. Without the work they all did I would have had a much harder job. One of the interesting things about studying family and local history these days is that more information becomes available on a weekly, if not daily, basis. I always said that I would only write this book if I could add to the wealth of information that my predecessors had published, and I feel very lucky that so much more is now available, allowing me to achieve this. I am also very grateful to all the people who allowed me to look at their photos and documents as well as sharing their own memories of Burpham through the years. Through my local history column in Burpham Pages I have made contact with people who have lived in the village for many years. The Facebook group Guildford Town Past & Present includes lots of current and past Burpham residents, many of whom have been willing to share their memories with me. Also, members of my Guildford U3A Local History Group have shared their stories and lent photos.

Reading and understanding old documents has been a bit of a challenge at times as the handwriting can be difficult, and sometimes illegible; language can be very different to modern ways of speaking; and often names change, so there is little consistency in following a series of addresses. I am grateful to the staff at the Surrey History Centre, whose knowledge of Latin and Medieval English has helped me to understand some of the writing, as my O Level Latin just wasn't up to scratch.

In Burpham the early census enumerators often just wrote London Road, or Portsmouth Road, or Bowers Lane and unless one knows when cottages or houses were built, and often demolished, it is difficult to be absolutely sure which dwelling was which. For instance, the houses known as Pimm's Row are recorded variously as Bowers Lane, Pims Row, Pimms Cottages, Pimms Row, or just Burgham or Bowers, some with numbers and some without - some much easier to identify than others. Often the census enumerator misspelt names, which caused confusion, and sometimes it was unclear about the direction that they went in to visit all the houses - there were occasions when it felt as if they were going around in circles. Kelly's Directories recorded the cottages as, for example, number 47 Burpham Lane South West Side. I have referred to both Burpham and Burgham, depending on how the source material spelled the name, so I apologise for swapping between the two.

Some cottages belonged to farms, some to inns, some to the mill, and it was not always clear how they relate to modern Burpham. Some guesswork has been needed and an occasional leap of faith has been required to take the research onward. Although this book is predominantly a local history I have attempted to include some social history as well, to give readers a feeling for what life would have been like in Burpham at different times, as well as some world history to give context.

At the time of writing this book there have been a wide range of historical anniversaries as well as many celebrations that won't be seen again for many generations. We had the Millennium festivities in 2000 and Queen Elizabeth II's Diamond Jubilee in 2012 – it will be a long time before anyone sees another monarch on the throne for sixty years, as only three monarchs have achieved this since 1066AD. Queen Elizabeth became the longest serving British monarch in September 2015, breaking Queen Victoria's previous record; in 2012 London became the first city to host the Olympic Games three times; King Richard III's skeleton was found underneath a car park in Leicester, then was re-interred in Leicester Cathedral in 2015.

2014 brought the commemorations of the start of the Great War and 2015 had a whole raft of anniversaries including 70 years since the end of World War II; 75 years since Dunkirk and the Battle of Britain; 200 years since the Battle of Waterloo; 600 years since the Battle of Agincourt; 750 years since Parliament first sat in Westminster; and 800 years since the Magna Carta was sealed. In 2016 it was 100 years since the Battle of the Somme and 950 years since the Battle of Hastings. Queen Elizabeth celebrated her 90th birthday, the first British monarch to achieve this. In 2017 she celebrated her Sapphire anniversary, 65 years on the throne, again the first British monarch to do so. The coming years will see more commemorations of events in the Great War and the Second World War.

I have tried to remember everyone who has helped with my research and to thank them accordingly, but if I have left anyone out then I hope that they will forgive me and know that I am very grateful for their input. I also hope that I have reported stories accurately, but again I hope that people will forgive me if I have made mistakes. It is possible that I could have found out more if I had continued my research for another couple of years, but one has to stop somewhere. Perhaps in the future someone will use my book as the starting point for their research to write another book about Burpham. Sadly, some of the photos are not as clear as I would have liked, but many were old originals or old newspaper cuttings that have not survived well through the scanning and printing process. However, I wanted to include as many as possible as they give an image of life 50 or 100 years ago. I have endeavoured to get permission to use photos wherever possible, but there are a few where I have tried but had no response. I have tried to give credit where I know who provided the photo. If I have made errors with historical facts then I apologise, and ask you to remember that I was never very good at history, but, with luck, I have improved.

I am still collecting memories and photos for my column in Burpham Pages. So if this book has brought back memories and you would like to contribute, you can contact me by e-mail at

<u>moira.macquaide@gmail.com</u>

Moira MacQuaide Hall

June 2017

WHAT, WHERE AND WHY?

What is Burpham? Is it a village, a suburb or what? One thousand years ago it was a Tything - a group of about ten households. For hundreds of years Burpham consisted of small groups of cottages, houses and farms along part of the London Road and Burpham Lane, with a mill by the river. For most of that time there was no church, no school, no village green, but for many years there were one or two public houses. As it grew it became a hamlet, then a village. A hamlet is defined by the Oxford English Dictionary as '*a small settlement, generally smaller than a village and usually without a church*'. Whereas a village is defined as '*a group of houses and associated buildings, larger than a hamlet and smaller than a town, situated in a rural area*'.

In 1986 the BBC launched an ambitious project to record a snapshot of everyday life across the UK, called Domesday Reloaded. As part of this there appeared a new definition of a village, '*To be a village a settlement must have: a church; a village hall or community centre; a school; some shops (including a post office); a village green; allotments; places to work; a public house; houses (including private, council/privately rented); and a parish council.*'

By having a church (1859), then shops (1905), a school (1908), a village hall (1922) and the playing fields (1956) - which could be viewed as the Village Green - it seems that Burpham eventually changed its status from hamlet to village. After becoming part of Guildford Borough in 1933, it is now more a suburb than anything else. Whatever it is called, the community still feels rather like a village, even though 'like Topsy, it just growed', and at the heart of the community are the people living there.

Where is Burpham? First of all it is in Surrey, not Sussex. First time researchers need to watch out that their investigations do not take them to the Burpham near Arundel in Sussex by mistake. The Surrey community lies about two miles from Guildford and about five miles from Woking.

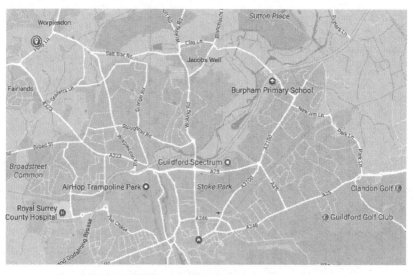

Google Maps 2017, showing Guildford, Burpham, Jacobs Well, Worplesdon, Merrow and Clandon

It is difficult to define the boundaries of Burpham as these have varied at different times. Originally Burpham was part of the parish of Worplesdon, which consisted of four tithings (Perry Hill, Burpham, West End and Wyke).

Design for Worplesdon Village sign
by Sidney Sime (Sidney Sime
Gallery, Worplesdon)

Until the building of St Luke's Church in 1859, the parishioners of Burpham had to travel to Perry Hill to attend St Mary's Church. Most old records showed people as living in Worplesdon, rather than Burpham.

For ecclesiastical purposes it was part of Worplesdon Parish until 1920, when it became Burpham with Sutton Green, then in 1954, probably to reflect the growing village, the Diocese made the decision for Burpham to become a parish on its own. For political and civic purposes the Ward Boundary goes along the Wey Navigation to the west, the railway line to the south east, Abbotswood conservation area to the south and Gosden Hill farmland to the north east. There is a Boundary Stone (marking the boundary between Guildford and Burpham, or Worplesdon Parish) on

Boundary Stone on
London Road

London Road, by the end of the Abbotswood Estate and the start of the Weylea Farm estate. Coming from Guildford along the London Road it is easy to think that Burpham starts at what is commonly known as 'the old AA roundabout', but technically this is

9

still Christchurch Ward up to the boundary stone at the end of Abbotswood. However, local estate agents show Burpham starting at the Guildford end of Abbotswood, thus including both that estate and Ganghill.

As part of the boundary changes in 1933 Burpham joined Guildford Borough Council and Gosden Hill Farm was included as part of Burpham. The original Manor of Burpham went out to the Woking Road, including Jacob's Well where Burpham Court Farm, Hurst Farm (now Willow Grange, the residence of the Bishop of Guildford) and Burpham Court House are located, as well as Burpham Lodge (now known as The White House) on White House Lane. The sale particulars from the 1905 sale of Onslow properties stated '*As between the Manor of Burpham and the vendor's adjoining Manor of Worplesdon the road from the Stoke Parish boundary to Hurst Farm shall be considered the western boundary and the road from Hurst Farm to Jacob's Well the north boundary of Burpham Manor.*' The 19th century census enumerators described Burgham as a tithing, part of Worplesdon Parish, and the area was usually the same as the old Manor. It is quite possible that Whitmoor Common, Stringer's Common and as far as Pitch Place were at some time part of the original Manor.

Why have Burpham? It may seem like an odd question, but it is worth looking at. It's not far to either Ripley or Guildford and both have plenty of facilities for the traveller. The Burpham community may have originally started due to its closeness to water (the River Wey), heavy clay soil and availability of sand for brickmaking and pottery, reasonably good farmland and ease of travel to larger communities such as Guildford. However, one of the big reasons was probably the route of the road from London to Portsmouth, which brought much traffic through the area. The public houses were licensed premises with stabling and accommodation, but were not coaching inns, which were part of the inland transport infrastructure. The Burpham public houses were not large enough to provide stabling for teams of horses for stagecoaches. People involved in the Navy would also travel between London and Portsmouth, bringing people, horses, equipment, etc along the road.

For many years the Manor of Burpham has been tucked in between the family seats of two influential families – the Onslows at Clandon Park House and the Westons at Sutton Place. Neither of these two great houses were part of Burpham, although the Lodge Gates for Sutton Place, on the A3, are included within the administrative boundary.

Clandon Park Gates on Epsom Road, Merrow

Sutton Place Lodge Gates on A3 London Road

So Burpham in Surrey was a hamlet, then a village, now a suburb. However, as well as the Burpham near Arundel in Sussex, there is a Burpham House in Great Bookham and in the 1950s there was also a racehorse called Burpham, which was quite successful.

ANCIENT BURPHAM

It all started with The Big Bang, or The Creation, or whichever version you prefer for the beginning of life on earth. However, the evidence of history for Burpham starts a lot later. Archaeological finds (many of which can be found at Guildford Museum) indicate ancient settlements in the area and include a Mesolithic flint pick (Stone Age, around 3,500 BC), a harness mount (Late Bronze Age, around 1,200 BC) and a Samian Bowl (Romano-British, around 157 AD), so the evidence suggests that there were definitely people living in the area

Samian Bowl - Romano British found in 1897 (Surrey Archaeological Society)

before the Norman Conquest of 1066. Roger Marjoribanks, in his little book 'Burpham, Norman Manor to Suburban Village', suggested that a small community lived behind the site of Weylea Farm Estate, making pottery from the local clay.

In 1897 a Roman burial site was discovered behind Pimm's Row - the Romans occupied much of Britain from 43AD – 425AD. Julius Caesar had invaded Britain a century before but he gave up due to determined British guerrilla resistance and a revolt in Gaul (France). Records suggest that a Roman road, called Stane Street, passed quite near to Guildford, but no remains have as yet been found in the area. It would have been nice to think that there had been a Roman road through Burpham, but it looks unlikely. However, in 1829 a Roman pavement was discovered at Broad Street Common, in Worplesdon Parish – more evidence of Roman inhabitation in the area. At the time of the Roman invasion Celtic Britain consisted of many tribes (such as the Iceni in East Anglia, ruled by Boudicca or Boadicea).

When the Anglo Saxons arrived from Europe in around the 5th Century the tribes developed into kingdoms, such as Wessex or Mercia. In the 9th Century Alfred the Great (House of Wessex) became the first King of England and, when he died, he bequeathed 'Gyldeford' to his nephew Etheldred in his will. This was the first written record of the town of Guildford. A Saxon buckle was found in the grounds of Winterhill Farm, suggesting that either there had been a settlement in the vicinity or perhaps there was a road passing through. Saxon Guildford was a thriving town that had its own mint, from which some coins still survive. However, the only extant building from that time is the tower of St Mary's Church in Quarry Street.

The Viking invasion of Britain began in the 8th Century and by 1013 the Danish King Sweyn Forkbeard had taken the English throne, followed by Cnut (Canute), and many reminders of these Norse

14

invaders can be seen in the northern counties of England, such as York, although they attacked all around the British coast. The Vikings and the English alternated through much of the 11th century until Edward III 'The Confessor' succeeded to the throne in 1042. In 1066 the Normans defeated the English, or Anglo Saxon, army at the Battle of Hastings. Clearly the melting pot of ethnicity has been mixed by the migration of people invading and settling around the world for thousands of years.

The name of Burpham comes from the Saxon – 'Burh' meaning an earthwork and 'ham' meaning a village or settlement, so probably a 'Fortification Hamlet'. Roger Marjoribanks also suggested *Fort in the Water Meadows*', which would fit with what is known of flooding in the local area.

Domesday Book entry about Burpham

The story of Burpham as it is known today started with the Norman Conquest in 1066. One of William the Conqueror's early decisions was to find out what he had won and, more importantly, what taxes were due to him as King. William died in 1087, so did not benefit from finding out this information. In 1086 the first official survey of England, the Domesday Book, written in Medieval Latin, was completed, and it gives modern day readers an idea of what Norman England looked like. Burpham, then spelt Borham, was part of the Woking Hundred and had a population of 10½ households, with 11 villagers, five small-holders and five slaves. The Lord of the Manor was Osmund of Eaton in 1066, but by 1086 this changed to Turald (Thorold) from Earl Roger de Montgomery of Shrewsbury. Ownership of land changed hands quite frequently, often being given either as a reward or in payment of a debt.

A Hundred was a division of a shire for military and judicial purposes, coming between the parish and the county. A tithing was originally one tenth of a Hundred and then a subdivision of a manor, often meaning a group of ten adult males, and usually denoting an area for church taxation. The value of the tithing of Burpham to the Lord of the Manor in 1086 was £8. Tax was assessed in hides (approximately 120 acres), that is the amount of land, measured in ploughs – which meant the area that could be ploughed using eight oxen with one plough in one day. The Domesday Book informed the King that Burpham had enough land for five ploughs and also meadows, a mill valued at 15s and woodland for 80 pigs as pannage – a form of payment for pasturing pigs - the right to pannage is still part of some modern forest laws.

One of the hides was called Wucha (or Wyke), which belonged to Godric, although it is quite a distance from modern day Burpham.

However, given that Thorold also occupied the Manor of Worplesdon, maybe it is possible that it was part of the Burpham Manor. Over the years the village name has been spelt in various different ways, including Borham, Burfam, Burcham, Burcgham and Burffam, but for the last 200 years it has been Burgham and Burpham.

THE MANOR OF BURPHAM

The traditional picture of a Manor is one of a compact area, at the centre of which is the Manor House, the Lord's residence. Clustered around the Manor House would be the village, comprising the humble dwellings of the tenants and, of course, the village church. This centre of population would be surrounded by cultivated fields and beyond these would lie common or waste land belonging to the Manor. However, not all Manors followed this pattern. It could be a group of scattered farmsteads, interspersed with land belonging to other Manors or wasteland. The Lord may have owned several Manors, only one of which would have been his normal residence, so many Manors never actually needed a Manor House.

There was also a view that a Manor was actually a system of social and economic organisation, based on tenants holding land from a superior Lord. One of the earliest handbooks on estate management, The Seneschancy of 1276, listed the different people in the Manorial hierarchy, enabling a sophisticated way of functioning in medieval England. There would be a Steward, who was the chief officer, perhaps working for a group of his Lord's Manors, a role that continued well into the late 19th century and possibly later. The Bailiff was the general manager, overseeing the day to day running of the Manor. The Reeve was the foreman, overseeing cultivation of the land and was usually a tenant, unpaid but not having to pay rent either. Then there would be other people taking on lesser roles, such as supervising harvesting, thus giving a medieval organisation chart.

According to the Manorial Society of Great Britain, Lords of the Manor would often apply to the Monarch for special rights within the manor. The most valuable of these was the monopoly to hold a market and fair in the manor. As there were virtually no shops in the early days, retailing was carried out at markets, thus the Lord regulated the activities of buyers and sellers, deriving some financial benefit. This was mainly from letting booths and stalls, but also from the profits of the justice his officers meted out in fines – for example, using short weights or selling watered ale. Burpham was too small to have its own market or fair, so its residents had to make do with travelling to Guildford or Woking for their retail opportunities. Droit de Seigneur, the alleged right of the Lord to have a bride on her wedding night, is fiction. The Society suggests that the myth was perpetuated in the 'Penny Dreadful' novellas of the 19th century. However, one of the 'perks' for the Lord of the Manor was to taste beer to ensure the quality, though usually the Lord appointed an ale taster to do this for him.

There are few surviving documents about the Manor of Burgham but some minutes of Courts Baron are kept at the Surrey History Centre. These courts were responsible for the internal regulation of the Manor, were chaired by the Steward and would have a jury, known as the homage. The main functions of the court baron were to:
- record copyhold land transactions;
- implement customs of the Manor and the charges to be levied, resolve disputes over property rights, damage, trespass, debt and defamation; and to
- regulate local agricultural practices.

Other business would include changes of tenancy, cases between tenants and payments of heriots (debts due to the Lord after a tenant died). One of the surviving minute books began:

'The General Court Baron of the Right Honorable Arthur George Earl of Onslow, Lord of the said Manor there held for the said Manor on Tuesday the 15th day of June in the 21st year of the Reign of our Sovereign Lady Queen Victoria and in the year of our Lord 1858. Before John Rand Capron, Gentleman, Steward there.

The Homage –   Arthur Pimm, foreman

George Burt'

Then went on to notify the Steward of changes, including:

'The Homage also presents that William Francis Pimm who held the freehold lands called Marlyns, also other parts of Marlyns estate, is dead and that his son Arthur Pimm now holds the same premises.

The Homage also presents that W Elkins who held the Green Man part of Marlyns is dead and that WE Elkins under the will of W Elkins now holds the same.'

John Rand Capron was a Guildford solicitor who acted as the Steward for the Lord of the Manor of Burpham for many years in the 19th century. He was also an amateur scientist, astronomer and photographer. He lived at Guildown on the Hogs Back and became an expert on spectroscopy. He also had an interest in crop circles and wrote to Nature magazine about early incidences of these, suggesting that they were caused by cyclonic wind action.

Some of the older documents are difficult to read and understand. Vocabulary has changed in 200 hundred years and the lack of punctuation adds to confusion. In the 18th century one said about the Manor of Burgham in the County of Surrey '*Be it remembered that on the first day of January one thousand seven hundred and eighty seven James Notridge of Cranley in the County of Surrey personally came before Thomas Sibthorpe Gentleman Deputy of John Chandler Gentleman Chief Steward of the said Manor and surrendred by the Rod into the hands of the Lord of the said Manor by the acceptance of the said Deputy Steward according to the custom of the said Manor all that his copyhold cottage and two acres of land with the appurtenances be the same more or less lying in Terresworth within the said Manor of Burgham and formerly in the occupation of Henry Ripley and since of John Westbrooke and James Stringer or their assigns held by the yearly rent of one shilling, Herriot certain one shilling and Fine certain one shilling To the only proper use and Behoof of Henry Howard of Worplesdon in the said County Yeoman his heirs and assigns forever and to or for no other use intent or purpose whatsoever.*' However, it is possible to find the names of people who lived in Burpham and have left their mark in the names of farms or roads, such as, in this case, Stringer.

The surviving minutes of the 1645 Court Baron were written in Latin and are hard to decipher. One or two names are recognisable as families in the Burpham area, such as Ripley.

Lordship of the Burpham Manor was included in the sale of Onslow properties in 1905 (see chapter on Burpham Court Farm), but no documents have been found showing who bought it at that time. An item in the Surrey Mirror in June 1905 reported that Burpham Court Farm and the Manor of Burpham were sold for £4,000, but did not say who was the buyer. Some Lordships become forgotten over the years. The Manorial Society advises interested purchasers '*It is no surprise to find several new or re-constituted websites offering to restore, claim, even to resurrect, what are described as "lost" or "discarded" or "forgotten" Lordships, and to offer them for sale to the unsuspecting. We thought that only Jesus Christ was resurrected.*' According to the Manorial Society, William, 6th Earl Onslow, was Lord of the Manor for Burpham in 1938, but as Michael, 7th Earl Onslow, was on the Society's Governing Council for about 15 years until he retired in about 2000, it is likely that he would have notified them of any changes. In the 1944/5 Kelly's Directory it was recorded that '*The manors of Worplesdon and Burpham belong to the Earl of Onslow*'. The 7th Earl died in 2011 so the title has probably been inherited by his son, Rupert, the current Lord Onslow. Unfortunately it has not been possible to get confirmation of this from the current Earl.

There is still a question about what and where was the Court referred to in Manorial documents. Burpham Court Farm seems to be a popular answer, where Norman Hamilton reported that the original Norman Manor House was situated. Many old maps just named it as Burpham Court. Another contender could be the current Burpham Court House, on the Woking Road. However, this has only been known by this name for a relatively short time, as it was originally called Hurst, along with Willow Grange.

THE MIDDLE AGES OR MEDIEVAL PERIOD

After the Conquest

There seems to be very little written history surviving about Burpham between the years 1066AD to 1550AD. However, the Victoria County History, a survey published in 1902 for the University of London's Institute of Historical Research, and dedicated to Queen Victoria, provides a wealth of information about life in Britain from the time of the Domesday Book almost to the end of Victoria's reign. Most of Britain's monarchs have reigned over battles and wars, many of which changed the face of society, and it is quite possible that young men from Burpham may have been sent off to fight for their country.

The Normans (1066 – 1216AD) and the Plantagenets (1216 – 1485AD)

[Conflicts included the Crusades, 100 years War, Battle of Agincourt and the Wars of the Roses]

At the time of the Battle of Hastings and the Norman Conquest, deer roamed free all over Surrey, but when the Normans arrived, with their love of hunting, they created the first parks designed specifically for that purpose. The Norman Kings ruled for 150 years, including two Williams, two Henrys, Stephen and Richard. In the 12th century Henry II reduced the whole of Surrey to the state of a forest, part of the Royal Forest of Windsor, and converted the Royal Manor of Guildford into a deer park, hence Stag Hill. The next five Kings, Richard I, John, Henry III, Edward I and Edward III gradually reduced the bounds of the forest, leaving Surrey parishes west of the Wey and north of the Hog's Back as a purlieu of the forest, known as the Surrey Bailiwick. Guildford Castle was built shortly after 1066AD but by the

23

late 14th century it had fallen into disrepair and today only the Castle Keep survives as a ruin. Henry III had favoured Guildford Castle and often took up residence over the Christmas season. He spent a great deal of money on upgrading the buildings. Trials were held at the Castle and the Keep served as the gaol for the counties of Surrey and Sussex for many years.

The influence of the Normans settling in Britain could be seen in the wealth of French names that appear in all parts of the country. For most of the 13th century Thurstan le Dispenser held lands in Burgham, enough to support him, his family, his esquires and servants. In 1276 Adam le Dispenser gave Burgham Manor to William de Wintershull and Beatrice his wife. According to Roger Marjoribanks it was described in 1287 *"in a fashion that sheds an interesting light on feudal society. Burpham Court itself, with its plum and apple orchard, is valued at 2s 0d a year; 100 acres of farmland were valued at 4d an acre, 12 acres of meadow at 2s 0d the lot and three acres of wood and one of 'underwood' are not given a specific value. In rents he received £4 6s 8d (corresponding to about 260 acres) in money and three cocks and six hens in kind; other valuable considerations included the labour of free and customary tenants, fishing rights (5s 0d), a water mill (20s), tenants' inheritance duties (heriot) and the pleas and perquisites of his manor court. The whole value was reckoned at £9 6s 9d, a modest but not inconsiderable estate (giving an annual value equivalent to well over £1000 in modern money or, more realistically, a workman's wages for about two years; more importantly, it gave William the status of a gentleman, one of the tiny proportion who had influence in local and sometimes national politics)."* [These details can be found in The

24

Topographical History of Surrey, which is available either online or at the Surrey History Centre.] This description seems to fit best with the size and attributes of what is now known as Burpham Court Farm.

From 1216 the Plantagenets ruled for almost 270 years, including four Henrys, five Edwards and two Richards, overseeing the Hundred Years War, the Battle of Agincourt and the Wars of the Roses. In 1349 the Black Death had a devastating impact on many communities across the country – a third to a half of all people in the country died - and it is likely that Guildford and its surrounding villages were also affected.

At that time the old Manor of Burpham seems to have centred on the houses at Hurst, on the Woking Road, and Burpham Court Farm. Jim Miller wrote that in 1290 *'William le Frances of Worplesdon granted to Agnes de la Hurst his tenement which Robert de la Hurst her father formerly held...'* and it is thought that this was a building in that area, though no longer standing. In 1332 *'Roberto ate Hurst in the Villata of Burgham'* was assessed for tax of 8d.

The Victoria County History of Surrey explains the, at times quite long-winded, story of how ownership of the Lordship of the Manor of Burpham was passed down through the families. In 1385 Alice de Burgham, wife of Thomas de Wintershull, Lord of Burgham, made a bequest to Guildford Friary, arising from land at Wintershull. For around 200 years the Manor passed through the generations of Wintershulls, through a convoluted family history, coming in 1420 to Agnes, wife of William Bassett. She conveyed Burgham to trustees, probably to keep it in the family, and it passed back to another Thomas Wintershull, but then through the Bassett line to Sir Anthony Windsor in 1548. His son, Edmund Windsor, who had inherited the Manor aged only four years old in 1566, conveyed it to Sir John Wolley in 1592. It is likely that the name of Wintershull gradually evolved into Winterhill in Burpham, but out towards Horsham there is also the Wintershall Estate (home to the Wintershall Players) who were possibly from the same family originally.

By the 14th century, what had been the Forest of Windsor was gradually filling up with smallholders. Most cottagers cultivated their tiny plots, more like kitchen gardens than farms, sowing a little winter and summer corn in regular succession. St Catherine's Fair started in Guildford in 1308, an annual affair lasting for several days, to which people from all around would travel to buy and sell goods and produce. According to the website for Ye Olde Ship Inn, on the Portsmouth Road, *"an old charter allowed pubs in the area to sell beer without a licence at the fair, so there was no lack of lubrication for festivities"*. However, by the mid 19th century there were riots and the fair ended around the time of World War I. JMW Turner painted 'St Catherine's Hill near Guildford' in 1808, showing the ruined medieval chapel at the top of the hill. The fair is likely to have been an attraction for Burpham residents each year, although it would have been quite a trek of about three miles, up and down hills, taking around two hours to walk there.

The main industry in medieval Guildford was the cloth trade. Farmers would keep sheep and send their wool to the various mills by the Town Bridge in Guildford. However, by the mid 17th century this was in decline and would affect nearby villages, such as Burpham, where producing wool would have been an important source of income. After the creation of the Wey Navigation, cloth would have been transported by river to London and other towns. Tradesmen in the town used tokens instead of money for buying and selling between each other. The Guildford tradesmen's tokens used to have an image of a woolpack on them, referring to the importance of this trade to the town. Local woad plants, plentiful along the Wey Valley as well as being imported from abroad, provided the blue colour used for dying cloth.

THE 16TH CENTURY

The Tudors (1485 – 1603AD)

[Conflicts began with the Battle of Bosworth Field and included the Spanish Armada]

King Henry VII started the Tudor dynasty when he defeated King Richard III at Bosworth, and reigned for 24 years, followed by Henry VIII who reigned for 38 years. Then there was Edward VI and next came three Queens: Lady Jane Grey, Mary I and Elizabeth I, who reigned for 45 years. John Wolley, who only owned Burpham Manor for three years before he died in 1596, is known for having been the Latin Secretary to Queen Elizabeth, translating official communications with foreign governments into Latin and translating the replies into English – a job held by the poet John Milton 50 years later.

John Wolley was a member of parliament for Surrey in 1596, having represented various other constituencies for the previous 20 years. He had been a Privy Councillor from 1586, was knighted in 1592 and was one of the commissioners who tried and sentenced to death Mary, Queen of Scots. He died at his house in Pyrford and his wife, Lady Elizabeth, held the Manor in trust for their son Francis. Lady Elizabeth was the daughter of Sir William More, of Loseley, and she was also one of the ladies of the Privy Chamber for Queen Elizabeth. In 1597 the settlement between Lady Elizabeth Wolley, widow, and George More, stated that her Manors of Burpham and Wisley and Manors and lands in Pyrford were hers for life, passing to her son Francis Wolley and his heirs.

Sir Francis Wolley was elected to Parliament for Haslemere. He lived in Pyrford and when the poet John Donne was released from prison (after his clandestine marriage to Francis' cousin Ann More) Francis gave the young couple refuge and '*supplied their worldly wants*' until his death in 1609.

Prior to the Spanish Armada in 1588 men were needed for fighting and the records show that almost 8,000 men came from Surrey. Some would volunteer but in many cases their landlords or masters would put them forward. Sadly the records do not include the level of detail needed to determine how many men came from Burpham, but it is possible that there were some. Ships from Portsmouth formed part of the British fleet that drove off the Armada, so it is probable that traffic along the London to Portsmouth road travelled through Burpham and may have stopped off at a local inn. From around 1589 to 1613 William Shakespeare was writing his plays and other works, most of which were performed at theatres in London.

Several Tudor buildings, or parts of houses, still survive in and around Burpham. These include Sutton Place, Burpham Court Cottages, Burpham Court House and Willow Grange. Also in Jacobs Well are Watts Cottage, Stringers Barn and Jacobs Well Cottage, all of which were built during the 16ᵗʰ century. Sadly, the four Tudor cottages, next to the Green Man on Burpham Lane and believed to be part of Green Man Farm, were demolished in 1971.

England was a Catholic country until the 1530s when Henry VIII separated from Rome, setting up the Church of England. Following the Reformation (dissolution of the monasteries) England officially became Protestant in 1559 and Catholicism was deemed to be illegal for most of the next 230 years. Those who wished to continue following the Catholic faith survived mostly in secret congregations. Many of the Catholic gentry had houses with secret chapels and hiding places (priest-holes) for clandestine celebrations of the mass. The ordinary villagers were expected to attend the new Protestant church services.

George Abbot was born in the parish of St Nicholas in Guildford in 1562. He was educated at the Free Grammar School and then went to Balliol College, Oxford before going into holy orders in 1597. He was the Vice Chancellor of Oxford University in the very early 1600s before becoming Bishop of Lichfield and Coventry in 1609, then in 1611 he became Archbishop of Canterbury. He founded his Hospital at Guildford (Abbots Hospital) in 1619 and died in 1633. His grave is at Holy Trinity Church.

Burial and will records tell something of the story of Burpham in the 16th century, but Jim Miller's history '*Jacobs Well - How the name got its village*' is also very informative, based on census and parish records. Living at Hurst Farm (now Willow Grange and Burpham Court House on the Woking Road), at the houses on either side of the road, were two families, the Russells and the Crosses. Linked in with these were the Attfield alias Ripley family, who appeared in both parish and will records for the area over more than 200 years. The use of 'alias' in a surname is possibly an early version of a double-barrelled surname. Alternatively it could be that some of the

Attfields came from the village of Ripley nearby. The use of 'alias' seems to have stopped by the 19ᵗʰ century.

Jim Miller wrote that the earliest Russell identified with Burpham was '*Thomas Russell of Birpham*', mentioned in the will of '*John Russell, the eldest, of Worplesdon*', in 1582. Possibly this was Old Thomas of Hurst, but no evidence has confirmed this so far. In 1593 '*Young Thomas then of Burgham*' married Joane Dawlton and they had four daughters and three sons. Young Thomas died in 1619 and made his will on his deathbed. One of the first baptisms in St Mary's, Worplesdon, parish records was in December 1594 for Alice Russell, daughter of '*young Thomas of Burfam*', followed a few weeks later by her burial, then the baptism of her sister Agnes shortly afterwards. Also in 1595 was the burial of '*Alice Russell, widow of old Thomas of Hurst*' and it is possible that '*young Thomas of Burfam*' eventually became '*Thomas of Hurst*'. The family lived in the house that is now known as Willow Grange.

Wills can give a fascinating insight into life at the time, often including an inventory of belongings as well as identifying family members. A very famous example is William Shakespeare's will in which he left his '*second best bed*' to his wife. In the case of Young Thomas, he gave donations of five shillings each to the parish church and to the poor. He also gave 20 shillings '*to be bestowed at my burial in bread and beere*', clearly wishing friends and family to enjoy a good wake in his memory. As well as money and land he gave various items to his son Thomas, including '*a Joyned Bedstead, a Joyned presse, and Cupboard and Bedstead, flockbed and all other furniture belonging to the said Bed which I now lye on, in the*

31

Chamber over the hall. And also, my Bullen Brasse Furnace, my biggest brasse pott saving one, one great Iron spitte my greate dresser Table standing in my kitchen with all settles and forms in the same'.

The earliest mention of the Crosse family was in 1521 when Harry Crosse died. He was clearly a good Catholic leaving money to the church, including *'four pence to mother church; to high altar four pence; five masses at burial and at month's end; five masses at Christmas; to church three shillings and four pence to help buy a new cross'.* Then in 1568 William Crosse of Worplesdon, Yeoman, died, leaving *'...daughters Joan Cockes and Alice Russell two pounds per annum on land called Carters which I bought from Arthur Bryckett in Burpham for ten years'.* He also left his houses in Burpham, Merrow and Stoke next Guildford to his son Thomas. In 1593 the Lay Subsidy assessments for Worplesdon mentioned William Crosse, who was also named in a register of Burgham Rentalls dated 1610. Jim Miller assumed from this information that it was the same *'William Crosse of Burfam'*, who died in 1614, leaving two sons and a daughter. Agnes, the daughter, had married Henry Triggs, possibly associated with Triggs Lock on the Wey. His son, William, lived in the house now known as Burpham Court House.

The Attfield alias Ripley family first appear in will records from 1572, when Henry Atfeilde alias Ripley of Burpham, Yeoman, died. Among other bequests he gave ten shillings to building and finishing the Free Grammar School in Guildford. In 1574 Agnes Atfylde alias Ripley of Burpham, widow, gave *'twelve dozen loaves, six cheeses and a kilderkin of beer'* for friends and family to remember her by. She also left three shillings and four pence to the poor of Worplesdon, one shilling and eight pence to the poor of Merrow, and '*three shillings and four pence to ringers at my burial*'.

In 1563 the Mayor and aldermen of Guildford wrote to William More of Loseley Park requesting that St Catherine's Hill Fair be cancelled in order to prevent the spread of plague infection. In 1576 a letter to Sir William More reported that Queen Elizabeth would probably not visit Loseley that summer as the plague had spread to Weybridge. No proof has been found of the plague in Burpham but it is quite likely that the disease could have spread to the village.

THE 17TH CENTURY

The Stuarts (1603 – 1714AD)

[Conflicts included the English Civil War]

During the reign of King James I Guy Fawkes was arrested and hanged for being part of the Gunpowder Plot. Charles I reigned for 24 years but was beheaded during the Civil Wars, which started in 1642. Then followed the Commonwealth and the Protectorate, when the county of Surrey supported the Parliamentarians under Oliver Cromwell. Sir Richard Onslow was one of the most prominent of the Lord Lieutenant's subordinates. The county was important, mainly because of the gunpowder mills at Chilworth. Richard Weston, of Sutton Place, was a Catholic and a Royalist, best known for being the creator of the Wey Navigation, and presumably not popular with Cromwell's government. His property was sequestrated during the Civil War and he took himself into exile, travelling around Belgium and Holland.

After England's one and only attempt at republicanism, the next 50 years saw Kings Charles II and James II, Queen Mary II, King William III and Queen Anne ruling the country. Around 100 people died of the plague in Guildford in 1644. Then in 1665 the worst outbreak of the plague since the black death in the 14th century broke out across England and London lost about 15% of its population, with over 68,000 deaths recorded. King Charles moved to Oxford, as did Parliament and the courts. All trade with London was stopped and this must have affected rural communities. In 1666 the Great Fire of London destroyed many of the buildings across the capital. No records have been found about the impact of the plague on Burpham, although five children were recorded as dying of this disease in Worplesdon. However, Londoners travelling south may have stopped off on their journey so there was a risk of spreading the disease. Perhaps the newly opened Wey Navigation was affected, in the hope that the disease would not be brought to the community by water.

When Francis Wolley died in 1609 he bequeathed the Manor of Burpham to his illegitimate daughter Mary. His will, dated that year, said *'I leave the Manor of Burpham and lands at Chagden to my infant daughter christened by my wife and Mrs Bridget Weston in Pyrford Church and called by the name of Mary Wolley'*. He also gave £4,000 for the erection of a sepulchral monument in St Paul's Cathedral, London, for his parents and himself. Maintenance of the monument was to be funded through a rent-charge on his estate of Burpham of £10 per annum, but the monument was destroyed in the Great Fire of London in 1666. Mary Wolley married Sir John Wyrley but after her husband's death the Manor passed to her half-brother Robert Wroth, who was a Member of Parliament for Guildford in 1704, 1707 and 1717.

There are very few buildings in Burpham surviving from the 17th century, but these include New Inn Farmhouse and possibly parts of The Anchor and Horseshoes public house, though the only records for the pub that survive date back to the 18th century.

Wills again provide more information about people living in Burpham in the 17th century. Emma Bannister of Burpham, daughter of Richard

Bannister, died in 1609. In the same year Hugh Tewsley of Burpham, Husbandman, died, leaving money for the poor of Worplesdon, Stoke next Guildford and Merrow. Additionally, he left ten shillings '*to mending of road between Chagden Hatch and Wynter Hill*' as well as leaving ten pounds to his godson Thomas Atfeild alias Ripley, son of Thomas of Burfam, Husbandman. Presumably Hugh lived somewhere along the London Road and felt that improvements were necessary – some things never change. The will of 1614 for Henry Ripley alias Atfield of Worplesdon, Yeoman, stated that amongst other bequests he left '*his wife to have a room in my house in Burpham Court for lease if she lives that long, the standing bed, trundle bed and bedding... if she dislikes staying they [sons John and Thomas] to pay her five pounds per annum during the rest of the lease*'.

The following year John Attfeild alias Ripley of Worplesdon, Yeoman, died leaving to his brother Henry '*...and two other parcels of land abutting upon London highway for rest of lease of Burpham paying twelve pounds per annum to my brother Thomas and three pounds per annum to my mother in law Agnes Attfeild alias Ripley*'. Also in 1615 Thomas Marline alias Cooper of Burpham, Yeoman, died leaving '*the messuage and tenement I live in with all its lands except four closes or crofts of nine acres... to wife for twenty years to bring up the children, then to my son Thomas Marline alias Cooper to have the house and land at Burpham*'. Just 20 years later his son Thomas, Husbandman, died leaving '*...to my wife Alice Marlyn alias Cooper my messuage...in which I live and fourteen and a half acres of arable land in Burpham for eleven years...*' This was the first mention of anyone named Marline or Marlyn and it is possible that the house

Marlyns was named after him or his family. Thomas Coxe of Burpham, Yeoman, died in 1616, leaving *'ten shillings to his sister Agnes Dendye, wife of Thomas Dendye of Burpham'*.

In 1614 William Bannister of Worplesdon, Yeoman, died leaving to his son William Bannister *'the house I live in and land in Burpham'*. Two more Attfeilde alias Ripleys died in 1626 and 1629, Thomas and Henry both lived in Burpham and were clearly men of substance. Henry's will said that he left *'my house and land at Burpham Cross to my son Henry, sixteen acres of land in Ganghill adjoining the common...'*. Is it possible that the land at Burpham Cross included what later became the Green Man? In 1663 Jane Crosse of Burpham died, leaving money to her son Thomas and daughters Jane Lee and Elizabeth Gilbertson alias Derrick. In 1681 Denis Taylor of Burpham Court, Gentleman, died, his will stating that he should be buried in the chancel of the church.

Also in 1681, George Toft of Burpham, clothier, died, leaving money to his granddaughter Elizabeth Toft of Reigate as both her father and uncle (a clothier in Godalming) had already died. One might wonder what a clothier was doing in Burpham – the term usually meant someone working with cloth. As the hamlet was very small at the time he could have travelled to and worked in Guildford. Alternatively, he could have worked from his home, possibly employing people as local weavers. Clothiers were fairly wealthy and important members of the community. George had at least two sons, George and Joshua, who were also clothiers. There were a lot of Tofts in Guildford and Godalming and it is a possibility that George was related by marriage to Mary Toft, known as the Rabbit

Woman of Godalming. Mary was born in 1703 and married Joshua Toft, a journeyman clothier, in 1720. Her story was that she gave birth to a number of rabbits. This became a national phenomenon, which was reported in newspapers at the time. She was eventually found guilty of a hoax and was imprisoned. She died in 1763 in Godalming. Mary Toft was immortalised in an engraving by Hogarth called 'Cunicularii or The Wise Men of Godliman in Consultation' in 1726.

Jim Miller wrote that William Crosse granted passage to Richard Weston in 1619 for his 'new river', which had been dug to carry water from the River Wey at Stoke to irrigate the grounds of Sutton Place – it appears that William of Burfam had leased this property from the Lord of the Manor of Burgham in 1591. More on this can be found in the chapter on The Wey Navigation. Jim also reported that in 1661, after the restoration of the monarchy, Parliament called on the population for a 'Free and Voluntary Present' to King Charles to help to reduce the substantial debt that he had incurred during his exile. Donations in the Guildford area included ten shillings from William Crosse, Yeoman, and fifteen shillings from Thomas Crosse, Yeoman (a Yeoman being a prominent citizen, such as a farmer). One William Crosse, who had been born in 1641, became the Constable of Worplesdon in 1668.

A surviving document at the Surrey History Centre is a lease for 16 years made in 1641 between John Wyrley and Thomas Bower of Worplesdon. The property consisted of Burgham manor or farmhouse with two acres called the Little Park and several other named parcels in Worplesdon. There were exceptions to the lease –

'*the Great Parlour and chamber over it, stable room for two geldings and barn room for two loads of hay, are reserved for Dame Mary Wyrley'*, also hunting and fishing rights, rights of entrance to cut timber, dig turf for making charcoal, make weirs for catching fish and set up any kind of mill, reserved to lessors. Despite this last restriction could it be possible that Bowers Mill was named after this Thomas Bower? He seems to have been a man of wealth as in 1664 the Hearth Tax records show '*Tho Bowers Gent'* of Burpham being liable for paying tax chargeable for six persons, presumably his family and household.

The Court Baron minutes of 1645 recorded several names of people who probably lived in Burpham at the time. These included Ripley, Cooper, Underwood, Gilbert and Ellyott. One interesting name was that of Thomas Entiknapp – despite much searching it has not been possible to find any other records of Entiknapps in Worplesdon or Burpham. The family seems to have lived in the Chiddingfold and Dunsfold areas only, so what was Thomas doing as part of the Burpham Manor minutes? Perhaps he owned land in Burpham, but no land tax records have been found.

THE 18TH CENTURY

The Georgians (1714 – 1837AD)

[Conflicts included the Jacobite Rebellion, the American War of Independence and the Napoleonic Wars]

Four King Georges and King William IV were next to rule the country. George I came from Germany to the English throne as a result of the 1701 Act of Settlement, which stated that the monarch could not be Catholic, and he was the nearest Protestant eligible to take the crown. Both he and his son George II faced opposition from the Jacobites when Bonnie Prince Charlie raised an army of rebellion in Scotland, culminating with the Battle of Culloden Moor in 1746. The mid 18th century also saw the start of the Industrial Revolution, which would affect rural communities across the country. The late 18th century brought an influx of French refugees to Britain during the French Revolution. George III's reign saw Britain lose many of its colonies in North America, and it is likely that men from Surrey joined the army to fight in the American War of Independence in 1776. Ireland joined Great Britain to become the United Kingdom. George IV was Prince Regent from 1811 to 1820 and it was at this time that Britain and France fought the Napoleonic wars.

There are few buildings in Burpham surviving from this time, but the Listed Buildings records include Pimm's Row cottages as a good example.

The late 18th and early 19th centuries saw the rise of the Industrial Revolution, bringing enormous changes to the way of life for agricultural workers, such as many of the Burpham community. New manufacturing processes were invented to take the place of hand production methods, bringing in steam power as well as changing from wood to coal. Another benefit was the introduction of gas lighting so that people no longer had only oil or candles to light their homes and workplaces. During the 1760s and 1770s Captain Cook led his expeditions to the Pacific and became the first European to see Australia, New Zealand and Hawaii. He produced maps of much of the Canadian coastline and almost discovered Antarctica.

Catholic worship became legal in 1791 and from then on Catholics were allowed to build churches.

When Robert Wroth died in 1720, Thomas, 2nd Baron Onslow, bought the Manor of Burpham and it then passed down through the generations of the Onslow family, until much of the estate was sold in the early 20th century.

Again wills provide information about people living in the area. In 1710 George Garment of Burpham, Butcher, died, leaving substantial amounts of money and land to his children. The land included '*two closes, Cursie Crofts of three acres, four closes Cottesfurlong and Cottersland, Burpham fifteen acres and meadow adjoining all in my occupation*'. Sadly none of these names match with plot names from the 1838 Tithe Maps, so it is impossible to tell where they were in Burpham. This was the first mention of such a trade in Burpham and it is not known whether a butcher would have a shop or would work on a farm. He could have worked in Guildford, but it seems like quite a long journey each day. Then in 1739 George Garment of

Send, Yeoman, left to his '*sister Elizabeth Spratley, wife of Job Spratley of Guildford Butcher, all my messuage in Burpham near Broadoak twenty acres*'. It is interesting to note that on a map of Green Man Farm in 1791 there is a plot of land recorded as belonging to Mistress Spratley approximately between the current Marlyns Drive and Pimms Row Cottages.

In 1723 Richard Butler of Burpham, Farmer, died leaving money to his sons and granddaughters, but also to his son in law, Lewis Goodger of Alton, as '*residuary legatee including rights in the River Wey*'. John Slifeild of Chobham, Yeoman, died in 1728 leaving to his son John, after the death of his sister in law Ann Atfeild, '*all my freehold messuage and ten acres in Burpham in the occupation of William Gilham*'. Then in 1756, John Attfield alias Ripley of the Green Man, Worplesdon, Victualler, died leaving his estate to his cousin Henry Attfield alias Ripley, Yeoman of Worplesdon, and to his children. In 1758 John Stanbridge of Burpham, Papermaker, left part of his estate to his '*late wife's niece Mary Heath, wife of George Heath, to divide between the family and her*'.

The daughter of another William Crosse, Elizabeth Leeves, died in 1771, by which time the Crosse property had shrunk to only 60 acres. His granddaughter inherited the estate but leased Great Hurst to farmers of Worplesdon, then in 1826 it was sold to Richard Sparkes, thus ending the connection of the Crosse family with this area.

THE 19TH CENTURY

The Victorians

(Conflicts included the Crimean, Zulu and Boer Wars)

Queen Victoria came to the throne in 1837 and reigned for 63 years. During this time the population of England, Wales and Scotland rose rapidly, almost doubling in numbers, mainly due to better living standards, allowing people to live longer and to have more children surviving infancy. Many Victorian families were large. However, in Ireland the population halved due to the Great Famine or Potato Famine in the mid 19th century. More records survive from this period of British and local history, which makes it easier to research and learn about life in Burpham and its surrounds. As the digital age grows it is possible to access information from home, using computers, such as census records from 1841 to 1911, electoral registers, tithe maps, newspaper reports and a wide range of other information available to those wishing to investigate families and local areas.

The Industrial Revolution changed the lives of thousands of people from the late 18th to mid 19th centuries. Machines took over many production methods, affecting milling, farming and manufacturing processes. Cement was new for the building trades, gas lighting allowed factories and shops to stay open for longer hours than had been possible with candles or oil lighting. Transport had been difficult when roads were so badly maintained by parishes, but these were improved with the introduction of turnpike roads, which charged tolls to pay for maintenance. Canals had been built across the country, enabling supplies to be shipped between towns. The railways came to the Guildford area in the mid 1800s, bringing even more change and eventually the demise of the canal system for carrying freight.

There are several buildings surviving from the Victorian age, including St Luke's Church, the Old Chapel and many of the cottages along London Road and Burpham Lane.

A few minutes of the Burpham Manor Courts Baron survive from Victorian times. In 1858 John Rand Capron was the Steward and Arthur Pimm, son of William Francis Pimm, was Foreman of the Homage. Various changes to ownership or tenancies were reported, including the death of William Francis Pimm, who held freehold lands called Marlyns, and stating that Arthur Pimm had taken these over. Also, W Elkins, who held the tenure of the Green Man part of Marlyns, had died and his son W E Elkins had taken this over.

In 1855 Kelly's Directories reported that there were 325 inhabitants in the tithing of Burgham but by 1890 the population had only increased to 337. There were farmers, publicans and the blacksmith, all of whom provided employment in the community. Whereas in 1841 the majority of working men in the hamlet were agricultural labourers and others were employed by the mill, by 1861 there was more variety to employment. Gardeners, carpenters and domestic service became more visible and there was even a lawyer lodging at the Green Man Inn. Female employees were often laundresses, dressmakers, nursemaids or other household servants. By 1871 tile makers and tile labourers appeared, along with brickmakers, heralding the start of the brickmaking industry in the area. In 1891 there was an engine driver living on London Road, but whether this was related to the railways or something else is not clear. Other jobs that appeared at that time included a butcher, a road labourer and two men in the Army Reserve.

THE 20TH CENTURY

The Windsors

(Battles included the 2nd Boer War, World Wars I and II, Korea, the Falklands, the Gulf Wars, Afghanistan and Kosovo)

Queen Victoria died in 1901 after reigning for 63 years and her son Edward VII succeeded to the throne, but having been Prince of Wales for many years he only lived until 1910 when George V became King. George V changed the name of the royal house from Saxe-Coburg and Gotha to Windsor in 1917 due to anti-German feelings during the Great War. He died in 1936 and was succeeded by Edward VIII, who abdicated later that year in order to marry Wallis Simpson. George VI then became King but he died in 1952, to be succeeded by his daughter Elizabeth II, who celebrated her Diamond Jubilee in 2012, her 90th birthday in 2016 and Sapphire Jubilee in 2017.

The 20th century brought enormous change to the country. Aviation, though attempted in the previous century, began with the Wright Brothers' Kitty Hawk in 1903. By 1976 supersonic travel became a reality with Concorde, but after some accidents this marvellous aeroplane was retired in late 2003. One of its farewell flights came over Burpham and a number of school staff watched it fly away for the last time. Ocean liners were the main method of international travel from the mid 1800s until the 1950s. In 1907 Cunard launched the RMS Lusitania and RMS Mauretania, but in 1910 White Star Line launched the RMS Olympic, followed by RMS Titanic and HMHS Britannic. However, the tragic sinking of the Titanic in April 1912 brought great changes to shipping regulations, including rules that all liners should carry enough lifeboats for all passengers and crew.

Railway networks expanded, motorcars became the vehicle of choice for many people, along with new industries to support these changes. Two world wars brought opportunities for women to step up to jobs that had previously always been held by men. Advances in science and technology have impacted on all areas of life, from medicine to leisure, with computers at the forefront of communications as well as underpinning travel, banking and manufacturing.

Queen Elizabeth II has seen incredible change during her reign. In the 1950s pre-fabs were the answer to the demand for housing; young men could expect to do two years National Service; rationing did not end until 1954. Television sets were new and quite rare at the time of the Coronation in 1953. The 1960s brought pop music, mini skirts and flower power. The first landing on the moon was in 1969. The 1970s were a time of strikes and industrial strife. Foreign holidays grew popular and affordable. Margaret Thatcher became the first woman prime minister. In the 1980s mobile phones appeared; Live Aid raised millions of pounds for starving Africans; the Falklands War took place; and Sky satellite TV was launched. The 1990s saw the death of Princess Diana and the return of a Labour government to power. Following the Millennium celebrations, new technology gradually took over, with Google, Facebook, YouTube and Twitter. In the 2010s there are over 65 million people in the UK and around 100 different languages are spoken across the country.

Census records for Burpham in the early years of the 20th century showed that the traditional industries still thrived – farming, milling and brickmaking, but there were also workers on the railway, coachmen and carmen. For the first time, white collar workers were living in the Burpham community, such as architects, surveyors, insurance agents, telephone workers and even a retired Indian Civil Service Judge.

It will not be possible to see any more census records until about 2022 when the 1921 census should be made available, and after that there could be no more for a further 30 years (the census for 1931 was destroyed and there was no census taken in 1941). However, the 1939 Register offers another insight into life in Burpham at that time. Similar to a census, its purpose was to gather information for identity cards, ration books and conscription at the start of World War II. It recorded everyone's name, address, age, marital status and occupation.

Some of it makes fascinating reading, mostly because it gives more information about living and working in the area just before the war, but partly because, inevitably, there are some transcription errors, such as the 28 year old man whose occupation was recorded as '*expectant mother*'. The vote had only been made available for all women just over ten years earlier, but the large majority of married women were not in paid employment – they were recorded as '*unpaid domestic duties*'. Unmarried women worked mainly in offices, shops, or domestic service. Several women worked in either Arthur Love's laundry on Burpham Lane or at Bower's Mill, which was

48

the laundry for the Duke of Sutherland, while a small number were teachers or nurses.

OS map 1912

The men of Burpham had a wide range of occupations. A few were still working in agriculture, and some were market gardeners. Sales representatives and commercial travellers were more common, along with work in offices and banks. There was still a need for plumbers, builders, bricklayers and carpenters, as well as electrical engineers, architects and surveyors. Men worked in aeronautics, and the railways, while lorry drivers, taxi drivers and chauffeurs worked on the roads. Other jobs included solicitors, teachers, accountants and one man who had retired from working at the Stock Exchange.

At the start of the 20th century Burpham was really still just two roads – London Road and Burpham Lane – almost everything else was farmland or common land. In 1912 most of the village consisted of the four main farms bordering the London Road – Winterhill, New Inn, Bower's and Weylea; plus the two farms on the outer edges, Burpham Court Farm and Gosden Hill Farm (which was still part of Send parish until 1933). On Burpham Lane there was little between the Tudor cottages next to the Green Man and Pimm's Row, apart from the two cottages opposite, where William Turner and his wife had their shop. There was a small scattering of cottages before arriving at St Luke's Church and the school, which had opened in 1908, and allotments lay between the school and the river.

Development of the village started after the Great War and by 1934 housing estates were being built - Paddock Road, Meadow Road, New Inn Lane, Orchard Road and Winterhill Way, with Briar Way and Hawthorn Way. However, Winterhill Farmhouse still presided over the far end of the village, where Great Oaks Park would eventually be built. Bower's Farm House stood opposite the end of Orchard Road, Weylea Farm House lay almost opposite the Anchor & Horseshoes, while New Inn Farm House is still there, the oldest building in the modern-day village. The swimming pool behind The Kingpost Restaurant could be seen clearly on the map and the old Methodist Chapel was no longer marked as it had been closed down several years before. Along Burpham Lane (or Jacobs Well Road as it was marked) the beginnings of Marlyn's Drive had three or four cottages. The Council Cottages, and the Village Hall next door, had been built in the 1920s and more cottages had appeared between Pimm's Row and the Church.

OS map 1934

THE ONSLOW FAMILY

The Onslow family were an integral part of the history of Burpham for many years. They were originally from Shropshire, but through the marriage in 1559 of Richard Onslow, M.P., Solicitor General and later Speaker of the House of Commons, to Catherine Harding of Cranleigh, heiress to the manors of Knowle, Bramley and Rowley, they became established in Surrey. They were a significant part of political life in England for many generations, with three Speakers of the House and many Members of Parliament in their midst. Apparently Richard became involved in a brawl in the Inner Temple in 1556 for which he spent a short time in Fleet Prison, but was readmitted after an apology was made. He and Catherine had seven children, including Edward, another ancestor of the Earls of Onslow.

His grandson, Sir Richard Onslow also became a solicitor and was elected as M.P. for Surrey in 1628, but only for a year as King Charles decided to rule without parliament for 11 years. When Civil War broke out in 1642 he raised a regiment for Parliament. He returned to Parliament under Oliver Cromwell and was elected as M.P. for Guildford in 1660, where he sat until his death in 1664. He was buried at Cranleigh. Richard and his wife had 14 children, and his second son, Arthur, became the 1st Baronet. Arthur married Mary, daughter of Thomas Foote, Lord Mayor of London in 1649. He also followed in the family tradition of the law and politics, becoming the M.P. for Surrey, then for Guildford in 1660.

Arthur's son Richard was created Baron Onslow and was also Speaker of the House of Commons and Chancellor of the Exchequer. Some

52

reports suggest that he was unpopular during his time as Speaker, being very pedantic so he was given the nickname "Stiff Dick". Then came Thomas, 2nd Baron Onslow, who married a Jamaican heiress, Elizabeth Knight, in 1708, which enabled him to buy Guildford Park, the manors of Somersbury, Baynards, Pollingfold, Burpham and Shalford. He also built Clandon Park House, which was completed in about 1730 and served as the family seat for many years. Thomas and his son Richard, 3rd Baron Onslow, were also M.P.s and both served as Lord Lieutenant of Surrey.

George, 4th Baron Onslow, was created Earl of Onslow and Viscount Cranley in 1801, and married Henrietta Shelley in 1753. According to Surrey History Centre records, he needed to sell the manor of Papercourt, Send to Peter Lord King in exchange for the manor of Wisley in 1785. Thomas, 2nd Earl of Onslow, sold the remaining lands in Cranleigh, reducing the estates considerably. Like his predecessors he was M.P. for Guildford and, allegedly, was friendly with the Prince of Wales. He played cricket and was known for driving four-in-hand (horses and carriage).

His son, Arthur, 3rd Earl of Onslow, who was not a politician, abandoned Clandon Park and became a recluse after the death of his wife and son. There was improvement in the management of the estates after his grandnephew, William Hillier Onslow, succeeded as 4th Earl in 1870, but during the late 19th and early 20th centuries much of their land near Guildford, including a large part of Burpham, was sold off for building development. This included the old Guildford Park, where Onslow Village was built in the 1920s, and which Richard, 5th Earl of Onslow, gave six acres on Stag Hill as a site for

Guildford Cathedral in 1928. In 1967 Guildford Corporation purchased the manor of Merrow, then Surrey County Council bought the manors of Worplesdon, Chobham, Bisley, Pyrford and Ripley/Send in 1968. William served in the House of Lords under Lord Salisbury and was Governor of New Zealand from 1888 to 1892. He was Under-Secretary of State for India for the next eight years and held various other government posts until his death in 1911.

Richard, 5th Earl of Onslow, made his career in the Diplomatic Service from 1901, working in Madrid, Tangier, St Petersburg and Berlin over the following six years. He joined the army in 1914, was mentioned in dispatches three times, received an OBE and the French Legion of Honour. In later years he was Honorary Lieutenant-Colonel of the 3rd Battalion Queen's Royal Regiment (West Surrey). After the war he took up his seat in the House of Lords, holding various posts, including Deputy Speaker of the House of Lords, until 1944. He died in 1945.

William, 6th Earl of Onslow, went to Sandhurst and was commissioned into the Life Guards in 1934. During the Second World War he transferred to the 4th County of London Yeomanry (Sharpshooters), winning the Military Cross. He was captured during the Normandy Campaign in 1944 and was a prisoner of war until May 1945. Following the war he was a member of Surrey County Council and Assistant Chief Conservative Whip in the House of Lords until 1960, then he joined the Liberals in 1965. He was also a Deputy Lieutenant of Surrey until 1962. He continued with the Territorial Army after the war and, as Captain of the Yeomen of the Guard, he took part in the funeral of King George VI and the coronation of Queen Elizabeth II. He died in 1971.

William was succeeded by his son Michael, 7th Earl of Onslow, who was an energetic member of the House of Lords, sitting on the Conservative benches. Although he fought against Tony Blair's proposals to strip voting rights from hereditary peers, in the end he was one of the 90 or so who elected to stay in the House of Lords after the 1999 Act. He was known for his love of carriage driving and could be seen driving a horse and trap in and around Burpham. He was the only hereditary peer to appear on the BBC programme "Have I Got News for You". The Guardian's obituary reported that he frequented the Onslow Arms in West Clandon, once chased a bullock down the A3 while riding a horse, and he bred canaries. Rupert, 8th Earl of Onslow, succeeded to the title on the death, from cancer, of his father in 2011.

Along with being politicians, there is a long tradition of the Onslow family being appointed as High Steward of Guildford. This was an honorary title bestowed by the council of certain towns and cities in England. Since the 17th century it has become a mainly ceremonial role. It is usually awarded for life and in some cases has become associated with a particular peerage title. According to a document in 2011 it was proposed, following the death of his father, to invite Rupert, 8th Earl of Onslow, to accept the office of High Steward for the Borough of Guildford. The reason given was to maintain the historic appointment of a High Steward. The role was described as *"an officer of great dignity and some influence, but with practically no duties or emoluments; usually a gentleman of high position, perhaps the owner or the patron of the Borough."* Apparently the only duty incumbent on the High Steward is the tradition of presenting a plum cake to any member of the Royal Family visiting Guildford.

PUBLIC HOUSES – 1 The Green Man

According to Norman Hamilton's History of Burpham the site on the corner of London Road with Burpham Lane, was subject to a one

The Green Man, postcard, about 1930s

thousand years lease, dated 25th March 1593, at a rent of two shillings and five pence. But in 1971 Courage Ltd, as occupants of the Green Man, were able to claim freehold possession of the site because the rent had not been paid or collected for over 20 years. Whether this was a lease for a building or just for the ground is not known. There used to be four Tudor cottages on Burpham Lane, next to the Green Man, so it is quite possible that the pub existed during the 16th century and it would have been the central point of the hamlet at that time.

A map, dated 1690 by John Seller, showed a New Inn on London Road in Burpham and this appeared to be on the site of the current

New Inn Farmhouse Surgery, but no records have been found to prove it to have been a public house before it was a farm. Often map makers put the name of the farm but without the word farm, so New Inn could have been the farm. Perhaps the name referred to the new inn on the other side of the road? Another map, dated 1762 by John Roque, clearly showed the Green Man at the crossroads. This was a prime site for a public house, being on the main road from London to Portsmouth and therefore offering refreshments for travellers on their long journeys. Both horses and passengers would tire and be in need of a break from travel. A photograph of the pub in 1901 showed it as a two-storey building with three gables and a large verandah extending round the front and one side.

The Green Man in 1901

The Green Man in 1901 (N Hamilton)

The will of John Attfield alias Ripley, dated 1754, recorded him as Victualler of the Green Man, Worplesdon. This is the earliest paper trail of publicans at the inn that has been found so far. However, Henry Atfeild alias Ripley's will in 1643, presumably an ancestor of John's, left *all my houses, land, etc at Burpham* Cross' to his son, also called Henry. Is it possible that he owned not only houses and land, but also an inn at that time? From 1785 to 1798 the licenced victualler records for the Green Man listed Laban Morris as publican and Henry Attfield was shown as the owner in the land tax records of 1790. He appeared in various land tax records for the Burgham Tything for several more years and died in 1832. He was buried at St John the Evangelist, Stoke, Guildford. The Tithe Map of 1838 showed the Green Man Inn on the corner of London Road and Burpham Lane, and there were three buildings on the plot. The landowner was recorded as William Elkins and the pub was occupied by James Cox. At that time the village was only a small number of houses, farms and inns on and around London Road and Burpham Lane, so this would have been the centre of the community.

In 1881 the census recorded John (or Jonathan) Dudley as publican, with his wife Martha Tarrier. He was born in Leighton Buzzard in 1846 and they had seven children, four of whom were born in Burpham. Martha died in 1884 and was buried at St Luke's, then John married Maud Ellen Durrant Marshall of Chiddingfold in 1888 and they had four more children. It is likely that he had come to the Green Man by 1877 as their son John was born in the parish. Kelly's Directories had John as publican up to 1907, but for 1909 and 1911 Alfred Jacob was recorded at the pub. Then the 1913 entry had John back until 1922, but by 1924 Robert Brown had taken over the pub.

Quite why John took time out from running the pub and then came back is not known. The 1911 census recorded that he and Maud were living in a house in George Street, Guildford and he was recorded as a building contractor. He died in 1927, aged 81 years, and was buried at St Luke's, with his final address shown as Cornflower Cottage, Burpham. Maud moved to Woking at some point and died there in 1936, but was also buried at St Luke's with her husband.

Jonathan Dudley's gravestone at St Luke's (Gravetone Photographic Resources)

According to Mark Sturley's book The Public Houses and Breweries of Guildford, '*the sign of the Green Man is an ancient one and as most of northern Surrey was at one time within the bounds of Windsor Forest it is not surprising to find inn signs to the forester in this area*'. In 1890 the Green Man was recorded as one of the properties belonging to Richard Elkins, the Guildford brewer, but it had belonged to the Elkins family since at least the 1830s. In 1890 Elkins' brewery and its licensed houses were sold by auction and purchased by Hodgsons Kingston Breweries, who in turn were acquired by Courage in 1967.

It was Hodgsons Kingston Brewery Company who, after buying the Green Man, rebuilt, in an Arts & Crafts style, creating the building that many people still remember, by replacing the former old three gabled and tile hung house. Apparently the cellars and outbuildings seemed to have been retained at that time. There have been some reports of an underground tunnel running from the cellar of the Green Man, but there have also been contradictory opinions, including the last publican Brian Wheeler, who said there was no tunnel. The romantics among us might imagine that there was an escape route, possibly for Catholics at the time of the Reformation or for Royalists at the time of the Civil War. Sadly we will never know, but it's a good story. An old stained glass window, with the crest of Hodgsons Kingston Brewery Company Ltd, survived in the old barn next door to the pub and this area was restored in order to be used as a restaurant. The barn, which was demolished in 1984, was

Stained glass window in Green Man
(N Hamilton)

timber-framed with 'ancient timbers'. Sadly, at around that time, the stained glass window that used to be in the barn was broken.

In the late 19th century there was a large private house called The Paddocks on London Road adjacent to the Green Man and this, with some associated cottages, formed the Paddocks Estate. This estate was also acquired by Hodgsons Kingston Brewery: the house in 1930, the cottages numbers 1-4 in 1935, and numbers 5-6 in 1936. The Paddocks Estate also passed to Messrs Courage in 1967. The 19th century house was used firstly as a café for coaches, then as a function room for wedding receptions and other community events. Eric Voller remembered that the West Surrey Big Band Society played in the Paddock Rooms.

The cottages on Burpham Lane, situated about 150ft behind the barn and set back from the road, were a two-storey block of four dwellings. They were Grade II Listed and dated to at least the 16th century. However, after the second-world war they fell into disrepair and various correspondence between the Council and the Historic Buildings and Antiquities Office between 1959 and 1971 recorded significant debate about what to do with them. In the end it was decided that, due to the dilapidated condition of the cottages, there was no objection to them being demolished and finally this went ahead in 1971. Looking at old maps, especially the plan of Green Man Farm of 1791, it seems likely that the cottages had originally formed part of the Green Man Farm buildings.

Census and Kelly's Directory records for the 19th and 20th century show that management of the inn changed hands at various times, with the publicans being:

1841 - Robert Harripen

1851 - Charles Herrett

1861 - Charles Pantry

1871 - James Collyer

1881 - John Dudley took over the inn and his name was shown as publican for the next 41 years, apart from a short break for

1909 - Alfred Jacob

1913 - John Dudley was back and stayed there until 1922.

1924 - Robert T Brown

1930 - Archibald H Selfe

The Green Man showing the café and off licence, c. 1930 (G Dye)

Green Man Roadhouse and Off Licence managers:

1950 – C G Murphy

1953 – O Wilkinson

- Roger and Jo Norris

1964 - Brian and Sylvia Wheeler

1984 – Harvester Steakhouse

In the records of the Guildford Petty Sessional Division of 1892 about licensed premises the Green Man was described as *'fully licensed; owned by and tied to Hodgson & Co (the brewery company); the licensee was John Dudley who resided on the premises; having accommodation for travellers and persons requiring refreshment other than drink; stabling provided; for the use of the general public'*. In 1904 the public house was still tied to Hodgson's Kingston Brewery Co and the licensee was John Dudley; trade was described as good but by that time there were no bedrooms and stabling for only one horse.

Brian and Sylvia Wheeler remembered that people used to say that the Green Man was built on a pond, but no evidence of this has been found as the more detailed of the old maps all show the pub on the site. However, the map of Green Man Farm in 1791 shows the pub building on the corner, so it is quite possible that there had been a farm pond there at some time.

Many local residents still remember when frequent coaches, travelling between London and Portsmouth, stopped off at the Green Man for refreshments. At one time travellers going north stopped at the pub and those going south stopped at the Kingpost opposite. Both had cafés, giving passengers a chance to stretch their legs and have a cup of tea, as licensing laws at the time would have prohibited the sale of alcohol during much of the day. The car park at the pub was extended in order to make space for the coaches. At one time there were 28 coaches all arriving at around the same time. However, when the coaches left on one occasion it was found that a lot of the pub's glasses had gone too. The police were called and the Wheelers went with them to try to get back their property, but only one was retrieved. When coaches arrived the pub staff would be called on to serve, including those who were off duty, or even having a shower. In earlier years many sailors would use the Burpham pubs as they travelled between London and Portsmouth, as this was an important route for naval business. When the breathalyser came into use in 1965 pub trade was hit hard. With the Burpham Traffic Centre nearby there were often police cars parked opposite the pub, but mostly they were there as a deterrent.

Ice cream was sold from the Green Man and many local children worked there during the school holidays. Several people recalled buying a block of ice cream, wrapped in newspaper, to take home in the summer.

Many people remembered spending New Year's Eve at the Green Man, when the celebrations usually included singing Auld Lang Syne and doing a conga around the roundabout.

Coaches in the car park, about 1970s (B Wheeler)

The Green Man was a popular place for the local community, but at various times some well-known celebrities stopped there as well. Brian Wheeler remembered that Joan Collins popped in to use the loo and Mick Jagger played on the fruit machine during his visit. Hank Marvin of The Shadows visited, as did Reginald Maudling M.P.

In 1980 the north-eastern end of the site, where the coach house for The Paddocks estate was located, was sold to McCarthy & Stone for development as sheltered housing, becoming West Court. Brian and Sylvia Wheeler called their last 'Time, ladies and gentlemen, please' in 1984 and moved to the Bull's Head at West Clandon. There were two parties to say goodbye and the pub ran out of beer, having to borrow more from another pub. It is rumoured that 'Wally Windows' (the window cleaner) wanted a souvenir of the pub when it changed into a Harvester, and at about the same time the pub sign from the corner of London Road and Burpham Lane disappeared. Of course, there is no proof that he took it, but it would have been a good souvenir to have.

The Green Man as a Harvester (B Darnton)

The Green Man inn was again rebuilt and the function room, called the Paddock Rooms, was demolished in order to convert to a 120-seat restaurant by a subsidiary company of the Courage Group, with a new name of the Harvester Steak House. For a while they kept the bar at the front of the pub, allowing some of the pub atmosphere to be retained, but eventually that too disappeared to convert more dining space. There were plans submitted to the Council in 2005 to build 70 flats on the site, but these were refused. John Boon recalled that the Harvester company used to film their advertisements at the Green Man.

Demolition of the Green Man 2008 (J Rickman)

The Guildford Borough Council's Honorary Remembrancer at the time, Roger Marjoribanks, reported in 2005/6 that The Green Man took part with 200 other Harvester restaurants across the country in a project to raise money for the Make a Wish Foundation by releasing 400 balloons, costing £1 each, with the assistance of the Mayor Councillor Tamsy Baker. This was the best result in the country. Sylvia Wheeler remembered that when they were there they did a lot of charity work, including raising money for the Royal Surrey County Hospital and Guide Dogs for the Blind. Thousands of pounds were raised for good causes over the years. They also did lunches for the Round Table groups.

In 2006 the site was sold for development and was bought by Aldi Stores Ltd to build a supermarket there. The site deteriorated to a derelict eyesore over the next two years and in late 2008, following major water ingress, the remaining buildings were demolished on health and safety grounds. Thames Valley Archaeological Services Ltd carried out their archaeological evaluation on behalf of Aldi in July 2014 but, possibly due to the piles of rubble deposited over the footprint of the pub building, they were not able to find any archaeological features or any items of interest, recording that all the walls and floors were relatively modern. Given the known history of the Green Man site, it is somewhat surprising, and very disappointing, that nothing was found. One would think that at least some reminder of past life would have been found and identified.

Sculpture of Green Man on Aldi wall

Apparently there is a restrictive covenant on the site, preventing it from being used as a pub in the future, possibly put there by the pub owners to avoid competition for the Horse & Groom in Merrow.

Burpham and Merrow residents objected to plan after plan submitted by Aldi, but in early 2014 the Council eventually gave the go-ahead and the new store opened in November 2015. On the corner of the building, overlooking the roundabout, there is a plaque about the history of the site and artwork depicting the Green Man. The sculpture was designed by Nick Bates and made by Burrows Lea Forge in Shere. '*The artist describes the Green Man Public Artwork as elemental, always in the background, ever watchful. The leaves and foliage are larger than life and grow vigorously from his head and body. His body is powerful but indistinct, forever moving and with urgency, elusive but still keen to see what going on in the space he's vacated.*' Apparently the artwork is referred to by some as the bearded lady of Burpham.

Outside the Green Man 1975 (P A Cloney)

PUBLIC HOUSES – 2 The Anchor and Horseshoes

This pub has been known as the Anchor, the Horseshoes, the Three Horseshoes, the Horseshoes and Anchor or the Anchor and Horseshoes over the years. It is not a Listed Building but, according to Mark Sturley's book, The Breweries and Public Houses of Guildford, it possibly dates back to the 17th century, although he said that the earliest record of it as a public house is only from the 19th century. Looking at the side of the building from the car park it seems likely that it was built in the early 18th century.

Anchor & Horseshoes side view 2015

However, it has now been possible to track the Heath family, in the Licensed Victuallers records dating from 1785 to 1826, as publicans in Burpham. The earliest records show George Heath running a public house in Worplesdon (there were only three in the parish – the New Inn, the Green Man and the Anchor & Horse Shoes) from 1785 to 1793, followed by his son James Heath until 1826. From 1822 the records include the name of the pub so as James Heath ran the Anchor and Horse Shoes it is most probable that George Heath, his father, was running it in 1785. Research into the Burpham Blacksmith's history established that George Heath, his son James and grandson James were all blacksmith's on the London Road. According to the Surrey History Centre it was quite common for people to have two jobs, and publican and blacksmith went together rather well.

There are two cottages next to the inn immediately to the east and two cottages immediately to the west and these have been known variously as Horseshoes or Horseshoe Cottages, Anchor Cottages and more recently as nos. 196/198 and 190/192 London Road. They were built sometime between 1839 and 1873 on the site of what seemed to be a former stables and probably a blacksmith's shop. Three horseshoes was the usual sign for a blacksmith or a farrier and the anchor was a familiar sign on the old Portsmouth Road as there was much traffic of naval personnel between the coast and London.

Norman Hamilton wrote that there was a story that the inn originally was sold by the Earl of Onslow, Lord of the Manor, to a tenant for one guinea. If there is any truth in this then it is likely to have been at some point between 1720, when Lord Onslow bought the Manor from Robert Wroth, and 1785, when George Heath was recorded as publican.

The earliest known mention of the pub on a map was from 1822/3, by C and I Greenwood, where it was marked as the Anchor, but on the Wey Navigation Map of 1823 it was marked as the Anchor and Horseshoes. On the 1838 Tithe Map of Worplesdon parish the inn was shown, but named only in the details rather than on the map, when the landowner and occupant of the Horseshoe Inn was given as William Baker. As William was married to Lois Heath, the sister of James the blacksmith next door to the pub, it is possible that he either bought the freehold property from her father or was given it after they got married in 1833. The 1841 census also showed William and his family living at the inn - they had two children, William and Lois. Young William became a carpenter, married, had six children and lived either at the pub or next door in either Horseshoe or Anchor Cottage. The latter was where he was living with his widowed daughter (Helen or Ellen) and two of her daughters (Elsie and Doris, who attended Burpham Primary School) at the time of his death in 1911. Young Lois married Richard Harding, a miller, they had ten children and lived for a while at Bower's Mill Cottage, but then moved to Ifield Mill in Sussex. She died near Rudgwick in 1915.

William Baker was born in 1801, possibly the son of William Baker who ran The Anchor public house in Woking. The Tithe Maps of 1838 recorded him as owner of the freehold for the Anchor and Horseshoes pub, at a time when very few people in the community actually owned their homes. Clearly he was fairly well off and an important member of the community. When William died in 1844, aged only 45 years old, he was buried at St Mary's in Worplesdon. In his will he directed that all his debts and funeral costs be paid and then '*I give and devise unto my dear Lois Baker and her heirs all that my freehold messuage tenement or public house and premises bearing the name or sign of The Three Horseshoes and Anchor and the stables one whereof was lately a Blacksmiths shop outbuildings garden orchard and land with the appurtenances thereto belonging or appertaining situate at Worplesdon aforesaid and now in the occupation of myself and John Vick'.* The plot seemed to include a pond to the east, two cottages to the west and outbuildings to the rear. Unfortunately there doesn't seem to be any other record of who John Vick was or exactly what property he occupied.

A year after William's death, Lois married James Allwright, born in Shinfield, Berkshire in 1800. He took over as publican, but they only had nine years together before he died in 1855. James was presumably married previously as in his will he left £100 '*of lawful money of Great Britain to be paid*' to his daughter Mary Allwright Bridger. He left everything else to Lois including '*all that my messuage or tenement orchard and garden together with the appurtenances situate at West Horsley in the County of Surrey, and which I lately purchased of Hannah Cumber to hold unto my said wife Lois her heirs and assigns for ever*'.

According to census records Lois then ran the pub on her own until she died on 26th April 1889, being a central part of the Burpham community for over 50 years. She was buried at St Luke's Church. Her gravestone says '*In Loving Memory of Lois Allwright. Who died on April the 26th 1889. In the 83rd year of her age. Resting in Hope*'.

She left the pub, along with the adjoining cottages on the site of the former stables and blacksmith's shop and pond, to her son, William Baker.

Lois Allwright's gravestone (Gravestone Photographic Resources)

On 12ᵗʰ October 1889 William leased the inn to Messrs Lascelles Tickner, the Guildford brewers, for 21 years at £52 p.a. Then the following week he mortgaged the property to John Reeve for £458, but when Reeve died two months later it was reconveyed to William. Having paid the first mortgage William then took out a second mortgage on the property, this time for £550. In September 1909 William, then described as a publican of Merrow, sold the Horseshoes and Anchor by auction at the Lion Hotel, Guildford, for £1820 to Farnham United Breweries. The sale included the inn, stables, outbuildings and garden, but not the land with the cottages and pond to the east of the property. The inn was described at the sale as consisting of a public bar, bar parlour, private bar, tap room, private sitting room, kitchen, scullery, cupboard under the stairs, larder, five bedrooms, attic, cellar, clubroom, stable for four horses with a loft over and a well. When William died in 1911 he was described as a retired carpenter. He had six children. Three of them sold the two cottages by auction for £470 to their cousins, William and Charles Harding, sons of Lois Baker and Richard Harding, who were millers, of Ifield Mill, Sussex. Charles left his share of the cottages to his brother, whose widow sold them to Farnham United Breweries in 1934, so that the company then owned all of William Baker's former property at the Anchor and Horseshoes. Farnham United Breweries were acquired by Courage & Co Ltd in 1927.

In the years after Lois died there was great change with people running the pub for two or three years and then moving on. The census of 1891 shows Lawrence Lickfold, his wife Mary and two sons living at the pub, describing him as victualler and carpenter. It is possible that he was employed by Messrs Lascelles Tickner and took over after Lois's death in 1889 and was still there in 1895.

In the records of the Guildford Petty Sessional Division about licensed premises in 1892 the Anchor and Horseshoes is described as '*fully licensed, owned by the Executors of Mrs Allwright; the licensee is Laurence Lickfold, who is residing on the premises; being a free house; having accommodation for travellers and persons requiring refreshment other than drink; stabling provided; for the use of the general public*'. A later record in 1904 said that the public house was tied to Lascelles, Tickner & Co and the licensee was Henry

Johnstone; trade was described as fair; it had four bedrooms; and stabling for four horses.

Publicans at the Anchor & Horseshoes changed fairly regularly over the years following Lois' death:

1899	Alfred Kent
1901	Edwin Blake
1903	Henry Johnstone
1905	George Tilbury
1907	William Henry Ivins
1909	Charles Best
1911-1915	Frank Sawyer
1918-1922	Benjamin Gravenstock

Anchor & Horseshoes c. 1930 (G Dye)

In 1924 the Horse Shoe & Anchor public house was managed by William F Lintott until the early 1930s, then Mrs Mary Lintott for the next ten years and Robert Lintott, presumably their son, during the 1950s. Possibly this was the same family who had run Bower's Mill in 1881. There was also a Herbert Lintott, recorded as a beer retailer in Wood Street in 1927, so maybe the family had brewing connections. Kelly's Directory didn't record who the publican was during the 1960s and 1970s, but later managers included Roy and Kay, Edward Gibson and Simon Watson.

Anchor & Horseshoes c. 1980s (BCA)

Since the 1930s various improvement schemes have been proposed for the London Road and one, in 1932, would have put a new road to the south of the inn and through its garden, marooning the pub on a traffic island with the existing road to the north. There were also plans to rebuild the inn entirely in 1934, but neither plan ever happened, although substantial alterations and extensions were made in 1968.

In 1954 a small plane crashed into the garden of the pub. Derek Oliver remembered, when he was a small boy, watching the fuselage being removed from the site. The Yorkshire Evening Post of 11th

January 1954 reported: '*COUPLE IN PLANE CRASH, SATISFACTORY PROGRESS. Mr Kenneth Owen, a journalist and his passenger, Miss Adam, were making satisfactory progress in hospital at Guildford (Surrey) today after escaping when their Gemini aircraft crashed on a flight from Yorkshire. Mr Owen and Miss Adam, who were returning to London from a weekend visit to Leeds, are expected to leave hospital in a few days. The aircraft was almost sliced in two when it crashed in the garden of the Anchor and Horseshoe Inn, Burpham (Surrey), after its wing hit a row of trees*'. John Oliver and Frank Phillipson provided more information, noting that the plane landed on the rose pergola in the pub garden; Kenneth Owen and Suzette Adam were thrown through the plane's windscreen on impact; and the St John's Ambulance and fire engine arrived quickly to the scene, colliding on the London Road (with no injury to the two crews). Kenneth and Suzette married in 1955 and were living in Godalming in 2005.

Oliver John Mason remembered that in the 1970s the pub was divided into two halves – the public bar and the saloon bar. His parents met in the pub, where his mother was a barmaid, and then they bought a house in Charlock Way. His father, Bob, was a local builder, who built the Old Smithy house almost next door to the pub. The Anchor and Horseshoes was a good meeting place if looking for building works, as most of the local tradesmen met there. Allen Mead and John Pidgeon remembered that it was also a meeting place for young people and was often the starting point for stag nights.

The modern pub is a managed John Barras pub restaurant and since 2006 has been the only pub in the village. Some extensions to the bar space were added in the 1980s, providing more space between the bar and the garden. The pub garden is a lovely area for people to enjoy the fresh air, to take children and, more recently, for smokers to indulge. There is a flourishing charity committee that organises events for fundraising, which have bought a range of resources for Burpham Homes, the Royal Surrey County Hospital and the Chelsea Pensioners among other charities. There are regular quiz nights and a Christmas draw as well as live music once a month and the pub offers good food for anyone wanting to eat there.

The new manager in 2016 reported that while looking in the attics of the pub building she had come across several horseshoes - possibly more evidence that the blacksmith's shop was part of the pub at one time? Around the same time part of the front car park collapsed and during the repair works it was discovered that there had been a well there, probably the well mentioned in old wills.

Anchor & Horseshoes 2015

PUBLIC HOUSES – 3 The New Inn

One last question remains about public houses in Burpham. On John Seller's map, dated c.1690, the crossroads of London Road and Burpham Lane was shown as Burpham Cross. Just below there was a New Inn marked, which was approximately where either New Inn Farm or the Anchor & Horseshoes are now. This could have been New Inn Farm and the cartographer left the word Farm off his map, or it could have been an inn. No other public house was marked for Burpham. So, the question is – does New Inn refer to New Inn Farm or a newly opened public house, and if the latter, then which one? Of course it is quite possible that the New Inn referred in fact to the Green Man and that it was there at the turn of the 16th and 17th centuries. The Licensed Victuallers records of 1785-1826 only have the Green Man and the Anchor & Horseshoes in Burpham.

As Mark Sturley noted in his book '*The site of the Green Man was subject to a lease for one thousand years, dated March 25th 1593, at a rent of 2/5d per suit of court and heriot*'. Was that lease for an inn or a farm or just a piece of land? Unfortunately it has not been possible to clarify who made the lease or whether it was for something specific. However, he also noted that there was a lease, dated March 10th 1752, from Lord Onslow to Thomas Longhurst, lately occupied by John Attfield. Thomas Longhurst was a farmer, of Longhurst Farm, in 1790 and John Attfield was the publican at the Green Man in 1754, so perhaps the evidence leans towards the New Inn being the Green Man about a century earlier. Or it could be that

the Anchor & Horseshoes was actually an inn in the 17th century. The
answer may never come to light.

John Seller's Map 1690 (Surrey History Centre)

THE VILLAGE BLACKSMITH

The village blacksmith or farrier was a central part of agricultural life and the forge was usually found in the middle of the community, often near to the village green. Until relatively recently, Burpham consisted of only London Road and Burpham Lane, and the blacksmith lived and worked on the London Road. The blacksmith made essential items such as tools and nails, but also repaired farm implements. Central to the blacksmith's work was the anvil, where he hammered hot metal in order to create whatever the community required. Usually dressed in a leather apron, to protect him from the sparks, he (and it was traditionally a man's job, though in modern times there are female blacksmiths as well) usually worked as a farrier as well, shoeing horses. In 1890 a scheme for registration of shoeing smiths was introduced, requiring farriers to pass an examination. In World War I many of these qualified shoeing smiths went to serve with the Royal Horse Artillery. After the war, with the increase in mechanisation of farm equipment and use of motor vehicles for transport, many garages and small engineering firms sprang up on former blacksmith's premises.

One of the earliest records of the Burpham blacksmith found so far was the Last Will and Testament of George Heath of Worplesdon, who died in 1772. He left most of his estate to his son 'George Heath of Worplesdon aforesaid Blacksmith'. Quite when the younger George became the Burpham blacksmith is not known, but in 1743 he was apprenticed to John Ledbetter, Blacksmith of Stoke, Surrey for a year, for the premium of £10 10s 0d. He was born in 1729 to

George and Mary Heath of Worplesdon. In 1755, he was recorded as living in Stoke next Guildford when he married Mary Birt. They had several children, one of whom was James, born in 1767. George's burial record at St Mary's, Worplesdon in 1793, clearly states that he was the blacksmith and lived in Burpham. However, as mentioned in the previous chapter, he had two jobs, being recorded in the listings of Jury Qualified Freeholders for Worplesdon in 1792 as an Inn Holder and in the Licensed Victuallers Register for 1785 as a publican in Worplesdon, presumed to be the Anchor and Horse Shoes.

Smithy on Chertsey Street (B Martin)

Little has been found about George's son James but he married twice, firstly to Elizabeth Howard in 1790 and then, following her death, to Hannah Jelley in 1801. Elizabeth died in 1798, aged 24 years, having had three children, two of whom died in infancy, but the third child, George, grew up to become the blacksmith in Chertsey Street, Guildford, possibly owning the smithy pictured. As with his father before him James had two jobs - the Licensed Victuallers Registers from 1793 to 1826 showed James to be the publican of the Anchor & Horse Shoes, whilst the Jury Qualified Freeholders listings for 1797 to 1824 showed him as Blacksmith. When he died in 1829, James' Last Will and Testament stated that he was a Blacksmith of Worplesdon and left his estate to his widow Hannah and all his children.

The oldest of these was also called James, born in 1801 in Worplesdon (most probably at the cottage next to the pub), and he had four sisters and five brothers, including step-siblings. One was Lois, born in 1806, who married William Baker and then James Allwright, and ran the Anchor & Horseshoes for about 50 years. Another was Hannah, born in 1803 but never married. She was living with Lois and William in 1841 and died in 1850. On the Tithe Maps of 1838 James Heath was recorded as owning and occupying a cottage and land on London Road, just along from the Anchor and Horseshoes public house. However, the map seemed to show two or three buildings on the plot of land so possibly there was a forge as well as a dwelling. Behind this was a field, belonging to the Earl of Onslow but occupied by Hugh Russell, called Horse Shoe Field. James was also recorded in the Land Tax Assessments twelve years previously, but although he owned the property he occupied it did not say that it was a blacksmith's forge, just a dwelling house and outbuildings.

In 1825 James married Ann Blishen at St Mary's Church and one of the witnesses was his sister Lois. They had 15 children, the youngest of whom was only a baby when her father died and three, including twin boys, had died in infancy. The census of 1841 showed the family living on Portsmouth Road (now London Road), but did not give a house name or number - there were eight children and a lodger living there with them. James died in 1846, aged 44 years, and by the 1851 census Ann was shown as Head of the Family, a widow of 47 years of age, living with four children, a nurse and a servant. Her son Samuel was recorded as blacksmith and the servant, George Steel, was his assistant. By 1861 Ann and three children had moved to Paddington and she died in 1882 in Wandsworth.

It is not known exactly how long Samuel continued as blacksmith, but according to emigration records he left for New York in 1855 and from there to Ontario in Canada. He married Mary Jane Burnett in Canada and they had eleven children. According to Canadian census records he continued working as a blacksmith until his death there in 1903.

By 1861 the census records showed the Burpham blacksmith to be Charles Puttock. Charles was born to Richard and Sarah Puttock in Albury in 1818. He was married in 1853 to Caroline Edmead, a widow. Her maiden name was Gosling, she came from Westcott and she had previously been married to Henry Edmead, a pastry cook. So started three generations of the same family, and the same name, working as the Burpham blacksmith. Charles and Caroline had one son, also called Charles, who was born in 1857. Caroline's son, William Henry Edmead and also a blacksmith, was living with them as well.

By 1871 the younger Charles was recorded as Assistant Smith at the age of 13 years. Clearly he had to grow up quickly, taking on responsibility for the business after his father was admitted to the Brookwood Asylum in October 1876, suffering from dementia. Perhaps the business was not doing well at the time, because he was described in the Brookwood records as a pauper. He died in the asylum in March 1878 aged 59 years and was buried at St Luke's. The young Charles was working with William Edmead, who by then was married to Rachael with three children, and living next door, recorded as a Blacksmith Journeyman. A journeyman was

Smithy on Upper High St in Guildford c. 1900
(D Rose)

someone who had completed their apprenticeship in a trade or craft, but was not yet a master. Charles the elder had been recorded as a Master blacksmith. No photos of the original Burpham smithy have been found but it is likely that it looked very like the ones in Upper High Street or Chertsey Street.

The 1881 census showed the young Charles as Blacksmith, living at Rose Cottage on London Road with his widowed mother, Caroline, and his nephew Henry Charles Edmead (son of William), who was also a blacksmith, aged 16 years. This Charles Puttock ran the smithy business for nearly 30 years. He married Mary Jane Hill in 1882 and they had two children, Charles Robert and Agnes Constance. Henry Edmead continued to work with Charles, living next door, firstly with his father William and family, then with his wife Mary and their son Basil. The Kelly's Directory of 1909 still had Charles recorded as blacksmith on London Road.

By 1911 the rise of motor vehicles (in 1915 the building now known as Chessington Tyres was owned by Joseph Binsted, Motor Engineer) meant that the smithing business was running down and Charles Puttock was recorded in the census of that year as a colt trainer, living at Addison Road in Guildford with his wife and children. However, Henry Edmead was recorded as living at Anchor Cottage, London Road and still working as a blacksmith, but it is not clear where he worked. In 1914 Charles was living at Bowers Mill Cottages, then from 1919 to 1936 he lived at Bowers Mill Lodge, first with his wife and son until 1923, then with his wife alone. The youngest Charles Puttock, who had been born in 1885, worked with his father as an apprentice blacksmith and then joined him working

88

as a colt trainer from Addison Road. He lived with his parents until 1923 and then dropped out of sight apart from a record of his death in 1976, aged 91 years. It is not clear whether or not he married but there was a Charles R Puttock living in Grantley Road with, presumably, his wife Susan M E Puttock in 1945, so this could have been him.

In June 1937 the Sunderland Daily Echo reported that *'As a plane was landing in Stoke Park, Guildford, last night in connexion with an air display to be given tomorrow in aid of Royal Surrey County Hospital it struck an 80 year old blacksmith, who died three hours later in that hospital. He was Charles Puttock, of Walnut Tree Close, Guildford. The pilot of the plane, Mr Enger Brand, aged 28, whose address was given as c/o Mayford Aerodrome, Colchester Road, Romford, had as passenger Mr Edward Cox, of the same address.'* Charles' wife, Mary Jane, had died in October 1936 and it seems that he moved to Walnut Tree Close afterwards, but still travelled back to Burpham, probably to drink at his old local pub, the Anchor & Horseshoes.

The Earl of Onslow was a good landlord who ensured that his properties were insured and in 1903 the Hand in Hand Fire & Life Insurance Society insured the *'dwelling house on London Road, brick built and slated and private in occupation of Mr Charles Puttock, smithy and outbuildings, brick built and tiled, for £325 at an annual premium of six shillings.* The big sale of properties owned by the Earl in 1905 included a small freehold estate, having a long frontage to London Road along with a dwelling house containing seven rooms with garden and pigsty. Also included were a farrier's shop with loft over, stable for two horses, a chaise house and arable and woodland attached. The cottage, smithy and garden were let to Mr C Puttock for a rent of £28 pa.

By 1915 the smithy building was the home for Binsted Bros, Builders and it seems that they stayed there until the Second World War.

During the second world war the smithy building was used to make prams. In 1944 an advert in the Surrey Advertiser told of Board of Trade Control of Perambulator repair prices. The old smithy was at the time known as the Utility Motor Company (Perambulator Dept), of London Road, Guildford. The advert went on to say that '*no matter how dilapidated your perambulator may be, we can renovate it like new*', clearly implying that the company complied with the legal prices whilst providing high quality.

In January 1953 sale particulars for The Old Forge, London Road, Burpham gave the address as 178A London Road, saying that the property was registered first with a possessory title in 1921. The freehold building had mains utilities on site (electricity, gas, water and drainage). The forge building was constructed in brick under a tiled roof, part of the floor was concreted and double doors opened directly on to the road verge, with a second set of double doors that opened onto a common right of way on the south side. The size was 1036 sq. ft., with a frontage of 25ft to the London Road and the depth was 30ft 3ins. Abutting to the rear was a brick built lean-to outbuilding with corrugated iron roof and concreted floor, with a single door to the common right of way. It had planning approval for light industrial work. It had a shared drive, for which the

90

maintenance costs were shared with Rose Cottage and also numbers 180 & 182 London Road, which were also being sold at the same time. However, the sale particulars for the latter two cottages made no mention of anything to do with either the blacksmith's business or the public house. They had three bedrooms upstairs with sitting and dining rooms downstairs, plus a bathroom and outside toilet.

The Old Forge and Rose Cottage in 2016

Kelly's Directories in 1955 showed Gerald Spyer, an Antique Dealer at that address, then from about 1957 to 1963 it was home for Peter Scarfe, Special Occasion Catering and Bakers. In the mid-1960s there was a company called Clear Design based there, but from 1967 onward Kelly's had no entry for this address.

Phil Dart remembered that a Mr Griffiths possibly ran a light engineering company there, then Mr McAdam ran a small print works there. In 1986 Mark Allen bought the property from a man who had a mail order business, for his company Guildford Signs, which has continued there until 2017. These days it is not possible to identify anything in the building as being part of the smithy. Improvements were made to the building, adding a new front and new floor. However, before the new floor was put down Mark says that the place where the forge would have been could be seen clearly. Then, when the owners of Rose Cottage, next door, wanted to dig up their drive a few years ago they discovered lots of old horseshoes and also the rings in the ground that horses would be tied to whilst being shoed.

BOWER'S MILL

The Domesday Book recorded that there was a mill in Burpham in 1086 but it wasn't until 1729 that it appeared on a map (by John Senex), then in 1768 (John Rocque), and both described it as a Paper Mill. It is interesting that the Burpham mill was not recorded on the John Seller map of 1690, when both Stoke and Clandon Mills were clearly marked. However, the Ordnance Survey map of 1811 showed an Oil Mill on the site. Oil-rich vegetables, such as linseed or sunflower, were milled, using millstones to crush the seeds, which could then be pressed to extract the oil. The Tithe Maps of 1838 show Bowers Mills on land owned by the Earl of Onslow with the

Tithe Map of 1838

occupier being William Francis Pimm, a noted land-owner of the time, but no detail was given about who was the miller. The electoral register of 1835 showed Samuel Kidd to be the occupier of the mill. It is interesting that the map clearly says 'Mills', so does this mean that there really were two mills on the same site?

During medieval times mills were governed by "milling soke", which was part of each Manor's charter. The mill was the property of the Lord of the Manor, who therefore had a monopoly over milling. Villagers were required to grind their corn at the Lord's mill, paying a toll, which was normally about 1/16th of the flour. Millers were often unpopular members of the community, being accused of taking more flour than they were entitled to. This led to changes in practice so that the miller bought the grain from the villagers and then sold the flour back to them. This then meant that mills had to be enlarged in order to have additional storage space.

Watermills generally consisted of three storeys. A hoist was used to lift the full sacks of grain up to the top floor, where they were stored in bins before being released to the middle floor. There the grain was ground between millstones, driven by the waterwheel. The flour was collected in bags on the ground floor. The miller's work was hard and skilled. He had to lift heavy sacks of grain and flour as well as maintaining the mechanisms of the mill. Millstones wore down, and needed to be 'dressed', a frequent job that had to be done in the evenings when the main work was finished. With the introduction of steam power, water and windmills started to close down as they could not compete with the new mills that began to dominate the flour trade in the 1880s, often using imported grain at the ports.

Three sources include some information about Bower's Mill, but some details differ between two of the accounts. According to Derek Stidder's book The Watermills of Surrey (1990), 'There is no documentary evidence to suggest that this was an ancient mill site and the first mention of the mill was in 1733, when it was apparently a Paper Mill. There was also a corn mill, for in 1779 the occupier, Daniel Eaton, insured the contents of both paper and corn mills for £1000.

Paper-making was discontinued soon after and in 1793 only corn was milled, by Benjamin and Richard Kidd. On the First Edition of the Ordnance Survey map of 1816 the site is marked as an oil mill and it was also marked as such on Froggett's map of 1831. It appears that linseed oil production ceased here soon after, since the site was recorded solely as a corn mill in 1831, in the occupation of Thomas Chandler. In the Tithe Apportionment of 1841, William Holden was the occupier, followed by Thomas Peerless in 1845, John Holden in 1847, until Edward Childs took over in 1870, with the firm of Lintott & Sons continuing until 1877. Towards the end of the 19th century it was converted into a roller mill, by the milling firm of Messrs Ranger & Burrows. A trade magazine chronicles the change in machinery and records it as a 'Turner Roller System' installed in 1890 and powered by the extant breastshot waterwheel, 16ft in diameter by 12ft wide. Messrs Ranger & Burrows were in control until 1899 after which the firm was renamed Ranger & Co, but by 1910 milling had ceased. The lease was advertised for sale but was never taken up.

A report on the state of the mill in 1932 recorded that it was timber-framed, rectangular and low, with brick up to the first floor then weatherboarding under a tiled roof, which was all in a state of disrepair. The mill building was demolished in 1945 and the timber removed to the estate of the Duke of Sutherland, who lived at the nearby Sutton Place. The building now on the site was originally built as a laundry for Sutton Place but was eventually converted to a private home.

Water power for the mill was provided from the River Wey Navigation at a point to the south of Bower's Lock. The lock gates bear the date 1933 and therefore it was probable that the mill race, and other associated watercourses, were removed at the same time.'

Bower's Mill about 1900 (W Durlacher)

According to the 1881 census Henry Lintott was still at the mill, with two pupil millers and one qualified miller working with him, so presumably he did not give up until after that date. Then in the Kelly's Directory of 1924 there was a William F Lintott managing the Horse Shoe & Anchor public house in Burpham. He must have died in the early 1930s as Mrs Mary Lintott was recorded as managing from 1934 to the late 1940s, when Robert Lintott took over, running the pub until the early 1960s. It is possible that this was the same family, diversifying with the demise of milling in the early 20th century.

J Hillier's book on Old Surrey Water-Mills (1951) says that '*although a paper-mill in Rocque's day, it began as a corn-mill (it is one of the Domesday mills) and, judging by the existing buildings, reverted to corn-milling in its last phase. The buildings still standing are of comparatively recent date, of that plain unadorned shape that seems to have been the rule for any mill erected after, say, 1880, with the staring red brick and graceless windows that belong to the completely "machine-made" mill, as contrasted with the earlier locally built mill, that had an individuality as decided as that of the village church. Traces of the older mill are visible on the end wall of the present building, and the present occupant of the mill cottage indicated where it stood, and the position of the wheel, just below the modern lock. The lock gates bear the date 1933, no doubt the date when the last traces of the mill-race, -wheel and older buildings were removed. The existing building is used, I was told, as a "laundry for the Duke"'*.

Alan Crocker's (Surrey Industrial History Group) information about Bower's Mill notes that '*the earliest known specific reference to this paper mill is a fire insurance policy taken out in 1733 by Thomas Hillyer. However, four years earlier a Thomas Hillyer papermaker of Worplesdon purchased a messuage called the Cyder House at Shalford. This house still exists and also features in the history of Stoke and Chilworth paper mills. Thomas Hillyer appears to have* died shortly after taking out the 1733 insurance policy as in November of that year Mary Hillyer, widow of Bower's Mill, insured her new paper mill called Down Mill. Then in 1783 John Hillyer of Bower's Mill papermaker, eldest son and heir of Thomas Hillyer late of the same place papermaker deceased, and Mary Hillyer of the same, widow, sold the Cyder House. Meanwhile in 1737 John Maidman papermaker of Worplesdon was at the marriage of Mary Hillyer of Bower Mill. This was presumably John Hillyer's sister and it is interesting that John Maidman also appears in the Shalford parish registers in 1716 and 1722.

The next papermaker was William Drury who in 1759 insured the household goods in his dwelling house and the utensils and stock in his brick and timber paper mill for £1000. Five years later he took on an apprentice Leonard Barker but in 1773 Daniel Eaton papermaker insured the contents of the house, mill and raghouses, including his wearing apparel, for £1,100. In a further policy of 1779 Daniel Isaac Eaton of Bower's Mill was described as a papermaker and miller when he insured the equipment and materials in his paper mill, corn mill, workshops, warehouses, raghouses and dwelling houses for £1,600. A year later when Eaton purchased the copyhold of the mill he was described as a mealman. In addition the land tax for the paper mill which was paid by Eaton decreased from £40 in 1780 to £10 in 1781. Between 1784 and 1789 William King paid the land tax "for ye paper mill" but in 1790 this was changed to "for land at ye paper mill" and from 1791 to 1798 it was paid by John Pimm. It is interesting that the 1794 Worplesdon land tax records are written on paper with the watermark "W King" but this could have been the William King who was at Alton Mill at this time.

In addition the Pimms were a well known family of papermakers at Bramshott and Barford and a "J Pimm" watermark occurs in the Stoke d'Abernon land tax paper of 1800. Also a booklet of lottery tickets has been discovered printed on paper with the watermark "EM" with the statement that they were used for E Marter by W I Pimm of Bower's Mill in 1794. However, it appears that papermaking at Bower's Mill died out in the 1790s and an insurance policy of 1793 refers simply to a corn mill at the site. This was rebuilt in the late 19th century and then converted into an attractive house.'

Bower's Mill by Bower's Lock 2015

However, a document from 1726 shows that a Grant of Annuity was given by the Rt Hon Thomas, Lord Onslow, to Vere Beauclerc, one of the brothers of the Most Noble Charles, Duke of St Albans: *'The two separate Manors and demesnes of Worplesdon and Burpham with the Manor House called Burfum Court with all its rights members and appurtenances in Burpham occupied by Richard Butler, the farmhouse, lands and appurtenances in the occupation of John Butler in Burpham and two watermills with appurtenances in the occupation of Hilliar in Burpham'.* The arrangement was that Beauclerc gave Onslow £3,500 and in return Lord Onslow granted him a life annuity of £310, payable annually in the common dining hall of the Inner Temple in London. This is the only reference found so far to there being two mills in Burpham and is also the oldest mention of milling in the vicinity apart from the Domesday entry. It does sound like Alan Crocker's description of Thomas Hillyer. Norman Hamilton wrote that *'The Hillyers were noted Guildford stationers.'*

Baptism records for St Mary's show that in the 1820s William Francis Pimm was the miller at Bower's Mill, when three of his four children were baptised there.

Census records from 1901 showed that Bower's Mill was home to the Miller and Corn Merchant, Robert Ranger and his family. Presumably they actually lived in Bower's Mill House next door as the mill was still working at that time. Robert's wife Emily, five of their twelve children and a nursemaid shared the house with William Russell Burrows, Robert's brother-in-law, who was recorded as a miller and corn merchant, as well as being a partner in the firm, and his wife. William Burrows was 20 years younger than Robert so may have moved away and worked somewhere else, but there is no record of him staying in Burpham by 1911. In the summer of 1909 the Ranger family suffered a family bereavement when their youngest son, Edward Sidney and only eight years old, was drowned in the river. He had been a pupil at the new Burpham Primary School since it opened the previous year. There are areas of sandy beach along the river from Bower's Lock so perhaps he had been playing there when the accident happened. Part of the school was closed so that his school friends could attend the funeral at St Luke's.

The firm of R Ranger & Co delivered their produce by lorry around the local community. Perhaps their drivers weren't as careful as they should be as a photograph from 1907 shows the lorry, which had crashed into a shop window - Edwins in North Street in Guildford (see chapter on Road, Rail and Transport).

Records in the Kelly's Directories still had Ranger & Co running the mill in 1909 but by 1911 the census recorded that the only occupier of the mill was Thomas Bicknell, who worked as the caretaker of the corn mill. The 1911 census showed Robert, his wife and eight children living in Sydney Road in Guildford, along with his son in law and two servants. He was 60 years old and recorded as a retired miller and corn merchant. What happened to Robert Ranger after that is not known, but he died in 1928, aged 77 years, and the record of his burial at St Luke's Church showed that his last address was Netherne Merstham. This refers to Netherne Hospital, which was founded in 1905 as the Surrey County Asylum, so perhaps he never got over his young son's death and the demise of his work. Robert's will showed his address to be Woodbridge Road in Guildford, and presumably that was where his family lived at the time. His wife, Emily, moved at some point to Walton on Thames, where she died in 1938, but was also buried at St Luke's.

Bower's Mill House, next door to the mill, is where the miller and his family lived. Over the years various mill workers lived in the cottages along what is now Bower's Lane, but was originally the Jacob's Well Road or Burpham Lane. The Duchess of Sutherland was very keen on providing a good standard of accommodation for the estate workers and was responsible for the installation of bathrooms in many of the workers' cottages. The Duke of Sutherland, who bought Sutton Place in 1919, living there until 1959, owned the mill and the mill house and used the mill as a laundry, with his laundry workers living in the house. Mamie Grover remembered that when he visited his estates in Scotland all the dirty laundry was sent by train to Bower's Mill for washing and ironing, and then back to Scotland by train. In 1915 the Surrey Advertiser told readers that The Mill House, Burpham, was '*to be let, unfurnished, with early possession*'. It was described as being pleasantly situated near the River Wey, with three reception, six bedrooms; stabling, garden, croquet lawn, cottage and about nine acres of grass land if desired.

Bower's Mill House 2015

In the early to mid 20th century Roy and Percy Howard, local Burpham builders, did most of the decorating in the mill. The brick building is now painted white but it is not clear if they did this as well. The Howards also did all the maintenance for Sutton Place, but had to give up when they became over-committed.

Bower's Lodge in 1950s (W Durlacher)

Mr & Mrs Raphael bought Bower's Mill in 1958 and were told that when the Duke owned the mill there was apparently a big barn behind the mill building. It is likely that this was where the corn was stored before milling or flour stored before delivery. The Mill is now owned by Mr & Mrs Raphael's daughter, Mrs W Durlacher. Mr & Mrs Eliott bought Bower's Mill House in 1957. Mrs June Eliott remembered that when they moved there Burpham Lane had a ditch on either side and was just fields all around. There is an old oak tree on the towpath by the mill with an iron band round the trunk, which Mr Eliott put there in order to hold the trunk together. The National Trust notice on the towpath says "*there is the hollow trunk of a large oak tree, bound by an iron hoop, thought to be 250-350 years old, which possibly started growing at the same time as the Navigation was built*". Oliver Mason recalled that the children used to call the tree 'the fairy tree'.

Oak tree on the towpath by Bower's Lock (T Bass)

Mr Vincent owned the old house right opposite the drive to the mill, with a field attached, and he did market gardening, but the house was demolished and rebuilt. When Clay Lane was built some of the Mill House's land had to be sold because the new road went straight through it. Mrs Eliott recalled how people used to play water polo in the lock in the 1950s and 1960s. She also remembered Mr Bollins, who lived in one of the old cottages on Bower's Lane and used to look after the polo ponies for the Duke of Sutherland. Also, she said

104

that the bridge over the river by Bower's Lodge, which was the main road from Burpham to Jacob's Well and Worplesdon, was a Bailey Bridge put in by the military during World War II. She remembered Sutton Place as a place to visit when it was owned by Paul Getty. Visitors could admire the gardens and musicales were held, open to anyone who wanted to attend an evening of musical entertainment. The Mill House is now owned by Mr & Mrs Eliott's daughter Ros Pollock and her husband.

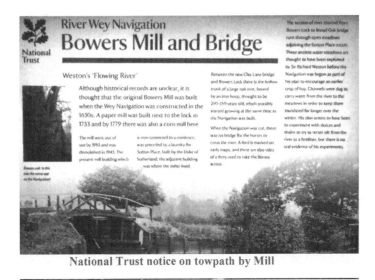

National Trust notice on towpath by Mill

All the information found refers to Bower's Mill(s), but who was Bower? The only possibilities found so far are for a Thomas Bower, whose name appeared in the Court Baron minutes of 1645 and also in the Hearth Tax of 1664, suggesting that he was a man of some wealth. There was also an indenture (legal contract) of 1641 between John Wyrley and Thomas Bower of Worplesdon. Assuming that these are both the same man, perhaps the mill was named after him?

BRICKMAKING

Bricks can be made wherever there is clay and sand, and brickworks were scattered throughout Surrey. Clay pits were often dug to make bricks for an individual house and some of these survive as ponds adjacent to the buildings. Women and children helped the men in the brickfields. In brickmaking the clay was dug and then left to weather prior to being put into a

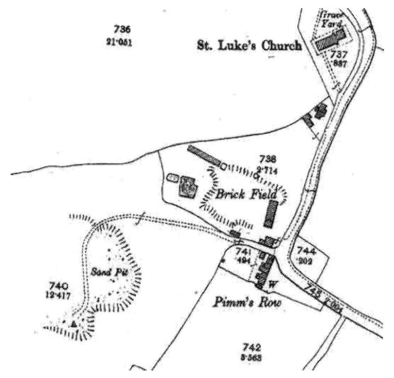

Brickfield on Burpham Lane 1895 (OS map) with sand pit

'pugging' machine, which cut and kneaded it. It was then thrown into wooden moulds from which the 'green' bricks were removed, ready for firing. The bricks were fired in clamps, in which the stacked bricks were covered with old bricks and turf. Fuel was packed throughout the stacks and then ignited. Since the bricks were fired at different temperatures depending on where they were in the stack, a wide variety of brick colours resulted. In the 19th century bricks were usually made near the sites of housing developments. Some farmers ran a pottery business on the side, using wagons to fetch the clay and deliver the pots to market for sale.

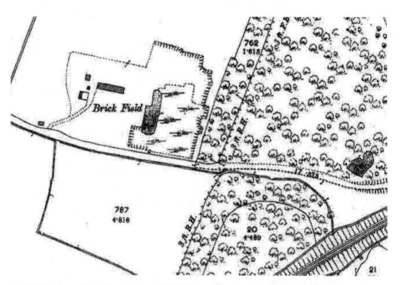

Brickfield on New Inn Lane 1895 (OS map) showing railway line in bottom right corner and pond in the woods on right

According to old Ordnance Survey maps there were two brickfields in Burpham by 1895, though there was nothing shown on the maps of 1869. One was on the left of New Inn Lane going towards Merrow and would have been part of the Winterhill Farm estate. The other was on the left of Burpham Lane going towards the church, just past Pimm's Row, where there are now cottages and their gardens. In the field behind Pimm's Row was the sand pit, providing an essential ingredient for making bricks. In 1905 the brickfield on New Inn Lane was included in the sale of Lord Onslow's properties. The description stated that the brickfield contained valuable brick earth including a large tile making shed. The plot was 17 acres and was let to Mr T Marshall and Mr G A Franks.

In December 1909 there was a clearance sale at the Burpham brickyard, due to the termination of the tenancy and dissolution of the partnership with New Inn Brickyard. Thousands of bricks, of various sizes and colours, both stock and ornamental bricks, were sold, along with 2,000 drain pipes. Mr C Standage of Clandon Estate Brickyard bought about 5,000 bricks.

In October 1883 there was a court case at the Old Bailey, in London, where George Dolley (aged 19 years) was accused of '*feloniously setting fire to a stack of furze the property of Thomas Slaughter*'. Although the furze stack in question seemed to have been on the Bower's Farm estate, one of the witnesses, George Stillwell, said '*I am a labourer at Worplesden, I was working in Mr Mitchell's brickfield at Burpham – I saw the prisoner coming along the road in the direction from the Green Man going in the direction of Burpham Church...*' presumably he worked at the brickfield near Pimm's Row.

Over the years many of the residents living in Pimm's Row Cottages worked in brickmaking. In 1871 William Jelley was

109

recorded as a bricklayer's labourer; in 1881 Henry Holt was a tile maker; in 1891 John Hoar was a brickmaker. In 1901 Albert Tidy was a carter in brickyard, Alfred Woods was a brickmaker, William Turner was a foreman brickmaker. In 1891 James Standage and John Mitchell, both living at Burgham Church Cottages, were brickmakers. Census records for Marlyn's Lodge showed William Lemon (1891) and George Thomas Howlett (1901/1911) as brickmakers, as was William Searle of Marlyn's Cottage (1881). The 1881 census entry for The Paddocks showed John Mitchell as a contractor brickmaker and perhaps he was the Mr Mitchell cited at the Old Bailey case, but clearly a man of some wealth and standing in the community.

In July 1899 the London Evening Standard reported '*Partnerships Dissolved. Wheeler and Hannay, Burpham Brickyard, nr Guildford, brickmakers.*'

BURPHAM COURT FARM

There had been some suggestion that Edward the Confessor's wife had owned the farm, but no evidence has been found to prove this. Part of the old cottages date back to around 1642 and many of the rafters in the barn look very ancient.

In 1641 Sir Francis Wolley leased Burgham Manor or farmhouse to Sir John Wirley and his wife Dame Mary (Wolley), and also to Thomas Bower of Worplesdon, gentleman. The lease included two acres called the Little Park and several other parcels of land in Worplesdon. However, there were exceptions to the lease, including: *'The Great Parlour and chamber over it, stable room for two geldings and barn room for two loads of hay, reserved to Dame Mary, also hunting and fishing rights, rights of entrance to cut timber, dig turf for making charcoal, make weirs for catching fish and set up any kind of mill, reserved to lessors.'* Possibly this was the Thomas Bowere after whom Bower's Mill was named?

In 1614 Henry Ripley alias Atfield died - he was a yeoman who owned various plots of land in and around Burpham. His will, as noted earlier, stated that he left to his wife use of a room in his house in Burpham Court *'for lease if she lives that long'*. In 1681 Denis Taylor died and his will stated that he was a gentleman living at Burpham Court. It is likely that both of these referred to what is now Burpham Court Farm.

Old maps of Worplesdon Parish showed Burpham Court Farm, but usually denoted as either just Burgham or Burgham Farm. The

Tithe Maps of 1838 showed Burham Farm with a number of buildings on the site, one of which was Burgham House, but there was no description for the other buildings. The Earl of Onslow owned the property and at that time it was occupied by William Francis Pimm, a local farmer and landowner. However, in the 1841 census he was also recorded as a farmer, living at Marlyn's on London Road, with his wife Mary and three children. It is likely that he was a tenant farmer for the Earl's land, but he actually lived at Marlyn's, while he employed people to live and work at the other farms. The same census recorded George Rothwell as an agricultural labourer at Burpham Court Farm, living with his wife Martha and two sons.

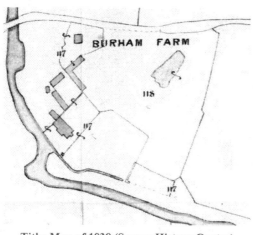

Tithe Map of 1838 (Surrey History Centre)

The layout of the farm buildings on the Tithe Map appear to show the two existing cottages and the barns, but not the current farmhouse. Various documents suggest that it is the cottages that are the oldest part of the farm and that the farmhouse is a Victorian addition. There also seems to be a pond near the road, probably the one currently by the entrance gate. The British Listed Buildings website records the cottages as early 17th century with 19th century extensions to the right end.

Burpham Court Farm cottages drawing 1977 (Surrey Advertiser)

By the 1851 census George Rothwell was recorded as being Farm Bailiff, so clearly had been promoted to look after the property and business for Mr Pimm. Not very long after that William Pimm decided to divest himself of some tenancies and John Christmas was shown in the 1861 census as farmer of 225 acres, employing seven men and four boys. John Christmas was born in Hampshire in about 1810 and his father was also a farmer called John Christmas. He married Jane Older in 1841 and they had four children, of whom his youngest and only daughter Jane was born in Worplesdon in 1854, so he must have been at Burpham Court Farm by then. Jane died in 1870 and John remarried in 1874, to

Eliza Older, a widow, in Effingham. She could have been related to Jane by marriage, but history does not record that detail.

17th Century house at Burpham Court Farm

Burpham Court Farm 17th century house (Norman Hamilton)

In March 1878 a document set out the letting of Burpham Farm by the Right Honourable William Hillier, Earl of Onslow, to John Christmas. This included plots of land around the farm buildings, bounded by the river on three sides and down to the back of the Chagden (Weylea) Farm fields, but not including Bower's Mill. The yearly rent was £170 in quarterly payments. The document was very specific including the following agreements by John Christmas '*I will cultivate and manage the whole of the said lands in a good husbandry like manner. I will not sow more than two crops of corn or pulse in succession on the same land. I will not sow more than half of the arable land with corn in any year; I will keep the whole land clean and free of weeds; cultivate annually with turnips, rape and mangold wurtzel; I will bring back one waggon load of good dung for every ton of hay or straw sold; not cut down any timber, fruit or other trees; not dig, procure nor sell any mines, minerals, chalk, gravel, stones; not grow more than half an acre of potatoes in any year.'*

The Christmas family stayed at the farm for around 40 years, with John's son Andrew recorded in the 1891 census as being the farmer. John had died early in 1890 and was buried at St Luke's. Andrew married Charlotte Hooker in 1890, just months after his father died, and they stayed at the farm until about 1895 and the next record put them living in Manor Road in Guildford, then Grange Road in 1911. Andrew died in 1912.

Bread oven on outer wall of
Burpham Court Farm house 2015

By 1895 Kelly's Directory recorded that Richard Blake was the farmer at Burpham Court. He was born in Cornwall in 1863, was married to Mary and they had two daughters. Having helped on his father's farm in Cornwall until the mid 1890s he then turned up in Burpham, where he ran Burpham Court Farm until about 1911, the last time he was mentioned there in either census or Kelly's records. By 1913 William Heard was the farmer and he remained there until about 1930. In 1916 the Surrey Advertiser reported that

William had been summonsed for *'exposing for sale in the Guild flesh of which after slaughter would be unfit for human consumption'*. The Town Clerk explained that the animal for sale had been suffering from parasitic gastro-enteritis. After pleading guilty William Heard had to pay costs of £1 5s.

The Hand in Hand Fire & Life Insurance Society records show that the Earl of Onslow insured Burpham Farm in 1903, including the house, brewhouse, barn, cattle shed, piggeries, shed, stable, coachhouse, cart shed, cowhouse, granary and cottage. Burpham Court Farm was one of the lots included in the big sale of Lord Onslow's properties in 1905. It was described in the sale particulars as *'Freehold manorial estate known as Burpham Court Farm and the Manor of Burpham, including an old manor house built of brick and tile roofed, containing two attics, four bedrooms, dressing room, two sitting rooms, kitchen, scullery, larder and cellars, with wash house, coal shed and tool shed outside...two cottages each containing four rooms and larder let to Mr R Blake at £174 p.a.'* It also said *'there will also be included in this lot the manor or reputed Manor of Burpham, with its rights and privileges'* though it didn't explain quite what these might have been. The rent roll of this manor showed nine freehold and five leasehold tenements held by the manor. The new Lord of the Manor would also have responsibilities as *'the owner of the Manor is liable for the repairs of two bridges crossing the River Wey'*. Finally, prospective purchasers were told that this was *'a very desirable purchase as a secure investment'*. The suggested price for this lot was £4,000 and notes on some sales particulars seem to say that it was been sold to someone called Soggel, but the records are not clear on this.

Burpham Court Farm outbuildings 2015

In the amendments to the Tithe Maps in 1920 the owner was recorded as the Duke of Sutherland. He bought up quite a large number of the Onslow properties, including this farm and the mill along the road. As William Heard was recorded as being farmer it is likely that he was a tenant farmer for the Duke. When the Duke sold Sutton Park and his other properties in 1959 ownership of the farm passed to Paul Getty for several years.

More recently, Peter and Mary Hill were recorded in the Electoral Register of 1965 as living at the farm. Perhaps they were tenant farmers under Paul Getty? By 1974 Nick and Alison Maiklem had taken over and stayed until about 1990, before moving down to the West Country. They ran a farm shop from the farm, selling produce. He would drive his cattle over the little bridge to get to the field in order to calve. Several people remember being held up on the road while the cows came over the bridge and that he had a bull called Angus.

Rafters in the barn at Burpham Court Farm 2015

The most recent history of the farm was reported in the Surrey Advertiser from 1992 onwards. Guildford Borough Council had acquired the land to save it from development *'we originally bought the land to protect a particularly vulnerable piece of green belt from development, having turned down a number of planning applications'.* Bob Dearnley took over as tenant farmer, setting up a rare breeds farm. Bob, with his then fiancée Margaret, brought in animals from around the country, including Manx sheep (brought over by the Vikings), Portland sheep (the rarest breed in Great Britain), Baggot sheep (brought over by the Crusaders), Middle White pigs and White Park cows (imported by the Romans). In later years there was also a family of llamas occupying the front paddock by the pond. Initially it had been very popular with over 20,000 visitors each year, but money was needed for renovation work and repairing damage. Many of the children from Burpham Primary School walked along the road to visit the farm and see the animals - such a wonderful opportunity for town children to learn about many of the farm animals that used to be part of everyday life in Burpham.

By 1995 the Surrey Advertiser reported that Bob and Margaret faced financial crisis and had to close the farm to visitors, selling endangered species for slaughter. It was a bad time to be selling stock as the lack of winter fodder had left many farmers offloading surplus animals. There were a number of problems with the farm, which included flooding, damage to farm roads and rabbits. According to a report in 1996 there were '*hordes of rabbits breeding on Slyfield, which systematically strip the grass from a quarter of the farm's pastureland*'. Once this was resolved it was possible for the farm to reopen that year and Bob hoped to replace many of the rare breeds that had been sold.

The summer of 1997 saw some rather different activities on the farm when:
'*musket fire shattered the peace of meadows where lambs normally frolic, when Napoleonic soldiers stormed the meadows of Burpham Court Farm at the weekend. Infantry resplendent in early 19th century scarlet uniforms, swelled by a smattering of smartly turned out cavalry, re-enacted some bloody skirmishes from Napoleon's campaigns*'. There were hundreds of sightseers watching the event and it was noted that firepower was restricted to muskets, not cannon. Bob penned his stock well away from the action for the day.

Burpham Court Farm Farmhouse 2015

In 1997 a sponsorship campaign started to raise money to cover the costs of keeping the animals, by which visitors could sponsor an animal for one year, receiving a certificate and ticket enabling them to visit the animal several times during the year. In 1998 Bob alleged that part of the farm had become polluted by the adjoining Slyfield landfill site. He said that 14 lambs had died and many had been born deformed due to contamination.

By 2006 Bob was claiming against the National Trust for flooding in his fields, saying that the farm had flooded 15 times in the 13 years to 1996 but the river had burst its banks 37 times since 2004. Sadly, all the problems and arguing led to Bob being declared bankrupt in 2006, after losing the court battle, and he was required to vacate the farm by September 2008. He said *'That's what they're saying but we won't be going anywhere. We're still fighting tooth and nail'*. With Bob's sudden death in May 2009 the farm was closed and all the animals were re-housed.

At the time of writing the farm is currently closed to visitors. In early 2016 Guildford Borough Council, in partnership with the Surrey Wildlife Trust, proposed to develop a Nature Reserve on the site, but there are also proposals to run the Clay Lane Link Road across the farmland. Local residents in both Burpham and Jacobs Well are fighting the idea of the link road.

CHURCHES

Church of England

St Mary's Church, Worplesdon

Before 1859, being part of the parish of Worplesdon, it was necessary for Burpham residents to travel about four miles to St Mary's Church in Worplesdon for their services. The booklet called A Brief History of St Luke's Church, Burpham explained '*Old parishes in Surrey were very large and Burpham was separated from its parish church by Whitmoor Common and the marshy valley of the Wey – the road liable to flood every winter. How they managed in the old days we do not know; but although Burpham was a small place a century ago, they had evidently decided that the distance was too great. They would have a church and a burying place of their own.*

A subscription list was opened, headed by patrons of the living of Worplesdon, The Provost and Fellows of Eton College. The Earl of Onslow gave the site, part of a field called the Short Seven Acres in Bowers Lane, measuring about three quarters of an acre in area, and work began in August 1858. The architect was a Mr

Woodyer of Graffham, and the builder Mr William Swayne of Stoke Road. The whole church was built for less than £1,000.

On a fine morning Tuesday 24th May 1859, the Lord Bishop of Winchester came over from Farnham Castle for the consecration (the diocese of Guildford was not formed until 1927). St Luke was chosen to be the Patron Saint, for reasons that are not recorded.

For the next sixty years, while Guildford and Woking were growing and other new parishes were being formed, St Luke's remained a Chapel of Ease to St Mary's Worplesdon. This enabled the farm workers and their families to attend church.

St Luke's Church 2015

In 1920 it was decided to make the separation from Worplesdon. As it did not seem practicable to join Burpham to other parts of *the growing neighbourhood of Guildford, it was joined instead to the southern part of the parish of St Peter's Old Woking (Send). It was not until 1954 that Burpham was formally made a Parish, and St Luke's approved by the Church Commissioners as the Parish Church.'*

It is not a big church, the nave measuring 75ft by 25ft and the chancel 26ft by 16ft. The walls are Bargate stone and the outside window facings, quoins and door facings are made from Bath stone. There is a small vestry on the north side of the chancel with an entrance from the outside. Originally there was a chalk stone pulpit but this was demolished in 1958, being replaced by an oak pulpit purchased from a parish in Bristol for £10. To start with, the organ was a pipe organ, which came from the Bishop's chapel in Farnham Castle, but this has now been replaced with an electronic one. However, a one-time worshipper at St Luke's remembered *'we had an elderly organist, who played an equally elderly harmonium in the chancel (later to be replaced by a small organ at the back of the church).'* The church porch was added in 1961, given by Mr & Mrs P Howard of Burpham. A lot of renovation was done inside the church before the centenary in 1959, mainly by T Swayne & Son Ltd, the successors to the original builder. Electricity was installed in the 1930s.

The church performed both baptisms and burials from the beginning and the first child to be baptised there was 'Lucy Chapman, daughter of James, a labourer, and Lucy Chapman of Burgham on 17th July 1859'. The first burial must have been a very sad occasion as it was a two year old child, Edward James

Alexander of Winter Hill Bottom on 30th June 1859. There doesn't seem to be any other record of this family in Burpham so perhaps they moved away after their son's death.

The Churchyard has some quite old tombstones that are still legible, including Lois Allwright of the Anchor & Horseshoes pub, John and Jane Christmas of Burpham Court Farm, Joseph Choat of New Inn Farm and Henry Graham Lintott of Bower's Mill. Among these is the grave of Sir William Stuart who died on 1st April 1896. His stone reads 'Knight Commander of the Order of St Michael & St George. Envoy extraordinary of Her Majesty the Queen in

St Luke's Church interior (Burpham 2000)

Athens and at The Hague'. Sir William never actually lived in the village itself, but at Sutton Park Cottage. Presumably it was felt that Burpham was the nearest Church of England church, though it is not known if he worshipped at St Luke's. His wife Georgina, who died in 1901, was also buried at St Luke's.

The War Memorial is just inside the main gate to the church, on Burpham Lane. It commemorates those in the community who lost their lives in both World Wars – 18 in the first and 11 in the second.

In 1921 St Luke's was licensed for the solemnization of marriages by the Lord Bishop of Winchester and the Common Seal of the Provost and College of Eton was affixed to the licence.

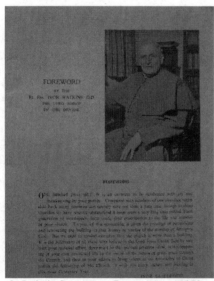

St Luke's Centenary Programme 1959 – Foreword (Surrey History Centre)

In 1957 a Conveyance between 'The Most Noble George Granville Sutherland Leveson Gower Duke and Earl of Sutherland KT PC, Royal Bank of Scotland, Church Commissioners for England and the Reverend Arthur William Henry Theodosius, incumbent of the Benefice of the Vicarage of Burpham with Sutton in the County of Surrey and Diocese of Guildford' set out the arrangements for a new vicarage in the village. This consisted of a 'parcel of land in the parish of Burpham in the County of Surrey containing .5 of an acre or thereabouts and

126

having a frontage of one hundred and twenty feet to Jacob's Well Road and a depth of one hundred and eighty feet' (opposite the entrance to Burpham Primary School). The cost of the land was £75 to come out of the Commissioners' 'Parsonage Fund'. Revd Theodosius left Burpham in 1957, moving to Hascombe, and it was his successor, Revd Douglas Bryant, who took on the project of building the vicarage. Later on a new Vicarage was bought in Orchard Road, then before Colin Matthews retired in 2011 the Vicarage moved to London Road, between Great Oaks Park and Mead Way.

BURPHAM

CHURCH SERVES 5,000

On Sunday St. Luke's Church, Burpham, had its 99th dedication festival. At the family Communion service in the morning the Archdeacon of Surrey, the Ven. A. J. de C. Studdert, gave the dedication sermon. In the afternoon there was a children's festival service. Evensong was conducted by the Vicar, the Rev. D. W. Bryant.

In his sermon the vicar pointed out the great change in the size of the congregation. When the church was built 100 years ago it was to serve a small rural hamlet, but it was now the parish church for about 5,000 people, and the number was still expanding. The church cost only £900 to build, and now they needed at least £500 for the centenary appeal to have it renovated.

The first offering day was held on Saturday for the centenary appeal, and money from collecting boxes brought in on that day and over the week-end amounted to £142. The second offering day is at the church's patronal festival on October 18th.

St Luke's 99th Dedication Festival 1958 (Surrey Advertiser)

In 1958 the church celebrated its 99th anniversary with a dedication festival. Noting the growing size of the community the church needed to raise funds for renovations and the vicar, Revd D W Bryant launched the Centenary Appeal.

1959 brought Centenary celebrations for the church and the programme set out a range of events between 31st May and 29th November. These included a Civic Service of Thanksgiving on Wednesday 3rd June, where the sermon was preached by The Revd Canon Roger Lloyd of Winchester. Then in 2009 there was a special 150th Anniversary Service held on St Luke's Day, led by the Right Revd Ian Brackley, Bishop of Dorking.

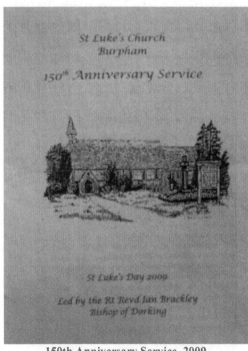

150th Anniversary Service 2009
(Surrey History Centre)

By this time it had become clear that with the village growing fast and spreading out along both sides of the London Road, the little parish church was quite a distance from housing estates like Glendale Drive and New Inn Farm so a second church was needed.

Parish papers from 1960 showed just a church hall on the New Inn estate. Revd Bryant asked for more money on the basis that if Burpham grew to a population of 5,000 then more financial help would be available. As the Great Oaks estate had just been built it was clear that the village would reach that number sooner rather than later. In September 1961 there was a Service of Dedication for the New Burpham Church Hall and Chapel of the Holy Spirit in New Inn Lane, led by The Lord Bishop of the

Church of the Holy Spirit from the back 2015

Diocese. Then in November 1965 came the Dedication of the Church of the Holy Spirit, led by the Lord Bishop of Guildford.

In the 1990s the children of Burpham Primary School held their annual Carol Services and Harvest Festival Services in St Luke's, until the numbers grew too great and it became necessary to move to the Church of the Holy Spirit as there was more room there.

In 2015 the Church of the Holy Spirit celebrated its 50th Anniversary. In recent years there have been many improvements made to the church and the adjoining hall, so that now all areas can be accessed from the same door.

There have been many curates and priests looking after the parishioners of Burpham since St Luke's opened in 1859. Their names appear in the registers of baptisms and burials.

Parish of Worplesdon:

Revd A W Thornton	1859 – 1867	Curate
Revd J Norton	1867 – 1869	
Revd N L Watson	1869 – 1871	
Revd H D Wyatt	1871 – 1877	
Revd W W Garrett	1877 – 1880	
Revd I E Horsley	1880 – 1888	
Revd J W Collett	1888 – 1913	
Revd J W Clarke	1913 – 1922	Priest in charge

Parish of Burpham with Sutton Green:

| Revd E C Storr | 1922 – 1927 |
| Revd A W H Theodosius | 1927 – 1954 |

Parish of Burpham:

| Revd Arthur W H Theodosius | 1954 – 1957 |

Revd Douglas W Bryant	1957 – 1971	
Revd Martin Hughes	1971 – 1988	
Revd David Williams	1988 – 1995	
Revd Canon Colin Matthews	1995 – 2011	
Revd James & Revd Jo Levasier	2011 –	Joint Vicars

Revd Theodosius 1952 (Surrey Advertiser)

Norman Hamilton reported people remembering Revd Collett, as the curate from Worplesdon, coming on a tricycle to take Sunday services at St Luke's Church. Apparently he would come for the early service and then have his breakfast in the vestry before taking the later service. Revd Arthur William Henry Theodosius was the Vicar for the people of Burpham for 30 years. He was born in Whitstable in 1895. His father was also a Church of England priest, who died in 1903 when Arthur was only eight years old, according to probate information '*in a railway carriage en route from St Moritz to England*'. Revd Theodosius lived for many years at the Vicarage at Pyle Hill in Sutton Green and was part of the agreement to build a vicarage in Burpham in 1957, although he didn't ever live there. He moved to become Rector at Hascombe, where he stayed for several years before retiring to live in Send from about 1967. He died in 1975 in Suffolk. His wife Margaret was another pillar of the Burpham community. She was one of the School Managers for Burpham Primary School and regularly went into the school to check the registers, a job that she continued after her husband moved, until her death in 1965.

Revd Douglas W Bryant (Surrey History Centre)

Norman Hamilton noted in his History of Burpham that Revd Theodosius *'used to run a car which was kept on the road with some difficulty by the Pantiles Garage, and was known to ring up at odd hours to announce that he was stranded without petrol.'* Another Burpham resident remembered him going round the parish on a push bike.

In 2015 Burpham Church celebrated the 50th anniversary of the Church of the Holy Spirit and the Surrey Advertiser reported on the weekend of celebrations. There was a dedication service, a birthday party, including hog roast, barn dance and talent show, followed by a celebration service led by the Bishop of Guildford, the Right Revd Andrew Watson. Revd James Levasier said *'The nice thing about having a church that is only 50 years old is that a lot of the people who were here right at the beginning are still around, so we could invite former parishioners and vicars to come along.'*

50th Anniversary of the Church of the Holy Spirit 2015 (Surrey Advertiser)
(At the back, Revd. Colin Matthews, Paul Bryant, Revd. Jo Levasier, Curate Jasmine Runnacles, Revd. Martin Hughes and Revd. James Levasier. At the front, the Bishop of Guildford, the Rt Revd. Andrew Watson, and the suffragan Bishop of Jarrow, the Rt Revd. Mark Bryant)

According to one report the Chapel of the Holy Spirit '*was intended to be the church hall, but in the meantime, while the church was being built, services were held there, using the vestry as a chancel, which was screened off when the hall was used for more social events. When the church was finally finished it was known as the Church of the Holy Spirit. As we then had a church with an adjoining hall and with all the amenities lacking at St Luke's, the life of the parish was centred at the church of the Holy Spirit, and St Luke's was only used for early communion services, occasional weddings, funerals and baptisms.*' In the late 1990s there were plans to attach an extension to St Luke's, in order to provide a church hall facility there as well, but these never came to fruition.

According to Kelly's Directory for 1913, Revd J W Clarke, the curate, lived at Bower's Mill House. In 1918/9, he was recorded as living at Marlyn's Cottage, on London Road. Then in 1924/5 Revd E C Storr, the first Vicar of Burpham with Sutton Green, was also recorded as living at Marlyn's Cottage. It is likely that the house was therefore used as a temporary vicarage until such time as a more permanent solution could be found. Though quite why Revd Storr didn't live at the vicarage in Pyle Hill, as had Revd Theodosius, is not recorded.

The old rectory on Burpham Lane, pre 1990 (Christopher Robin Day Nursery)

The number of clergymen required for a large parish such as Worplesdon does not seem to have been set in stone. In 1915 a newspaper reported on the meeting of the Worplesdon Vestry Assistant Clergy Fund. Mr A Birks was appointed as pro-warden for Burpham. There was some strong feeling about the appointment of another curate, '...*an assistant curate was absolutely essential. In the old days the curate worked the whole of the parish in a wonderful way. The work, however, was too much. It stood to reason that if one clergyman was at Burpham then they must have two at that end of the parish. Remarking that he was afraid he must be rather personal, the Rector (Revd. J C Bruce) said he very willingly paid the stipend of the assistant curate at Burpham, but when it came to paying the stipend of the other priest of the parish it was taking practically the whole income of the benefice. He suggested that a circular letter appealing for help be sent round the parish. Winchester Diocesan Fund quota was £25-£30 for Worplesdon and £5 for Burpham.'*

In 1916 the newspaper reported that Mr E Beeney had been presented with a handsome marble clock by the parishioners of Burpham, in recognition of 21 years service as organist at St Luke's Church.

Roman Catholic

Before 1876, the chapel at the Sutton Place Manor House was the centre of Catholic worship. Subsequently, the nearest Catholic church for the Burpham residents was St Edward the Confessor on the Sutton Park estate, which had been built in 1875 in the early English Gothic style and is a Grade II listed building. The architect was Charles Alban Buckler and he is buried in the cemetery that surrounds the church. When the church opened in 1876 the parish priest was Arthur Hinsley, who later became Archbishop of Westminster and a Cardinal. The church was consecrated in May 1950 by the Bishop of Southwark. Up to the 1950s the journey to St Edward's was not an easy one for the Burpham residents, when few people owned cars and public transport was infrequent. Some of the owners of Sutton Place allowed these worshippers to walk

Parish Still Alive?

The first Sunday Mass in Burpham 1953
(M P Hornsby-Smith)

through the estate, from the Lodge Gates to the church.

Michael Hornsby-Smith, in his book 'Parish still alive?' in 2009, explained that Fr. Gordon Albion, the parish priest at Sutton Park, requested permission for Burpham to become a Mass Centre. He first said a Sunday Mass in the home of two sisters, Ann and Nell Leonard, at 79 Glendale Drive on 21st June 1953. It was attended by 51 people. This must have been quite a crowded location as the Mass soon transferred to the Kingpost, which was loaned free of charge to the Church. Michael reported that '*Pat Burroughs (Veale) recalls it was very cosy, but a bit cramped, and even had a tiny gallery which held about ten, and also a small very old harmonium with mouse-proof pedals!*'. Fr. Albion tried to buy the Kingpost but the Diocese felt that the price of £4,400 was too high.

Then in 1958 he asked for permission to buy Orchard Cottage in New Inn Lane, which he funded through a successful appeal for money. Michael Drakeford, in his book about Abbotswood, recorded that there was local opposition to building a church on Orchard Cottage's land, which resulted in a public appeal hearing against the possible nuisance, from which they obtained a music restriction. Planning permission was granted in July 1959 to build a church on the land, subject to the condition that the building '*shall not be used for the holding of private or public dances*'. This was to cost about £12,000, so the Burpham Catholics raised more money through a range of fundraising events.

St Mary of Pity (M P Hornsby-Smith)

By December 1959 the congregation had grown so much that the Sunday Mass needed to move to larger premises, so the coach party room at the Green Man was used and *'the scent of incense mingled oddly with that of stale beer'*. On 10th June 1960 the new church, called St Mary of Pity, was opened. The hall was used as a Montessori school during the mornings, and was available as a general community amenity at other times. St Edward's donated a pieta for the new church and two stained glass windows were also donated and installed. The house in New Inn Lane had been in a terrible state, previously occupied by an old man who kept chickens in the loft. After being cleaned up a retired

St Mary's Presbytery, Orchard Cottage (BCA)

138

couple moved in as tenants and church caretakers. It wasn't until 1973 that the house was lived in by the priest.

In 1973 the newly opened St Pius X in Merrow merged with St Mary's to form the Roman Catholic Parish of Merrow with Burpham. However, by 2003 St Mary's had a long list of maintenance works that were needed for both the church and the presbytery. Following various meetings the Bishop decided that no more money was to be spent on St Mary's. The Closing Mass was held on Sunday 7th September 2003 and the site was sold. For several years the buildings were left empty and suffered from vandalism. Eventually a planning application to erect houses on the site was approved and by 2013 Raynham Close occupied the land.

Methodist

The Old Chapel on London Road 2017

The Old Chapel on London Road was originally built for the Methodist church in about 1888. According to Roger Marjoribanks '*Apparently the Alchin family were the prime movers; the 1881 census record, though very sloppily written, makes it clear that there was a chapel at Marlyns House and appears to describe Alchin himself as "Protestant Minister". Certainly the blacksmith's shop, leased to Charles Puttock, on part of whose land the chapel was built after the Alchin's retirement to Sussex, had been bought by Mary Ann Alchin, his wife, in 1876 and was now sold on for £60 to the trustees of the Guildford Circuit of the Primitive Methodist Church. The foundation stone was laid by Rev. George Cripps of that circuit and a house for the minister built next door (170 London Road).'*

Postcard of the Methodist Chapel c. 1900 (D Rose)

On the OS map of 1895 the building is clearly marked as Mission Hall, but on the OS map of 1912 it is marked as Methodist Chapel Primitive. By 1934 the building is still shown but with no description.

Roger Marjoribanks wrote *'The Methodist Chapel does not appear to have long survived the First World War; certainly, on oral evidence, it had ceased to be a place of worship by the late 1920s. The chapel and minister's house were sold separately by the trustees in 1951; the chapel has been used for a variety of business offices and the house as a private residence.'* Norman Hamilton gave some added details saying *'Later it was to be used as a furniture depository, a drawing office and then a shipping office.'* Kelly's Directories from 1955-75 showed the chapel was used as a warehouse by Kelly's removal contractors. In about

141

2000 James Rackham bought the building as a wreck and restored it, winning an architectural award in the process. It is now used as offices for Emporia Brands Ltd, part of the Rackham wine business. They still have the foundation stone engraved 1888 'Primitive' Methodist Church. For more information about the boar sculpture in the photograph, see the chapter on landmarks.

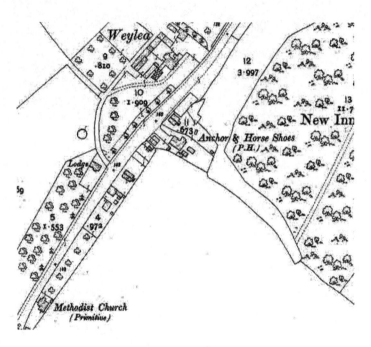

OS map 1912 showing Methodist Church

THE POOR, THE NEEDY AND THE SICK

The Poor Law Act of 1388 came out of the labour shortage after the Black Death, fixing wages and restricting the movement of labourers. Historian Derek Fraser noted that *the fear of social disorder following the plague ultimately resulted in the state, and not a 'personal Christian charity', becoming responsible for the support of the poor.* The laws against vagrancy were the origins of state-funded relief for the poor. The mid 1500s saw a legal distinction made between the genuinely unemployed and the idler – not so different from the current day. The Poor Relief Act of 1576 established the principle that if the able-bodied poor needed support then they had to work for it.

The Workhouse system started in the Georgian era when parishes were allowed to reduce the cost to ratepayers of providing poor relief. There were two types of poor relief. Outdoor relief was given in the form of money, food or other necessities, to people living in their own homes and this was funded by a local tax on the property of the wealthiest in the parish. Indoor relief was by obliging those who sought poor relief to go into a Workhouse and undertake a set amount of work, in return for very basic board and lodging. Think of Oliver Twist and the image of life in a workhouse comes to mind. Conditions were grim, but sufficient to keep the inmates alive. According to the St Luke's Hospital Heritage Project *'The rationale was to make life inside the Workhouse worse than that of a basic agricultural worker in the world outside.'* By the 1830s, most parishes had at least one Workhouse and legislation in 1834 brought in the concept of Poor

Law Unions, based on parishes and each having a union Workhouse. Several parishes joined together to form the Guildford Union and the new Union Workhouse was erected at Stoke-next-Guildford *'for the reception of those who are so unfortunate as to be subjected to the restraints now inflicted upon poverty.'* This Union included Worplesdon, which was the third largest parish after Guildford and Woking. The total cost for the poor of these parishes in 1840 was over £12,000.

The first meeting of the Board of Guardians of the Guildford Union took place in April 1836 in the town's Council Chamber. The Right Honourable Lord King was the Chairman of the Board and George Smallpeice was the clerk, who was paid the sum of £130 per year. Three Relieving Officers were appointed, paid £120 per year each, who would evaluate the cases of all persons applying for medical or poor relief and authorise any emergency relief or entry to the Workhouse. During this meeting it was noted that *'the Worplesdon Workhouse would hold one hundred inmates'* they debated the need to erect a Union Workhouse rather than continue with the existing Workhouses. However, they also resolved that all aged and infirm throughout the Union be removed to Worplesdon Workhouse – presumably this was only a temporary arrangement as the building was put up for sale the same year.

The poor and needy residents of Burpham, though they seemed to be few in number, probably went to the Worplesdon Workhouse before the creation of the Union. Almost no information has survived about life there, but the website

144

'Normandy Historians' said that Samuel Cork was the Master of the Worplesdon Workhouse in 1824. Then a description of the buildings came from sale particulars in 1836, which offered two lots for sale. *'By order of the Poor Law Commissioners for England and Wales, and the Board of Guardians of the Guildford Union. Lot 1 – A large brick-built messuage or dwelling house (the timbers of which are as good as new) with a productive grapevine attached. There are eight convenient bedchambers on the first floor, with a passage and store room, on the second floor are three large bedchambers with good flooring. On the basement is a large dining room and stone-paved kitchen. Adjoining the dwelling house is a substantial brick-built brewhouse and oven, and a pump of good spring water, also a large cellar and a Hog Cistern. Detached from the dwelling house is an extensive range of well-timbered buildings and divided for stabling, fuel house, cart houses and pigsties.*

Lot 2 – A brick-built dwelling house formerly used as the Pest-House, with two good chambers, a paved kitchen and a wash-house and cellar.' The Pest-House would have been used as a minor hospital facility for those suffering from infectious diseases, especially the Plague.

In order to attract potential buyers the sale particulars went on to say that *'The above freehold property is on the healthy and elevated site of Perry Hill, commanding beautiful views of the surrounding country, has a right to a large and productive commonage, is distant about three miles from the respectable market town of Guildford, and within two miles of the London and*

Southampton Railway, and is well worth the attention of Capitalists, Builders and others, the land being remarkably well-adapted for building purposes.

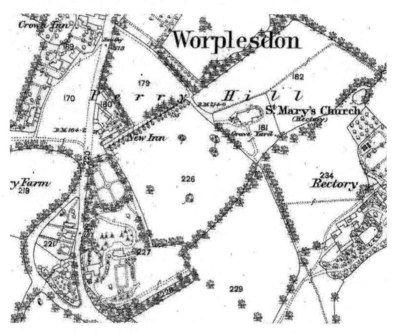

Perry Hill area of Worplesdon - OS map 1870 (the workhouse was not shown on this map, probably demolished by this time)

The materials of the dwelling houses (particularly the brick-work of the walls which is 14 inches thick up to the plate) are in the soundest repair, the same having been erected within a few years.'

A year later the Board of Guardians accepted Mr William Haydon's offer of his field in the parish of Stoke for the site of the new central Workhouse for the price of £150 per acre. This was erected in 1836 and would accommodate up to 300 inmates. The building included a chapel, accommodation wards and utility rooms such as the laundry. There was an infirmary at the back but in 1856 a new hospital was added and a school, with a casual ward as well. After 1930 the Workhouse became St Luke's Home and the infirmary was taken over by Surrey County Council to become Warren Road Hospital, a military hospital during the war, and then after the war it was renamed St Luke's Hospital, becoming part of the National Health Service in 1948.

The Spike - grilles for pushing broken rocks through - 2016

The casuals ward, built in 1905, is the only part of the Guildford Union Workhouse to survive. Known as The Spike, it is now a Heritage Centre and well worth a visit. Some of the cells where 'casuals', mainly vagrants or tramps, stayed have been preserved and four of them still have the grilles across the windows. One of the jobs for casuals was stone-breaking – they would break about two hundredweight of rocks into pieces small enough to be pushed through the grilles, in return for board and lodging. The broken rocks were sold off for road-making. Another job was taking apart old rope to produce oakum, which was then sold off – the origin of the phrase 'money for old rope'. The Workhouse opened its doors at 6.00pm each night and there would often be a queue of men, women and children outside the gates, hoping for a place for the night. There is no evidence of anywhere in the casuals ward for food to be prepared, so it is assumed that anyone seeking lodging for the night would already have found some food and drink before going to The Spike.

There were opportunities for young boys and men in the Workhouse to join apprenticeship schemes or work abroad, though it is probable that life for them would not differ much from that of the convicts being transported to Australia. A letter to the Guildford Board of Guardians in 1846 said '*We are in receipt of your letter dated 18th inst. respecting some boys you are desirous of apprenticing to the Sea Service. In answer thereto we beg to state that we have apprenticed several boys for the parish of Dorking and shipped a number of men at nominal wages to be paid off at Port Philip, Adelaide, or some port in South Australia and have provided them with board lodging and outfit after their arrival in London for the sum of £7 but we find this sum does not pay us as we hold Mr Southon, in future our charge would be £8. Upon these terms we shall be glad to apprentice any stout boys but not under 15 years of age and to provide passages for any men that are inclined to work their* *passage to South Australia. We should mention in addition to the £8 the men who go to South Australia have paid to the Captain £2 each to be given to them on their arrival so that they may not be left entirely destitute. If these terms meet your approbation we shall be glad to know the names, ages of the boys and men and as we require them we will send for them. We remain Sir, Yours obed*, Messrs Symonds & Co.'.*

Life in the Workhouse was hard but it is interesting to look back and see what was provided for the residents. In 1901 a Ready Reckoner for Workhouse Provisions was published for everyone to be consistent in feeding the poor. This included ingredients for a range of meals, stating amounts depending on the number of people to be fed. Thus 100 pints of Hotchpotch Stew required *'31 lb 4 oz raw beef, free from bone; 1 lb 9 oz flour; 1 lb 9 oz peas; 3 lb 2 oz scotch barley; 25 lbs carrots or turnips; 25 lbs cabbage; 6 lb 4 oz onion; pepper, salt and herbs to taste; stock or water a sufficiency.'* The image conjured is of enormous pots and pans being cooked and served. The Board of Guardians met in 1849 and agreed a weekly menu for able bodied paupers:

Breakfast	bread and gruel, with tea
Dinner	bread and soup (three days);
	meat / vegetables (four days), with beer
Supper	bread and cheese, with beer or tea

Bread would have been cooked in-house and beer brewed in the Workhouse's own brewhouse – water was often not fit for drinking, so beer was a cheap alternative for the inmates. A note in the minute book from 1877 stated that salaries for the Master, Matron, Assistant Matron, Schoolmistress, Porter and Female Nurse included beer money. However, the Clerk and Chaplain did not benefit from this, presumably because they didn't live at the Workhouse.

It was a sad fact of life that children were born in the Workhouse and people died there. The St Luke's burial records show 20 entries between 1889 and 1945 for people, mostly over 70 years of age, who had died at the Guildford Union Workhouse. These include a number whose families appeared in census records over many years, such as Collis, Faithfull and Worsfold. The records do not state where they lived before they entered the Workhouse, so it is surmised that they came from Burpham and Jacob's Well. Originally being destitute was the main reason for being in the Workhouse. Mass unemployment followed the end of the Napoleonic Wars in 1815, the industrial revolution brought in new technology in agriculture and milling, poor harvests, could all have resulted in people losing jobs and accommodation. Many cottages were attached to jobs and whole families could become homeless when they disappeared. The aim of Workhouses was to put off the able-bodied poor so that only the really destitute would apply to enter. Later on, Workhouses became refuges for the elderly, infirm and sick rather than able-bodied poor and by 1929 Local Authorities took them over as municipal hospitals.

Minutes from the Board of Guardians in 1864-1871 recorded the details of those receiving outdoor relief, not so different from modern-day Social Services benefits. William Collis, of Pimms

Row, received relief for his wife's illness, but by the turn of the century he was an inmate himself at the Workhouse, where he died. Elizabeth Wapshott, aged 77 years and wife of the Toll Collector at Green Man Gate, received 12 shillings per half year because she was partly disabled. Arthur Wyatt, aged 8 years and living at Pimms Row, received £1 16s per half year because he was an orphan. Susan Woods, aged 24 years of Burgham Lane, received £5 8s per half year for her children – but by the time of the 1871 census she was living at Pimms Row and was recorded as working as a charwoman, so hopefully she had turned her life around. Other reasons for receiving outdoor relief included part or whole disability and illness. Jane Ellis, aged 44 years and living on Burgham Lane, was described as a lunatic receiving £1 3s per half year, but in January 1867 she was sent to the Brookwood Asylum, where the admission records stated that she suffered from acute mania.

Before 1800 the mentally ill were often confined in their homes, chained or in small stalls. Some would become vagrants or in large cities a few hospitals, such as Bethlem in London, took them in. Few doctors had the skills to look after them. However, there were private lunatic asylums around Surrey and from 1774 to 1879 the nearest one was Lea Pale House in the parish of Stoke next Guildford. From 1817, Thomas Jenner Sells, the doctor who created the Charlotteville housing estate in Guildford, was one of the surgeons for the asylum. Mental disorders included mania, dementia and senile dementia, general paralysis, melancholia, imbecility, puerperal mania and epilepsy. Hospital records show that women, with lower social status, power and money could be

151

labelled insane and locked up for postnatal depression, alcoholism, the menopause, infidelity and even possession by evil spirits.

Brookwood Hospital opened in 1867 as Surrey County's second County Lunatic Asylum. It was originally intended to house 650 pauper lunatics, who could come from anywhere within the County, their maintenance being paid mostly by poor law unions. Over its 127 year lifetime the hospital grew with additional buildings, including a chapel and a library/ conference centre. By 1946 patient capacity had peaked at about 1,900. In the early days many patients arrived at Brookwood by barge on the Basingstoke Canal. There was a wharf at the edge of the grounds and patients were taken up the path to the main reception building. The hospital was self-sufficient, having a dairy farm, a cobbler's workshop, its own fire brigade, gasworks and sewage farm. Patients were encouraged to work as well as undertaking recreational activities. Local artisans were employed to teach skills and sports teams were created. Able-bodied patients were put to work around the hospital – in the kitchens, laundries and gardens – earning small amounts of money. Brookwood was a major employer in the Knaphill area for clinical, ancillary and other support workers.

Roger Hunt, in his book 'Rural Britain Then and Now' described the difficulties in finding medical treatment before the 19th century. *'Many people relied on patent medicines or dubious traditional remedies and herbal cures'*. Professional treatment was basic at best. Surgery was dangerous, despite advances with anaesthesia and antiseptics. Where there was a village doctor he was well respected, having the social standing of the gentry and clergy. Some charitable doctors would treat the poor and needy without any charges.

In terms of general medical and surgical care, life for the residents of Guildford and surrounding areas changed in 1866 when the Royal Surrey County Hospital opened on the Farnham Road site (now Farnham Road Hospital). It was designed with advice from Florence Nightingale. Queen Victoria became a patron of the building project. Prior to this there was a free dispensary on Quarry Street, where Olivio's Restaurant is now, which opened in 1860 but closed when the hospital was built. After 1930 the Workhouse infirmary, which eventually became St Luke's Hospital, became a second hospital for the residents of Guildford and surroundings. The National Health Service was set up after the second world war, providing free healthcare for everyone and growing to expand services through advances in medical science and technology. In 1980 the Royal Surrey County Hospital moved to its new home on Egerton Road and by 1996 all services from the St Luke's site had joined the new Trust Hospital. Many specialist services had been based at St Luke's, including Maternity, Cancer & Radiotherapy, Pathology and the School of Nursing. The first cottage hospital was in Cranleigh in 1859, providing local treatment for a small fee.

Telephone directories from 1936 to 1941 show that there was one doctor living at St Damiens in Winterhill Way, Dr Dermot Murphy. Jan Kemp remembered Dr D J Watson, who, according to telephone directories was living at Cheriton in Hawthorne Way. Perhaps they shared a practice? Peggie at the Drop-In Club remembered a Dr Evans, also in Winterhill Way in the 1950s.

Following the Second World War there were many people suffering the aftereffects of war and rationing. In 1950 a newspaper reported that Thomas Wilkinson, of Paddock Cottages, Burpham, was ordered to hospital for three months. He was described as being just skin and bone and his doctor said *'when I visited him it was obvious that he had had no food for a long time. His ration book had not been used for three months, neither had his pension been drawn.'*

However, community medical care changed in the mid-1950s when William Winzer sold New Inn Farmhouse and it was bought by Dr Derek Parkin, who became the Burpham GP, staying there until he died in 1987. In his latter years Dr Parkin was also the police doctor. Morris Kemp remembered him as being an interesting character, who was very good with children, but not so good with the elderly patients. Dr Leon Barbour bought the practice and, at the time of writing, still owns it, although he no longer works there. In 1992, Dr Barbour got permission to develop the outbuildings at the surgery into minor operations and treatment rooms. There are currently two GPs working at the surgery, supported by practice nurses, community midwives, community nurses and health visitors. In 2006 the Guildford Chiropractic Centre moved into the premises as well. For dental services, patients had to travel into Guildford until the practice opened in New Inn Lane.

For many years there were old people's homes, called Burpham Homes, in Coniers Way, off New Inn Lane. At the Opening Ceremony in June 1964 there were speeches by Lt. Col. H J Wells CBE, Chairman of the County Council, Alderman E B Nicklin JP, Mayor of Guildford, The Most Hon. The Marquess of Lothian, Joint Parliamentary Secretary to the Ministry of Health, and the Revd. D W Bryant, Vicar of Burpham. There were three buildings making up the Homes, named Abbot, Annandale and Astolat, each of which accommodated 40 residents - male, female and couples. Landscaped grounds, including gardens and woodland provided a nice environment for the people living there, and were '*adjoining school playing fields, where the elderly liked to watch the pupils at play*'.

A 'Friends of the Homes' group was organised locally to help with the welfare of the residents. The Burpham Friendship Club made visits, arranged outings for the residents, birthday gifts and cards, and a Christmas party. A sweet and book trolley was taken round the homes every week by members of various organisations in the village, including the WRVS. Philip Arthur Cloney remembered being a paper boy for the Homes in the 1970s, when he delivered newspapers and tobacco for the residents. Phil Dart remembered that '*On the first Sunday of every month, evensong was transplanted from the church next door to the dining room of one house, possibly in rotation. The organist, Albany Watkins used to lug a none too lightweight portable organ across on his shoulder and set it up, and residents were fetched from all three houses if they wanted to attend.*'

Burpham Homes Summer Fete early 1980s (D Kyle)

One of the annual events for the village was the Fete held at Burpham Homes, around the end of June or early July. Stalls were run by local organisations, such as the WI, and money was raised to support the Homes. Stalls included second hand books, jumble, hoopla, cakes, plants, hook a duck and, of course, a beer tent. Celebrities usually opened the fetes, such as Tony Hart (artist), Richard Baker (newsreader) and Joyce Grenfell (entertainer). Phil Dart remembered '*It NEVER rained. It was always opened by some local dignitary. The Sea Cadets band was always in attendance. People used to seek me out to win them a bottle of lemonade from a particular stall. A stick with some string hanging from it, with a metal loop on the end – it was a race to get the loop over the neck of the bottle before anyone else,*

156

thereby winning the bottle. My technique was finely honed and I was frankly unbeatable!'.

Andy Jackson remembered doing his Duke of Edinburgh award there in the 1970s. He helped with serving food after school and provided some companionship, but was a little too young to really understand the business of dementia. Lorna Bailey remembered that she lived opposite the Homes and used to visit a one of the residents, as well as doing a bit of shopping for them and helping out at the summer fete. Teresa Jane Rowe remembered visiting the Homes when she was in the Girl Guides and there were some very definite smells of over-cooked food.

In the 1970s the homes were the subject of media interest, when council officials investigated issues about expensive running costs and complaints about the conditions, including food and accommodation. Staff, unhappy with the suggestion that they did not do their utmost to make life happy for the residents, challenged the complainants to come and see what life was really like in the Homes. Funding was identified for improvements in 1979, including screening, curtains and carpets to make life more private and comfortable for the old people who had to share rooms.

In 1987 the Surrey Advertiser reported that two of the residents, with a combined age of 150 years, had met the previous year, fallen in love and then got married at the Church of the Holy Spirit. A wedding buffet and party was arranged back at the Homes, including a cake and champagne. Mr & Mrs William Webb

157

spent their wedding night at a local hotel, in the honeymoon suite, watching televisioin and drinking champagne, before returning to Abbot House, where they shared a room and were very happy.

There were more concerns about care later in 1987 after an elderly woman wandered out unnoticed, and was found the next morning lying dead in a ditch half a mile away. The Vicar, Rev. Martin Hughes, wrote to the council requesting redesignation of the Homes that would enable higher staffing levels and better pay for staff. It was recognised that there were more residents needing a different level of care to what had been acceptable. By late 1990 it had been decided to close Burpham Homes because it was outdated and too costly to refurbish. Residents would be moved into new homes planned for Merrow and Farncombe, while some would be encouraged to move back into the community. The shut down was phased over two years to fit in with building of the new homes. Staff were transferred to other social services departments, or took early retirement or voluntary redundancy.

Astolat building in 2017

In 1997 the Surrey Advertiser reported that six purpose-built houses, providing community living for 27 people with learning disabilities, were opened in Mallow Crescent. These took the place of some of the old Burpham Homes buildings, whilst the Astolat building remained as office accommodation for voluntary sector organisations, such as Surrey Community Action, Action for Carers, Surrey Independent Living Council and social services teams.

In 1988 McCarthy & Stone opened new retirement / sheltered housing flats at West Court on Burpham Lane. These include both one and two bedroomed apartments, with some shared facilities and a weekly social activities programme. There are resident management staff and a community alarm service. In 2017 new McCarthy & Stone assisted living apartments have been completed on the site of the old AA building on the way into Burpham from Guildford.

LIFE IN THE COUNTRYSIDE

Roger Hunt described life in the countryside in his book 'Rural Britain Then and Now', saying that up to Victorian times villagers usually stayed in and around the area where they had been born and where their families lived. Movement tended to be within five or ten miles of the birthplace and sons mostly followed their fathers in the type of work, on the land or in a trade. Census records give a fairly clear picture of this, but are only available with such detail from 1841. In Burpham there were many families who stayed in the area, moving around Ripley, Send, Merrow, Clandon and Guildford, and a few who lived for a very long time just in Burpham.

Before the 20th century this part of Surrey was mainly agricultural, with workers living on farms, in mills, or in cottages attached to the employer. Roger Hunt also said that *'most cottages were overcrowded and sparsely furnished. Until the late 19th century bread was generally baked at home, and it was this, cheese, swedes and turnips, which were the staples, with meat as an occasional luxury. Many families kept a pig; when slaughtered it supplied lard and meat. Killing the pig was a major event, invariably left to the travelling pig-sticker.*

Toil was never-ending. Cereals, fruit and vegetables were grown and harvested; livestock reared and killed; followed by skinning, preserving and cooking. Many cottages just had a single downstairs room, serving as kitchen, dining room and parlour.

*With the development of the village shop, at the beginning of the
20th century, a vast range of goods, including tinned products,
could be stocked in the community and the need for self-reliance
grew less.'*

Elected Parish Councils were established in 1894, providing a
local decision making process for rural communities. However,
Burpham has never had an administrative Parish Council, despite
becoming an ecclesiastical parish in its own right from 1954.
Ecclesiastical parishes date back to the Middle Ages and had great
influence over villagers' lives, both spiritual and social. Village
life was divided by class, with the agricultural and mill workers at
one end, then the craftsmen, tradesmen, teachers and clergy in
the middle, while the gentry and wealthier farmers were at the
other end. The middle and upper classes in the village saw it as
their duty to serve the community and care for those less
fortunate than themselves. They would become guardians of the
poor, rates assessors, highway surveyors, and parish constables.
Through the parish they would ensure that food and clothes were
distributed to the poor and needy, round up stray animals and
keep them in pounds, and maintain the local roads.

There was genuine hardship for many labouring families, which
were often large and children had to share bedrooms, or even
beds. Insanitary conditions often meant that disease could
spread quickly and children's illnesses such as whooping cough,
diphtheria and scarlet fever were common. Children would be
expected to work, spending hours in the fields scaring away
birds, or clearing stones, or helping with the harvest. Legislation

regarding children's work hours was often ignored and school would be missed, particularly at harvest time. The children would be sent out to scour the hedgerows for additional food, such as blackberries and other wild fruit.

The Office for National Statistics recorded that in 2014 nearly 20% of the population were aged 65 years and above. Roger Hunt suggested that in the 19th century it was only about 6%. However, the 1851 census for Burpham recorded only four people over 65 years, out of a population of about 350, rising to ten people in 1911.

Market day was a chance for people to do business, meet friends, and visit local shops to buy items that were not available in the village. Most Burpham residents would go to Guildford markets as these were nearest to them.

FARMING IN RURAL AREAS

Census returns used the term 'Ag Lab' to describe those working on farms and the Burpham records are full of them. With at least six farms around London Road and Burpham Lane there were plenty of opportunities for work and often the cottages were tied to jobs. According to Kay Handford in her book 'The Agricultural Labourer in 19th Century England', skilled labourers could be hired for a year at hiring fairs and they would bargain with the farmer for the best wage they could get. Unskilled or inexperienced labourers were 'casuals' and often hired by the day. Boys aged 12 or 13 would be hired as farm servants, living on the farm, provided with food and bedding (some did rather better than others), but expected to do anything required of them. General labourers had a wide range of duties, from mending fences and roads to sowing seeds for crops. In the summer there were maintenance tasks such as weeding or hoeing, followed by haymaking and harvest. Labourers' wives and children helped in order to ensure that the harvest was completed successfully.

Kay Handford said *'Women generally looked after cows and poultry on the farm, and did the milking, butter and cheese making. The work required physical strength; the pails of milk were heavy and strong arms were needed for making cheese and butter. Working outdoors was hard on clothes and boots, so women were glad to earn money by working at home, lace making, straw plaiting, spinning and glove making. A woman with small children of her own would look after infants for other women; many took in sewing or washing.'* She also said that *'During the years when their wives were able to work, and they had several children of working age still living at home, labourers were better off than at any other time. Cottage rents ranged from 1s 6d a week to 4s or 5s, depending on the number of rooms. With a garden for vegetables, free fuel, and a pig, families could expect to live fairly well. But, for labourers with no garden, hardship was worsened by continued enclosure of common land, where they had at least been able to gather fuel.'*

Many people kept animals to provide food for the family. In 1943 the Surrey Advertiser ran an advert for *'Hornless Nanny, with first two kids, week old; good milker, also 8 month old Nanny kid'*.

The seller of these goats was Harry Cutt, who lived on Burpham Lane and also sold hens.

Agricultural labourers often suffered with a poor diet. Breakfast for the poorest men was bread, soaked in hot water with salt and onion. Dinner was usually bread and cheese with cold tea, taken to eat in the fields. The evening meal with the family centred on boiled potatoes and other vegetables if they had them. A small piece of meat was an added luxury if it could be afforded. Tea was the normal drink, with sugar and milk if possible. Those who were fed at the farmhouses usually fared better, with a wider range of food and drink on offer. Sometimes men felt it was worth the risk to poach game from the local landowner's estate, but, if caught, they could be hanged, imprisoned or transported.

FARMS AND SMALLHOLDINGS

Market Gardens and Smallholdings

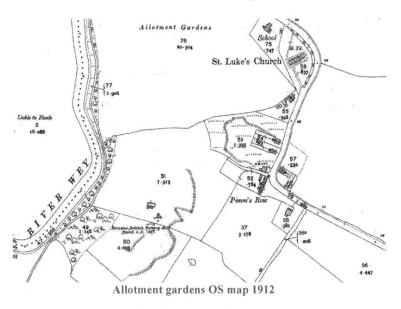

Allotment gardens OS map 1912

For most of its life, Burpham has been a mainly agricultural community. With Burpham Court Farm at one end of the village and Gosden Hill Farm at the other, there were also four farms along the London Road. At various times there have also been other people working on the land, either as smallholders or market gardeners. They lived in cottages along either London Road or Burpham Lane and grew their produce in their own gardens or in the market gardens area behind St Luke's and Burpham Primary School. Jan Kemp recalled that her father, uncle and grandfather were all market gardeners in Burpham.

Burpham still has its allotments down by the River. Some of the land was donated to the Council by Leonard Vincent, who lived opposite Bower's Mill Lodge, on the understanding that it would be for horticultural use only. Guildford Allotments Society manages Burpham and 13 other allotments, but there is a site representative for Burpham who manages the area and sorts out day-to-day issues. One of the Burpham allotment plots was the overall winner in the Allotment section of Guildford In Bloom 2015.

Burpham allotments 2016

In 1911 Alfred Marshall and John Howlett were recorded as smallholders on the census, then by the 1920s Kelly's Directory recorded that Richard Thomas (Nurseryman), Harry Tann and Silas Kilby (smallholder), Albert Russell and Alex Wheeler (Market Gardener), were all living around Bower's Cottages. Whilst up by

New Inn Farm, between 1924 and 1930, Albert Binfield and Eric Perry were poultry farmers, William Angus, Ernest Dann and Charles Stevens were smallholders, all living in New Inn Cottages on London Road. In 1938 Lucy Haydon was a smallholder at Winterhill Farm. Silas Kilby and Albert Russell continued until at least 1938, then in 1950 Leonard Vincent was recorded as market gardener until the early 1960s.

Silas Kilby's van (J Kemp)

In 1947 Burpham Primary School needed more land as it was growing bigger and a letter from the County Planning Department to the County Land Agent suggested converting a plot that was at the time used for market gardens. It was noted that this would affect Silas Kilby, who had pasture, arable land and a cottage; A & W Durrant, who had arable land and a cottage; and Guildford

167

Borough Council, who had allotments there. Then in 1950 a letter from the Education Department said '*the need for playing fields cannot be regarded as pressing...*' – a very different line of thought to the present day when playing fields are deemed to be very important by most people. Later in the year it was decided to give notice to quit to two tenants and that one acre of land would be appropriated for the playing fields. It seems that the proposed plot of land was at the rear of Pimm's Row and by 1951 it was decided that owing to the distance from the school and the age of the young children, it was unsuitable to provide playing fields there.

Then, in 1948 there was another difficulty when it was decided that new overhead electricity lines and pylons would affect Mr Kilby, Mr Durrant and Mr Isard, who all lived in Pimm's Row. Sadly, no further information was found on the outcome from this.

The mechanisation of farming began in the 18th century with the invention of Jethro Tull's seed drill in 1701. Gradually more machinery brought improvements, including threshers, tractors and grass cutting. However, horses were used well into the 20th century to pull farming equipment.

Farmers have always had difficulties to overcome with running their farms. In 1872 the newspapers reported an outbreak of foot & mouth disease, so no cattle could be moved or sold. In 1877 there was a cattle plague, a contagious disease that again restricted movement of animals. Then in 1879 it was reported that there was an outbreak of swine fever, another contagious disease restricting movement of pigs. In 1906 a newspaper reported that *'Farmers in West Surrey has sustained heavy losses through their sheep being worried by dogs. Mr George Gatley, of Bower's Farm, Burpham, Near Guildford, has lost 51 ewes and lambs in one night. The animals had been either killed or drowned.'* More recently, in 1938 most farms in the area were affected by an outbreak of foot and mouth disease in Worplesdon. The resulting standstill order affected farms across six counties.

In his book 'Rural Britain Then and Now' Roger Hunt described life on farms in the 19th century, saying that *'prior to the development of the railway network the average farm kept only two or three cows. Well into the century it was not unusual to see the milkmaid on her three-legged stool, attending to the milking in the field or farmyard. Most farms had a dairy run by the farmer's wife, who made milk, butter and cream for domestic consumption.'* Cheese making required rather more equipment than milk and cream so was not so widely undertaken. When the railways came, demand increased and large dairy herds dominated the landscape. Milking machines were first introduced in 1895.

New Inn Farm

New Inn Farmhouse (now Surgery) 2015

John Seller's map of 1690 showed New Inn on the London Road, but didn't say if this was a farm or an inn. However, many other farms were just marked as the name, without the word Farm, so perhaps it was the farm, which would fit with the age of the house. In 1752 Thomas Longhurst agreed a lease of 21 years on New Inn Farm from Lord Onslow, stating that the farm had previously been in the tenure of John Atfield, presumably a member of the Attfield alias Ripley family. At the time of the 1838 Tithe Map, the farm and surrounding area was owned by Lord Onslow and occupied by Hugh Russell, who farmed many acres of Burpham land, most of which he leased. Hugh Russell also occupied Chagden or Shagden Farm (later to be known as Weylea Farm), Although that was owned by William Sparkes, and land from New Inn Lane to Ganghill Copse along the London Road and up to where the railway line is now situated (the boundaries of the parish).

The 1841 census records showed that William Francis Pimm had New Inn Farm, although it is likely that he actually lived at Marlyn's, which he also owned. The electoral register of 1853 showed that Joseph Choat occupied New Inn Farm, with his wife Fanny and he continued to farm there until 1877. The 1861 census recorded that he farmed 200 acres and employed five men and two boys. He died in 1878 and was buried at St Luke's. In 1887 the Right Honourable William Hillier, Earl of Onslow, agreed a mortgage with H B Mayne, F E Beauclerk and J P Martineau for three freehold farms (New Inn Farm, Winterhill Farm and Burgham Farm). New Inn Farm was recorded as being part of Winterhill Farm, and was let to James and Henry Standage from 1880 for sixteen years at £190 p.a. rent. Kelly's Directory for 1890 had both James Standage and Henry Pitman-Smith recorded as farmers at New Inn Farm.

For the next 20 years from 1890, the farmer was Henry Pitman-Smith, who lived there with his wife Margaret and four children. While he was there, Lord Onslow put the farm up for sale in 1905. The sales particulars at the time described the farm as '*An attractive dwelling house, built of brick with partly tiled walls and tile roofed. It included an attic, four bedrooms, bathroom, two boxrooms and WC on the upper floor. On the ground floor there were two good sitting rooms, kitchen, scullery, dairy and larders. There was also a garden and orchard.*' It didn't sell and reappeared in sales in 1909 and 1912. In the sales particulars for the 1912 sale the description stated that the boxrooms had been turned into additional bedrooms, which probably was rather more attractive than the four in the original details.

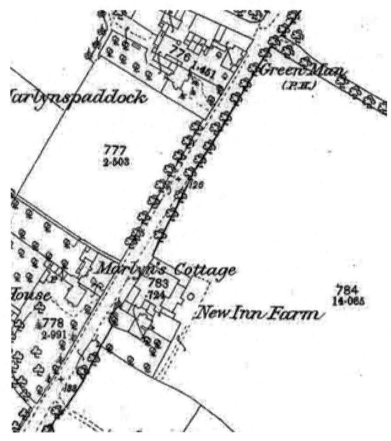

New Inn Farm (OS map 1869)

According to Kelly's Directories, William Winzer, originally from Somerset, took over with his wife Hannah by 1915, so perhaps he bought the farm though he may have been a tenant farmer. Some of the land stayed with Lord Onslow until 1920, when he agreed to sell it along with Ganghill, excluding a piece of land at the top of New Inn Lane beside the railway bridge. William and Hannah had three daughters, but Ivy died, aged only 19 years, in 1934 and was buried at St Luke's.

William must have had a great interest in sports as in 1914 the local newspaper reported that he was an official for a sports meeting at Chertsey. His role there was Clerk of the Scales and Official Measurer. William continued to farm the land until about 1950, well into his seventies, but sold up in the early 1950s and died in 1956 at Mount Alvernia Hospital. He and Hannah were both buried at St Luke's.

The farmland was developed in the early 1950s to provide space for the police estate, and later on George Abbot School. In 1952 the farmhouse was up for sale again and the details said that it was reputed to be about 400 years old. Described as a 16th Century old-world Surrey farmhouse residence, having *'quaint low beamed ceilings and brick fireplaces... it offers those seeking old-world atmosphere an opportunity of restoring to a charming country residence of character.'* Along with the farmhouse were included various outbuildings, such as a harness room, stables and a *'small hovel'*. A second lot offered other farm buildings including two barns, cowstalls, granary, bull-pen and a piggery. According to Kelly's Directories the farmhouse was used for a while by J Hartley, an antique dealer, before it was bought in the late 1960s by Dr Derek Parkin to be a doctor's surgery. Dr Parkin worked as the village GP until his death in 1986, when Dr Leon Barbour took over the surgery. The farmhouse is now the oldest building in modern Burpham and is Grade II listed. The Historic

England website describes Lilac Cottage (no. 202 London Road) and New Inn Farmhouse (no. 200 London Road) as 17th century with 18th century extensions and a 20th century addition at the rear.

New Inn Farm from the back c. 1952 (Surrey Advertiser)

Winterhill Farm

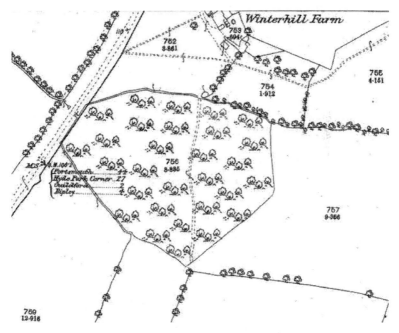

Winterhill Farm (OS map 1869)

At the eastern end of the village lay Winterhill Farm. It first appeared on a map in 1823, marked as Winter Hill Bottom. The Tithe Map of 1838 showed the full extent of the farmland, where the north eastern end of the farm reached almost to the Sutton Place Lodge gates, down to New Inn Lane at the south eastern end. Bordered by the London Road on one side and Merrow parish on the other there were two fields and a wood called Upfolds on the Merrow side. The land was owned by Lord Onslow and occupied by William Smallpiece, apart from one small plot that was occupied by the Revd George Bethell as Rector of

175

Worplesdon. This piece of land was marked as 'Glebe', which was an area of land within an ecclesiastical parish used to support the parish priest – often called the 'church furlong' or 'parson's close'.

Census and electoral register records showed Benjamin Budd as the farmer from 1849 to 1856, describing him as a farmer of 80 acres, employing three labourers. Born in Puttenham in about 1804, he only appeared in Burpham records for a few years. In 1851 he lived at Winterhill Farm with his wife Mary and his widowed father John, who had also been a farmer. The following years are a bit of a mystery as census records show only agricultural labourers living at the farm on those nights. Then in 1891, Walter Mitchell was recorded as the farmer, and he stayed there for the next 20 years. Walter was born in 1840 in Alfold and his father was an agricultural labourer. The last record of him at Winterhill Farm was in 1912 when he would have been about 71 years old. In the big sale of the Onslow estates in 1905, Winterhill Farm was described as let to Walter Mitchell for a rent of £61p.a., a *'pleasure farm'*, which included the house, outbuildings, arable and timbered pasture land of around 47 acres. There were five bedrooms, a box room, two sitting rooms, kitchen, scullery, larder and dairy. Like many other lots in the sale, this one did not attract a buyer either in 1905 or in 1909.

The OS maps of 1895 and 1912 both showed the brick field in the south eastern corner of the farm, on New Inn Lane. The sales particulars of 1912 said that there were two kilns as well as a stable, sheds and an office on the site. Between 1913 and 1927

176

Lymposs & Sons, later Lymposs & Smee, took over Winterhill, mainly as a dairy farm. They were a fairly big dairy business, operating from at least two sites in Guildford, providing milk from three farms that they owned.

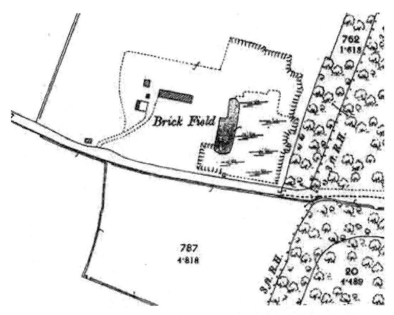

Brick Field on New Inn Lane (OS map 1895)

There was nothing in Kelly's Directory for 1930, but by 1934 Alfred Haydon was running the farm. He died in 1934 and was buried in St Luke's. His wife Lucy was recorded as a smallholder at Winterhill Farm in 1938 and it is not known for how long she continued there. The electoral register of 1945 showed that after her death in 1946 she too was buried at St Luke's. There were no updates to Kelly's during most of the war years, but in 1938 Percy

Gatley had moved into the farmhouse, where he stayed until about 1960. An item in the Surrey Advertiser in 1939 was for the sale of cow and pig manure, which would be delivered locally, on application to Gatley, Winterhill Farm. Percy had worked with his father, George, at Bower's Farm since about 1911, but moved over the road just before World War 2. Percy was married to Amelia Jessie Haydon, who appears to have been the sister of Alfred Haydon, so presumably this was all keeping it in the family. In 1960 Percy moved to a house in Orchard Road, where he lived until his death in 1971.

Mr Gatley at Winterhill Farm 1952 (Surrey Advertiser)

The first advertisement for housing on the Winterhill estate was in 1934 by Armstrongs Estates Ltd. Described as 'Charming', the prices ranged from £700 to £950 and buyers could decide how their house should look. *'Plans can be drawn by the Estate Architect to conform to your desires'* and *'all Winterhill Estate Houses, which are brick built, are designed by an eminent architect to suit individual plots and to catch the maximum sunlight'*. It is not known how long the farmhouse remained on the estate, but it looks to have been still there in 1945.

Orchard Cottage, which was occupied by Hugh Lancelot Robson, a fruit grower, lay between the brickfield and London Road. He was born in Guildford in 1882, one of four children born to John and Elizabeth Robson, and, according to census records, his father was a Clerk in Holy Orders. For many years from 1911, he was recorded in Kelly's Directory, although sometimes it said Lionel rather than Hugh Lancelot so it's not clear if this was the same man. The electoral registers recorded him as living on Merrow Lane whilst owning Orchard Cottage, though by 1919 he seemed to be living there. He disappeared from Kelly's Directories after 1924 but could be found living in Echo Pit Road from about 1932 onwards. He died in 1953 at St Thomas' Hospital in Hambledon, which, along with the George V Hospital and Milford Hospital, provided care for patients with tuberculosis. Orchard Cottage was bought to provide housing for a Catholic priest in Burpham in 1958, but was demolished in order for a small housing estate to be built shortly after the Millennium.

Weylea Farm

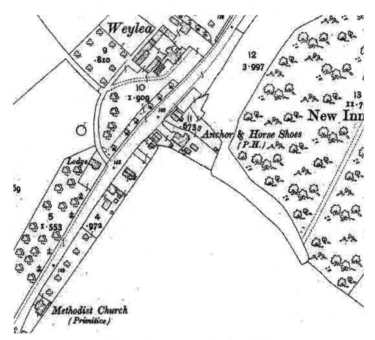

Weylea Farmhouse (OS map 1912)

Weylea Farm was known in the past as Chagden or Shagden Farm. Situated on the London Road, where the farmhouse was opposite the Anchor & Horse Shoes inn, the fields stretched down behind the land belonging to the Marlyns estate.

An early reference to the farmland was found in documents about the estates of Lord Onslow in 1785. A grant of annuity or rent charge was agreed between Lord Onslow and two bankers of Pall Mall, and William Smith Buckley of Polebrook, Northamptonshire. This included the Manor of Burgham, alias Bursham, with the

180

messuage known as Bursham Court; the *'messuage and 141 acres formerly in the occupation of William Yarrow and now Thomas Longhurst with 10 acres of meadow ground known as Chagden Mead in Worplesdon and Stoke'*; also *'Chagdens Farm alias Cowles Chagden, with lands comprising Shed Close, Eight Acre Close, Woodcock Close, the Barn Field, the Four Acre Hilley Field, Hinsley Wood, Chagden Meadow and the Hangers in the tenure of William King.'* However, the earliest reference to Chagden was in a document from 1603 held at the History Centre. This set out a rental agreement relating to the Manor of Burgham, written in Latin. Difficult to both read and understand this document gave the names of Henricus and Walter Ripley, Roger Gillam and Thomas Fox. Sadly further detail was not discernible. The name of Chagden clearly went back at least to the time of Elizabeth I.

At the time of the 1838 Tithe Maps the farm was owned by William Sparkes but occupied by Hugh Russell. Hugh leased land from Lord Onslow, from New Inn Lane down to the parish boundary, south of the blacksmith's shop, as well. He was born in about 1813 in St Nicholas parish, Guildford, and married Ann Lymposs in Worplesdon in 1834. They had seven children and at the time of the 1841 census were recorded as living in the parish of Stoke next Guildford.

By the 1851 census the farm was being run by Charles Gosden and his wife Ann. He was born in Leatherhead in about 1806 and was a successful farmer of 50 acres and employing four labourers. At that time, his brother Alexander, who was recorded as a 'proprietor of houses', and his sister Harriet were living with

181

him. No further information has been found about Charles, but it would be interesting to know if he or his family had any connection to Gosden Hill.

By 1861 Peter Watson had taken over the farm. At only 25 years old he was quite young to be farming a 50 acre farm, along with three men and a boy as labourers. Peter does not appear to have been married, but had three servants living with him at the farmhouse. One of these, Ellen Wapshott, was possibly related to the Burpham toll collector John Wapshott.

Peter Watson died in 1869 and the farm was advertised for sale in October 1869 at the White Hart Hotel in Guildford. The advertisement said *'This valuable estate: comprises a very pretty modern FAMILY RESIDENCE with a newly erected lodge entrance, carriage drive, pleasure grounds, lawn gardens and orchard, tastefully laid out and planted with ornamental trees, evergreens, and flowering plants. Very superior newly erected carriage house, stables, excellent harness room, comfortable enclosed farmyard, barn, granary, cow-house, sheds, piggeries, and other farm buildings...high state of cultivation, a portion of which is beautifully studded with fine growing oaks, presenting a park-like appearance.'* A month later the stock and equipment was put to auction, including three Alderney milk cows, five horses, a Sussex breeding sow with eleven pigs and white Dorking fowls. Equipment included ploughs, turnip cutters, scarifiers, oilcake crushers, chaff-cutter, sheep and pig troughs and a lawn mowing machine. There were also carriages, including a brougham and a phaeton.

Presumably it was not sold, because it was advertised again in 1870. Described then as '*50 acres of capital arable, meadow, and park-like land, with lodge entrance, convenient residence, capital stabling and farm buildings, orchard and vegetable garden. Weylea is suitable for a gentleman requiring a country residence, with a farm sufficient for the enjoyment of healthy and profitable occupation, and where access to the metropolis and inland counties is made easy and quick by railway accommodation...Apart from its residential character, Weylea recommends itself to notice for building purposes, having a frontage to the high road of 1,100 feet, and being within a short walk of the town of Guildford'.* Clearly this was seen as suitable for housing development nearly 120 years before it actually happened.

There was more change to come, as in the 1871 census the Head of the Family was recorded as Catherine L Ward, who was living there with her son and two daughters. She was American, born in New York in about 1808, but apparently she became a naturalised British Subject. Her son, Ernest Carroll Ward, was recorded as being a farmer of 50 acres, employing three men and a boy. The family had previously lived in Cheshunt, Hertfordshire, where two of the children were born. The 1861 census recorded Catherine as a Fundholder and her oldest son, Livingstone, was a Member of the Stock Exchange. The 1851 census had recorded that she was a merchant's wife living in Hackney, but by 1861 she had been widowed.

By 1891 Weylea Farm was run by Albert Coote and his wife Sarah. He was born in Huntingdonshire and was recorded as *'living on his own means'*. There was no mention of him being a farmer either in 1891 in Burpham or in 1901 in Shalford. In 1871 he had been living in Thruxton, Hampshire, where he was recorded as being a farmer of 600 acres, employing twelve labourers and three boys. Then, by 1911 he and Sarah had moved to Leamington in Warwickshire and at the age of 66 years he was recorded as a Gentleman Farmer.

Meanwhile the Kelly's Directory of 1899 recorded that Weylea was home to Percy Smeed, a farmer. He was born in Godalming in 1856 and married Rosaline Cooke in 1887. His father had been a brewer and in the 1861 census his widowed mother was recorded as an innkeeper. He was sent to boarding school in Temple Cowley, Oxford, then in 1881 he was staying with his brother William, also a brewer, in Portsea, but Percy was described as a retired farmer, at the age of 24 years. In the 1891 census he was living at the Angel Hotel in Guildford, where he seems to have been the hotel proprietor. He joined the Royal Alfred Lodge, Guildford, becoming a Freemason in 1899, where he was recorded as a hotel keeper. He stayed at Weylea for about four years, then the 1911 census found Percy, Rosaline and their five children living in Winchester, where he was recorded as being of 'private means'.

However, by 1913 he was recorded in Kelly's as being the farmer there again until about 1919. By 1926 Percy and Rosaline were living in Shalford at a house called Weyleigh. Did the house have that name before they moved there or did they want to call their new house the same name as the farm (albeit spelled slightly differently)? Rosaline died in 1935 and was buried at St Luke's. Percy died in 1941 but no record has been found of where he was buried.

Perhaps Percy rented out the farmhouse during his stay in Winchester, as from 1909 to 1911 there was a lady called Georgiana Skirrow Richardson living there. Described as a widow of private means, born in Marylebone in 1829, she lived with a companion, Adriana Greenhill from Bermuda, and three servants. She was married to James C Richardson, who was a merchant and ship owner from Durham. However, by 1881 she was a widow, living in Esher with her four children and by 1891 living on her own. Clearly a woman of some wealth she had four servants living in the house and possibly another one in the stables next door. In 1920 she was living in Bath where she died aged 92 years, but she must have had some fond memories of Burpham because she was buried at St Luke's.

There were few references to Weylea in the Kelly's Directories over the next few years. In 1927 a Frank Eve lived there; from 1950-1953 Robert Dickie was recorded as farmer; in 1955 Robert J Cox was the Weylea farmer. 1957 saw a new farmer, J S Heard, but he was recorded as living at Weylea Farm Lodge. However, he continued to be listed as the farmer until 1975. It must have been fairly soon after this that the farm was sold to developers and the farmhouse was demolished in order to make way for a

new housing estate. Sylvia Wheeler remembered that there used
to be donkeys at the farm, which her daughter Diane would ride.

View of Weylea Farm from Woodruff Avenue (P Gardner)

Bower's Farm

The land between London Road and Bower's Mill, on the north side of Burpham Lane, was just one part of the large estate either owned or leased by William Francis Pimm back in 1838. He owned the property on the south side of Burpham Lane, including Pimms Row, Marlyn's and Green Man Farm, but leased from Burpham Court Farm all the way back to London Road from the Earl of Onslow. This enormous area included Burpham Court Farm (then called Burgham House), Bower's Mill and Mill House, and all the fields, woods and meadows between the river and Burpham Lane. The 1841 census recorded William Francis Pimm as living at Marlyn's, but the Tithe Maps records show that he farmed all this land. William had died by the time of the 1851 census, but his wife, Mary, was still living at Marlyn's and was recorded as being the farmer of 370 acres, employing 18 labourers. Their son Arthur was shown as a corn dealer in 1851, but in 1861 he had moved out of Marlyn's though still living on London Road, and was shown as the farmer of 18 acres, employing two men and a boy.

The first mention of Bower's Farm as a separate property was in the 1881 census, when Thomas Slaughter was recorded as farmer. He lived there with his wife Agnes Armstrong, who he had married in 1880. He was born in Worplesdon in about 1852 to a farming family. He was still there at the 1891 census, by that time with five children, but then he seems to have moved to Worplesdon and then Normandy, where he died in 1940, aged 88 years.

By 1899 George Gatley had taken over the lease for the farm. George was born in Cornwall in 1868 to Thomas and Charlotte Gatley, who farmed 200 acres near Bodmin Moor and had nine children. It is not known what brought him to Burpham. He married Elizabeth Ann Blake in Launceston in 1894 but both his children, Percy (1895) and Ethel (1897), were born in Worplesdon parish. George lived at Bower's Farm until 1935 according to the electoral registers, but it seems that in 1918/19 he also farmed Bushes Farm at Wanborough and from 1921-36 he also ran White House Farm at Send. He died in 1936 and was buried at St Luke's along with his wife Lizzie, who had died in 1928.

His son, Percy, helped to run Bower's Farm from around 1911 until 1938, but by 1944/5 he had moved to Winterhill Farm, though he too seemed to hold onto White House Farm as electoral registers for 1937/38 recorded it as his property. In 1905 the Surrey Mirror reported an accident at Guildford Cattle Market involving Percy. It seems that he was standing near to an Alderney bull when the auctioneer was selling some fat bullocks. *'it is presumed that, forgetting the bull's proximity behind him in his interest in the sale, he came within the reach allowed the animal by its tether. At any rate the bull made a dash at Mr Gatley's back and tossed him violently some yards, goring him in the rear. The unfortunate farmer was picked up by his friends and conveyed to Mr Ernest H Ellis's office in the market, but refusing to go to the Royal Surrey County Hospital, he was driven away in a cab. It is feared that the injuries he sustained are of a serious nature.'* Clearly he survived this and went on to continue farming in Burpham until 1959.

188

In 1938, when Percy moved from Bower's Farm to Winterhill Farm, the stock was sold. The newspaper advertisement described the sale as '*70 head of cattle, viz.: the herd of 33 grand young dairy cows and heifers, roan stock bull, 10 roan shorthorn in-calf heifers, 20 choice roan shorthorn bulling heifers, 5 wean-year calves; five active cart horses; 20 head of poultry; excellent collection of modern farm implements and machinery, including waggons, carts, tractor, haymaking and barn machinery, binder, ploughs, harrows, rolls, drills, harness and dairy utensils.'*

Tony Mallard remembered that Mr Gatley used to buy up little pockets of land as development opportunities in the 1960s, and these included some garages in Recreation road. The rent was 7/6d per garage. He rode around on his bicycle and wore a blue mackintosh. His tenants had to go to the house in Orchard Road to pay the rent. From 1960 until his death in 1971 Percy lived in Orchard Road. He was also buried at St Luke's, along with his wife Amelia (died 1954), his parents and his sister Ethel (died 1964).

After the war, the farm was taken over by William Leopold Keene, known as Leo. He already owned Gosden Hill Farm and leased other farms in Burpham, Merrow, Send, Old Woking and Stoke Park. According to his daughter's book, '1934 to ?', at one time he had fifteen landlords. In 1945 there was an outbreak of foot and mouth disease at Bower's Farm. All the cattle, pigs and sheep had to be slaughtered at all five of his farms. It was a very hot summer, the ground was baked hard and there was no

189

machinery to bury the carcasses. Despite wartime fire restrictions they were given special permission to burn them after complaints about the smell.

Bower's Farm (D Keene)

During the outbreak, a policeman would stand at the farm entrance on Friday afternoons and Mr Keene had to throw the workers' pay packets across the road to be given to the men. There was no insurance or compensation in those days, so this would have affected his livelihood very badly. Early in 1946 he was able to re-stock. All the cattle at Bower's Farm were given names beginning with B – there was a pedigree Guernsey bull that was called Burpham Colonel.

Bower's Farm (D Seymour)

In 1958 Dorothy Keene and her husband Barry Jones took over Bower's Farm, which was rented from the Duke of Sutherland, and later on Paul Getty. She paid rent to her father and ran the farm. They had a farm shop to sell produce to local people. One day a donkey escaped from the field into the garden of the vicarage on Burpham Lane, through a gap in the hedge, getting out onto the road by the school. Dorothy's two children attended Burpham Primary School. In the late 1960s the Surrey Advertiser reported on the Bower's Farm sale of eggs stall at the Surrey County Show, describing the farm as '*150 acres of light loam soil, and 120 are into barley this year, this being the third consecutive season that an all-barley policy has been pursued. There are 600 head of breeding pigs on the farm, predominantly Wessex cross-Welsh...also Hereford cross calves and 1000 head of poultry.*'

In March 1970 Dorothy moved to Chippenham in Wiltshire, taking the pigs with her. The farm was bought by Sainsbury's to be their new store. In 1974 Leo Keene disappeared for eight days and there was a big search in all farm buildings and throughout the fields. Eventually his body was found, fully clothed, in the long grass at the river edge, believed to be at Bower's Farm. Although no-one will ever be sure, it was suspected that he had fallen into the river whilst helping an animal and then drowned because he had never learned to swim.

Gosden Hill Farm

Old maps of the area have shown Gosden Hill since 1768, though sometimes spelled as Gosling or Gosding Hill. Originally in the parish of Send, when boundaries changed in 1933 it joined Burpham to become part of Guildford. The farmhouse is dated 1876, but it is thought that the old farmhouse may have been located further up the lane, near to the farm buildings past Dillon Cottages. The first mention of the farm was as part of a marriage settlement between Thomas Onslow and Elizabeth Knight for *'one hundred and twenty acres be the same more or less commonly called or known by the name of Gosden Hill lying and being in Send aforesaid now or late in the tenure or occupation of George Tickner or his assigns or undertenants'*. In the late 18th century John Hale was the tenant farmer, but by 1809 George Street had taken over the tenancy, at a cost of £160 p.a.

Gosden Hill Farm house (D Keene)

In 1884 John Mitchell was the tenant farmer, paying £340 p.a. to the Earl of Onslow. In October 1881 a valuation of stock was carried out on the farm, showing a total value of £1,018 10s 3d. The stock included '*12 horses, three swine, 42 hens and roosters, 36 ducks, 30 live chickens and 12 fowls'*. There was also a range of farming equipment, including ploughs, drills, haymaking machine, carts and waggons. Census records for 1891 and 1901 showed that John Mitchell was the farmer, living with his son. In 1911 James Mitchell had taken over from his father, who was then

aged about 86 years and shown as a retired farmer. James, aged 50 years, and his wife Janet had two small daughters, and his sister Liza lived with them. Next door, at one of the Gosden Hill Cottages, lived Mrs J Munro, a widow of 69 years, living on private means, and her brother William Mitchell, aged 90 years. Presumably they were siblings of John

Outbuilding at Gosden Hill Farm 2016

Mitchell. Records show that there was a fire at the farm in about 1916.

The 1930 Surrey Directory showed that the farmer was Mr Paton and at that time William (Leo) and his brother Cecil (John) Keene were farmers in Send, but no farm name was given. By 1957

Keene Bros were the tenant farmers, paying £870 p.a. to their landlord for 346 acres, though sporting rights were reserved. The Earl of Onslow put a lot of his Clandon Estate and Merrow properties on sale in 1959 and this was when Leo Keene bought the farm.

Dorothy Keene, Leo's daughter, wrote a book, which told of life

Mr W L Keene (D Keene)

on the farm. Her father had never been to school but had worked on farms for most of his life. During the war the farm provided accommodation for girls from the ATS, WRAF and WRNS, who would hand over their food coupons in exchange for board and lodging. After the war there were pigs at the farm and these were grazed on common land along Merrow Lane. Two farm workers lived in Dillon Cottages, by the farm, working for the Keenes for many years.

When he died there was a eulogy published, which said '...*He served his country in the 1914-18 war and was in fact in Germany when the Armistice was declared. In the 2nd World War he served from its early days with the Milk Marketing Board. He* *was an original governor of Merrist Wood. He was a delegate to the NFU. He was particularly interested in the production of T.T. Milk. He gave support and encouragement to the Young Farmers Club. Some of his work was local, some national, but to both he brought the same qualities of extreme patience, courage and determination. And now his work is done...'*

After Leo Keene's death in 1974 the farm was sold. Noel Grant said that some estate agents were looking for a property with a large house for his parents, Mr & Mrs Martin Grant. They were both from farming families in Ireland and when they first came to Burpham they had beef cattle, battery chickens and farmed potatoes. The farm is currently owned by Martin Grant Homes, headed up by Noel. Burpham Community Association has been fighting planning applications by the company since about 1981 to build a huge housing development on the farmland. Guildford Borough Council's Draft Local Plan, published in 2016, proposed building 2,000 new houses, primary and secondary schools, community facilities and traveller pitches on the land. Time will tell what the outcome of this will be.

Green Man Farm

Very little is known about Green Man Farm, but it seems that it was on Burpham Lane, beside the Green Man pub. It is likely that the Tudor Cottages, where West Court is now, were the farmhouse and other buildings for the farm. At the Surrey History Centre there is a map of the farm in 1791, showing plots of land on the corner of Burpham Lane and London Road, around two sides of the pub. By the time of the 1838 Tithe Maps the farm had been subsumed into the Marlyn's estate and was owned by William Francis Pimm, recorded as cottages with gardens, farm yard and three acres of farm land.

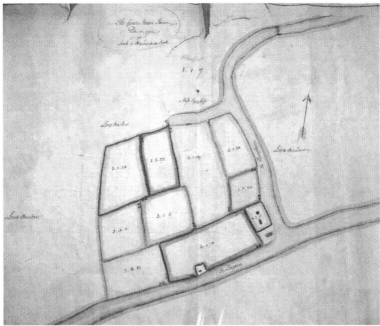

Map of Green Man Farm 1791 (Surrey History Centre)

197

ROAD, RAIL AND TRANSPORT

Gordon Knowles, in his book Surrey Roads from Turnpike to Motorway, described Surrey as lying between the Weald and the Downs. Most of the forests had disappeared by around 1700 and mostly uninhabited heathland was left. Settlements developed around farmland but many were isolated in bad weather as the roads were usually unsurfaced, not very wide, with no defined edges. Road maintenance had been infrequent, although landlords had responsibility for the upkeep of any public highways that ran through their land. In 1555 legislation was passed requiring each parish to repair the roads within its boundaries and this remained in place until 1835. *'Every fit male was required to contribute his unpaid labour several times a year to help and to provide his tools and a horse and cart if he had the means. Wealthier citizens bought out their contribution, as they often did for military service in time of war.'* By 1575 amendments to this legislation were made so that local Justices of the Peace could raise rates to repair roads.

Burpham was built around the London to Portsmouth road, which was an important route for naval and military travellers. Sadly for the parish of Worplesdon, this meant that there was a high volume of traffic on this road and therefore it needed more effort to keep it roadworthy. Parishes with small populations often carried an unfair burden and this was clearly the case for Burpham and Worplesdon. Matthew Alexander, local historian and Guildford Remembrancer, said that the basic method of road repair was simply to bring gravel in carts and the workmen would shovel it into the ruts and potholes to produce a (temporarily) smooth surface. However, the local geology was unfavourable, with London Clay soil contributing to the sticky mud in winter and there was little good roadstone available nearby. Peter Brandon, in his History of Surrey, commented that in the days before the late 19th century the roads in West Surrey were so bad that often wagons could not pass because of the wet clay soil. Farmers had to resort to using pack horses in order to get produce to market along bridle roads.

From 1653, when the Wey Navigation was opened, much of the heavy freight traffic moved onto the waterways, especially that serving local mills. Canal boats were horse-drawn. The decline of this form of transport started with the coming of the railways in the mid 19th century, then with the growing use of road haulage in the 20th century only very few canals survived until the mid 1960s. Renewed interest in the 21st century has brought projects to restore canals and a new leisure industry has built up around travelling on narrow boats.

In the 18th century it became clear that the arrangements for maintaining roads were not adequate and Turnpike trusts were formed (the name came from the pivoted bar which originally acted as a gate). Essentially, these were privatised main roads, where toll fees were collected from travellers at tollgates. By 1830, about 22,000 miles of turnpike roads operated in England. Milestones were made compulsory at the new turnpikes so that travellers could calculate their toll, which was based on mileage for the journey. There used to be a milestone on the London

Road, about half way between Orchard Road and Winterhill Way, but either it has succumbed to the undergrowth or was lost when houses were built and the road widened. It told travellers that it was 44 miles to Portsmouth, 27 miles to Hyde Park Corner, 2 miles to Guildford and 4 miles to Ripley. There is still a milestone at the corner of Boxgrove Road and London Road. Signposts on roads were mandatory from the late 17th century.

Money from the tolls, along with the local rates set by the Justices, provided the funding for maintaining the roads. However, the toll system was often abused and frequently some of the money would end up in the toll keeper's pockets. The Portsmouth road through Burpham was taken over by the Kingston and Sheetbridge Turnpike Trust in 1749 and continued until 1870. This Trust also had responsibility for the road right into Guildford and down the High Street.

Coaching inns were frequent along the roads, where coaches could stop to change horses and many also provided food, drink and accommodation for the travellers if required. Locally there was one in Ripley and several in Guildford. Horses were very important for travellers, either to be ridden or to pull carriages. The advent of motor cars in the late 19th century brought with it a reduction in the need for blacksmiths who were also farriers. Many converted to be motor engineers instead. The use of horses for travel and on farms decreased until, in the 21st century, there are very few shire horses left in the country and other horses are used mainly for leisure activities.

OS map 1869 showing Green Man Gate (just to left of no. 782)

Toll houses were a feature on toll roads and 27 still exist in Surrey. In Merrow there is still a little road off Epsom Road, called Tollgate. Burpham's toll gate was called Green Man Gate and seems to have been located about halfway between New Inn Farmhouse and the Anchor & Horseshoes. It can just be seen on the OS map from 1869 as a small building jutting out into the road. No images have been found for the Burpham toll gate but it is likely that it looked much like the one in the picture of the Toll Gate on Portsmouth Road.

In 1851 the toll collector was John Turner. He was born in Send & Ripley in about 1814 and at the time of the 1841 census he was collector of tolls for Send. He married Emily Pike in 1838 and they had two children, Emily and Walter. Young Emily was one year old in 1851 and was born in Ripley, so John and his family must have moved to Burpham not long before the census. By 1861 he was the toll collector at Artington on the Portsmouth Road before moving into Guildford, where in 1881 he was collector of rates in Bury Street. It is possible that the man in the photo of the Portsmouth Road Toll Gate was actually John Turner. According to the 1871 census, John was a cripple.

Toll gate on Portsmouth Road c. 1870 (Guildford Institute – Box 1C - 7007)

In 1861 the Burpham toll collector was John Wapshott, born in Ripley in about 1791. He married Elizabeth Worsfold in 1813 and

202

they had several children. In 1851 he had been a labourer on the turnpike road in Ripley and in 1841 he was just recorded as a labourer. Elizabeth was partly disabled and received poor relief in her later years. John died in 1869 and was buried at St Luke's. Elizabeth carried on the job of collecting tolls for a short while until the house was sold.

The auction notice for the Green Man Gatehouse and garden appeared in the Surrey Mirror in June 1870. The house was described as a brick built and slate roofed freehold property, with an excellent garden attached. The frontage to the turnpike road was 160 ft. For some reason the porch was not included in the sale. Elizabeth died in 1877 and was buried with her husband at St Luke's. It is not known when the house was demolished, though OS maps up to 1934 still appeared to show the building. No records seem to have survived to tell what the toll charges were at Green Man Gate. However, records show that in 1867 the Merrow Toll gate charged '*4d a horse; 10d per score of bullocks; 5d per score of sheep*'.

The coming of the railway to Guildford in 1845 affected traffic on the roads as both people and freight changed to using trains instead of horse and carriage. For a while, until the motor car arrived, often the fastest traffic on the roads were cyclists, and by the late 1890s cycling had become a major recreational pursuit. Ripley village was a very popular meeting place for cyclists in the late 19th century.

The main Guildford railway station was opened in May 1845 and was then enlarged and rebuilt in 1880. The New Guildford Line, which used the London Road station, opened in 1885 and runs from the town behind Ganghill, George Abbot School and up to the Merrow Depot at the top of New Inn Lane. Development of the rail system brought electrification of the lines by the 1920s and many improvements in rail services. In the 21st century there are suggestions that the depot should be converted into a station to serve Burpham and Merrow, but whether or not this will ever happen is open to question.

In 1889 the new Surrey County Council had been created and control over main roads across the county was handed over to them. The Council arranged for roads to have new surfaces, using water-bound macadam, which was broken stone that was crushed by steam rollers and then by the wheels of the traffic to form a solid surface. However, in winter they turned to mud and in the summer they were mostly dust. In 1899 an advertisement appeared in the Surrey Advertiser & County Times seeking tenders for watering roads during the months of May to August. Messrs A & A Streeter submitted their tender of £135 8s per day per horse and man, but Mr A H Shotter's tender of £117 10s 7d per day per horse and man was clearly cheaper and the County Council, as is often still the case, accepted the lower tender.

During the 19th century there were developments in transport that would eventually lead to the motor car of the 20th century. There were problems in these early days such as The Locomotives on Highways Act of 1865, which restricted 'road locomotives', to include combustion-engine cars, to four miles per hour in the country and two mph in towns. All steam or petrol powered cars were required to have a man carrying a red flag walking in front to warn horse riders, drivers of horse-drawn vehicles and those on foot or the oncoming vehicle. By the late 1890s the speed limit was raised to 12mph and the requirement for a red flag had been abolished.

Burpham crossroads, looking towards New Inn Lane, c. 1950 (D Rose)

Gordon Knowles wrote that in 1900 the Surrey Chief Constable, Capt. Sant, appeared to hate motorists and issued *'A caution to cyclists and drivers of motor cars in respect of furious driving and riding on highways...Should this be insufficient I shall be obliged to have recourse to more stringent measures.'* He then set up speed traps, especially on the London to Portsmouth Road, where the stretch of road through Ripley was a particular hot spot. His efforts were lampooned in the national press and Punch magazine printed cartoons on the subject. Capt. Sant remained in charge until 1930 and after he left there was a less aggressive approach to motorists.

In the early years of the 20th century people were just getting used to motor cars and other vehicles on the roads. However, in 1907 there was an accident in Guildford, when one of the Ranger & Co's Roller Mills steam lorries rolled back into the window of the undertaker's shop, Messrs A E Edwins & Son, in North Street. According to the Guildford Dragon, the driver, Walter Lampard, was sitting at the steering wheel at the time, but was unable to stop the vehicle. The crash caused considerable damage to the shop, but it seems that the lorry was little the worse for wear.

Ranger & Co 's lorry crash in North Street (Guildford Institute – Box 17A 1a)

206

Considering that the speed limit in the early 1900s was only about 20 m.p.h. the idea of racing on the public highway seems rather far fetched. However, in 1908 Gustave Oscar Alson, of Burpham Lodge, and John Thomas Millett were accused of road racing at Ripley. They had started outside the Talbot Hotel and had driven at about 35 - 40 m.p.h. along the main road at a very busy time of day. The following day Mr Millett was found near the Green Man with a car that was smashed to fragments. Both were fined £10 plus costs. Perhaps Capt. Sant's speed traps were responsible for catching them, though the report in The Times stated that the police constable was in his house when he saw them lining up, with the landlord, watch in hand, who shouted 'Go'. Then, the police sergeant was sitting in the police station when he saw the two cars race by.

By 1905 tar macadam, a mixture of tar or bitumen and sand or slag, was being used on the Portsmouth Road near Esher and from 1909 tar spraying was carried out on an annual basis on many roads. In 1909 Lloyd George introduced a system of vehicle licensing and taxation on petrol 'solely to provide income for improving and maintaining roads.' The car was becoming more popular and traffic congestion on the roads became serious, leading to the construction of bypasses around towns. The speed limit was raised to 30mph in 1934. However, during the First World War there was a large increase in traffic due to troop movements, which inevitably broke up the road surfaces. Four miles of the Portsmouth Road was almost destroyed by traffic to and from Witley Camp.

The Surrey Advertiser reported a motor fatality in February 1916 on the London Road, between the two Burpham public houses. A labourer called Joseph Stacey, aged about 70 years, was knocked down by a motor car belonging to Lady Warmington, who lived in Kensington, and he died from his injuries. Norman Phillips, who worked as Foreman at the Guildford Fruit Farm in Burpham, identified the body and witnesses said that the victim, although he might have had a few glasses of beer, was certainly sober. The chauffeur said '*I had just passed the Anchor and Horse Shoe. Everything was all black, the trees overhanging the road at this point. I was driving at about 12 miles an hour, and did not see anything until I felt "a sort of a bang" in front of me"...*'. Norman Phillips also said that the piece of road was very dangerous owing to its slippery state, and there had been several instances of skidding during the past three weeks.

In 1934 there were major works on the A3 and the Guildford and Godalming bypass was opened. Much of the work was done as unemployment relief, the Council receiving Government grants in return for employing unemployed men from areas of the country where work was hard to find. In 1937 the Ministry of Transport took on responsibility for main roads but continued to delegate most of the work to county councils. The number of accidents increased, partly due to breakdowns of cars and partly due to pedestrians not realising how fast the cars were travelling. This caused great concern leading to improvements in footpath construction, child safety education and road layout. Steam locomotives, trams and trolley buses were all phased out by the

1960s, though by the early 21st century trams were making a comeback in parts of the country.

In 1939 A Streeter & Co Ltd, public works contractors, were laying the sewer in Burpham Lane. They asked for permission to tip the surplus from their excavations into a large hole about 200 yards from St Luke's Church and this was agreed. However, there were complaints from the County Lane Agent about the tipping not being in accordance with the agreement and there were problems with the maintenance of the track.

The first stretch of motorway in Britain, the Preston bypass, was opened in 1958, followed by the M1 in 1959. Access to Surrey from other parts of the country was made easier with the building of the M25, finally completed in 1986. Until 1934 the London Road through Burpham and Guildford was the main road. Then, in June that year the Guildford to Godalming By-Pass, after five years of construction, was opened formally by the Minister of Transport. A small group of Burpham Primary School children with a teacher attended the event. The A3 bypass in the 1980s was intended to reduce the volume of traffic coming through Burpham. However, in order to build this stretch of road there was a lot of debate about exactly where the route should go. Apparently one proposed route was successfully opposed by the billionaire Paul Getty, who lived at Sutton Place, because it would have gone across his land. Unfortunately, drivers cannot leave the A3 at Burpham when going north or join the A3 to go south, so there are still problems with volume of traffic at the Burpham junctions and along the London Road to get to the other Guildford junctions.

Clay Lane running over the river by Bower's Lock (BCA)

In 1969 there were proposals to knock down Pimm's Row cottages and eleven other newer houses. The County Architect wrote '*Although nominally eight cottages, originally two up two down, some years ago on the instructions of the Smallholdings Committee they were converted to form four dwellings and modernised by the provision of bathroom, toilet, etc. The accommodation now comprises a living room, parlour, kitchen, store and larder, with three bedrooms and bathroom above. There is also an outshut containing store, coalshed and outside toilet to each cottage. The cottages are built of red brick with plain tile roofs and a dentil course with eaves. The windows are wood casements. Nos 49 and 50, the two (now one) northern cottages, were probably a slightly later addition having a lower ground floor level with increased head room and a straight joint*

210

in the brickwork where adjoining the other cottages at the southern end. The loss of the cottages would be somewhat regrettable, as although of only modest character individually, they form quite a pleasant group and are in fair condition. They are included in the SCC list of antiquities and there is a fire plaque on the wall of no. 45.'

The Guildford to Godalming By-pass c. 1934 postcard

Courage Barclay & Simmonds Ltd objected to the proposals for the route on the grounds that trade for the Green Man and the Anchor & Horseshoes would be adversely affected. They wanted Guildford Borough Council to erect suitable signing on the new road to indicate the existence and position of both licensed premises. However, the Ministry of Transport replied that it was not their practice to erect such signs.

In 1974 there were objections from the owners of two Burpham properties that would be affected by the new road. Both Bower's

Mill and the Mill House lay beside the proposed route and the road would cut through part of their grounds. Alternative routes were offered by the Guildford Scheme, which would not cut the village in two, avoid having to demolish houses and would not affect the playing field. It was said that there would be less danger for school children. One alternative was to run the road through Weylea Farm. However, eventually it was agreed to take some of the primary school's playground instead and cut off the old Jacob's Well Road, leaving two cul-de-sacs on either side of the A3. A big concrete acoustic fence was built along the boundary of the school grounds in order to reduce traffic noise, but as the volume of traffic has increased over the years this has become less effective.

The new Clay Lane was built on the other side of Sutherland Memorial Park from the old Jacob's Well Road. Keith Powell remembered that when the A3 was built there were concerns about lead emissions affecting the children on the school playground and for a while they had to play on the other side of the school site. Oliver Mason remembered that when the A3 was being built some of the workmen lifted a pole that hit the overhead electrical cables and one of them died.

It will be interesting to see what happens in the future. Proposals for the Guildford Local Plan 2016 suggest that additional access junctions could be created to support the development of housing on Gosden Hill Farm. There has also been a suggestion that a tunnel could be a solution to congestion on the A3.

According to the Automobile Association there were 4.5 million cars on the roads in 1958 but by 2008 this had increased to 28 million. There were less than 200,000 miles of road in 1958 and nearly 250,000 miles of road in 2008, including 2,200 miles of motorway. However, the number of people killed in road accidents had halved during this period. In 1965 a speed limit of 70mph was introduced, reducing casualties as a result.

By the 1960s parking was becoming a problem and traffic wardens appeared for the first time in 1963. In the 1980s it was claimed that nearly 45% of Surrey residents owned a car. Sadly this has brought a decline in the provision of public transport.

Gordon Knowles summarised in his book that 'The Portsmouth road was the most important in the county during the Turnpike era, not least in military terms. By the early years of the 20th century the Portsmouth road carried some 2,000 motor vehicles daily near Esher. 80 years later the Esher bypass was taking well over 50,000 vehicles a day...The A3 is today virtually up to motorway standard throughout all the 68 miles from London to Portsmouth, except that unlike the motorways there remain numerous side roads entering and exiting from it, and, of course, there is no restriction on the type of user.'

Usually hot air balloons set off and land in open spaces, but in September 2014 the residents of Elder Close were rather surprised to find one coming down to them. Get Surrey reported the incident saying that 'A hot air balloon sponsored by Wonderbra was left deflated when it clipped a roof and a car as it came down over houses in Burpham. It seemed to struggle to stay airborne but dropped down, narrowly avoiding the roofs of some houses, it caught one roof and the back of a car parked in the road.

One would like to think that in the 21st century people would have some common sense about using motorways, but in 1987 a letter appeared in The Times newspaper from PC G B Oliver, of the Burpham Traffic Centre. *'Sir, Mr Bush (October 9) recommends fried puffball mushrooms. As a serving traffic patrol officer with the Surrey Constabulary on the M25, I would like to point out that pedestrians and stopping are both prohibited on the motorways (other than for emergencies). Motorway madness takes many forms, but please – no mushroom pickers in lane three of the M25.'*

It is interesting to look at the names of roads in Burpham and ask where do the names come from? London Road is the obvious example, being the road from Portsmouth to London, and at times it was known as the Portsmouth Road. New Inn Lane must refer to New Inn Farm, or perhaps the New Inn, if indeed it existed. Burpham Lane has variously been called Jacobs Well Road, Bower's Lane and Green Man Lane, all of which describe where it is or where it is going. Winterhill Way refers to Winterhill Farm, but Briar Way and Hawthorne Way may only refer to local hedgerows and plants. Orchard Way clearly relates to the orchard that used to be part of Winterhill Farm and then was Guildford Fruit Farm. Merrow Lane was the road to Merrow from the old London Road. Gosden Hill Road is close to Gosden Hill Farm whereas Great Oaks Park, Oak Tree Close and Oak Hill probably

214

refer to the trees that used to grow there. Raynham Close remembers Mr Raynham, George Abbot School's first Headmaster.

Weylea Avenue clearly refers to Weylea Farm, whilst Marlyn's Drive and Marlyn's Close were both built on land belonging to the Marlyn's estate. Paddocks Road was built where the Marlyn's paddocks were located, though it could refer to The Paddocks house, and Meadow Road refers to the meadow that was there in 1838. Some names may remember people of Burpham (though some may just be a coincidence), such as Howard Ridge (Roy and Percival Howard, builders); Pimms Close (W F Pimm, landowner and farmer); Elkins Gardens (W Elkins, brewer); Hodgson Gardens (possibly either Kingston Hodgson Brewery or the Misses Hodgson, who lived in Marlyn's Cottage for many years); Sutherland Drive (Duke of Sutherland); Gatley Drive (George and Percy Gatley, farmers); Turner Close (William Turner, shopkeeper); and in 2016 the newest one was Wroth Place (Robert Wroth, Guildford MP and Lord of the Manor of Burgham).

On Weybrook Park there are many references to the land's origin, such as Bower's Farm Drive. There are several names of farms in the vicinity, such as Ladygrove, Hazelhurst and Tythebarn. Newark probably refers to the now ruin of Newark Priory in Ripley. Dairyman's Walk must relate to the dairy farm, whereas Jersey and Guernsey may refer to the type of cows kept there.

When asked if there was a policy for naming roads, Guildford Borough Council said that there was nothing in place and

215

therefore it could be a bit haphazard. However, it is good to see that some of Burpham's residents are remembered in the names of the roads.

Over the years there have probably been numerous accidents on the busy London Road, including two in 1935. One was a lady driving out of New Inn Lane onto the main road, when she crashed into a motor coach. She was injured, as was one of the coach passengers and a pedestrian – all of them were taken to the Royal Surrey County Hospital. Also that year Bert Blake, who was the head gamekeeper to Lord Onslow, died in hospital after being knocked down by a motor car at Burpham. In 1953 Henry Charles Hunt was knocked down and killed by a hit and run driver while riding his bicycle out of New Inn Lane onto the main road. His grandson, Michael Hunt, said that this motivated the Council to build the roundabout by the Green Man.

Jan Kemp remembered that the bus from Guildford used to turn round in the Green Man car park before returning to the town. It cost 1½d (old pence) per trip for a child.

However, in February 2015 one of Burpham's best known landmarks was hit by a car. The King Edward VIII post-box outside Cycle Works on the London Road Parade of shops was hit when an elderly lady drove out of the car park, straight through the bollards and into the postbox, knocking it to a very jaunty angle. The lady sustained a leg fracture and was taken to the Royal Surrey County Hospital. Quite how she managed to miss the bollards is not clear, but apparently she was more concerned about whether or not she had hit anyone. The postbox was repaired within a month and the lady driver recovered.

In 2016 a trailer, carrying a Spitfire aeroplane to a 1940s weekend on the Isle of Wight, overturned on the A3. There have been a large number of accidents on this road in recent years, some due to speeding and some due to the high volume of traffic.

In 2002 several motorists rang the police to report a car crashed off the A3 by the Burpham junction. However, when officers went to investigate they found no new crash, only the wreckage of a Vauxhall Astra, which contained the remains of a man, very close to the reported crash site. The car was nose-down in the ditch and almost impossible to see from the road. It seems that the crash had happened almost six months earlier - the car's battery was dead and the body was badly decomposed. The incident has gone down in Surrey folklore as a ghostly story, because so many of the drivers who reported the crash had said that the car went off the road with its headlights blazing.

As a busy and important traffic route there have been times when the London Road has carried a range of interesting cargos through Burpham. In 1932 people lined the streets of Guildford to see the world's largest lorry carrying the rudder of the Cunard liner RMS Berengaria. It was being transported from Darlington to Southampton by road and the lorry was 41 feet in length, so could only travel at 5 m.p.h. Newspaper reports said that it arrived via Burpham '...and when it reached the roundabout at the

217

by-pass it took the right-hand bend, and traffic which had been held up was allowed to pass through along the left-hand bend.' Brian and Sylvia Wheeler remembered Sir Francis Chichester's boat, Gipsy Moth IV (which sailed around the world in 1967), coming through Burpham, so everyone sat on the wall of the pub to watch.

A3 traffic from Clay Lane 2016

In recent years there have been road closures for sporting events, such as the Surrey Half Marathon, and, in 2012, the Olympic cycle races. Although these have caused some disruption for local residents, they have also provided an opportunity to be part of both local and national celebrations of sport. However, closures of roads are not a modern phenomenon. In 1940 the Surrey Advertiser reported that due to the Burpham Main Drainage Scheme, New Inn Lane would be closed for twelve weeks. The report informed readers that the alternative route would be by travelling along Merrow Lane.

218

Many of Burpham's older residents will remember the quiet roads of years gone by. One of the BCA's early newsletters included a letter from Mrs I A Carr, who recalled what the village was like in the 1920s. '...On my way to Guildford, passing the olde village of Ripley with fields and farms each side of the road. Towards Merrow Lane, a large estate on the right – namely Sutton Place, property of the Duke of Sutherland. On the left the estate of Lord Onslow, this being orchards with once more farms and fields. Crops growing, cows and horses, sheep and chickens running free everywhere. Often a hare or rabbit hopping across the main road from field to field.

During this my first visit to the Surrey country-side, we saw coming towards us, at a trot, an olde fashioned stage coach. It had an open top painted black and orange. Ladies and gentlemen in costume, ladies in large hats tied under chin with ribbons. Gentlemen in top hats in open carriage, trumpeter in bright uniform, standing at the rear with a large post horn which he blew at intervals, onwards to the races.

No one travelled at speed. Coaches and lorries were seldom seen, mostly vans or cycle. Plenty of room on the roads, no parking problems! Progress continues! What of the Good Olde Days? Never mind, we still have our memories!'

WATER, WATER, EVERYWHERE

Roger Marjoribanks suggested that Burpham could mean 'Fort in the Water-Meadow'. This name would fit with the area that we know in the 21st century, where flooding is often a problem for parts of the community. The River Wey and Wey Navigation provide the northern boundary for the village, whilst the stream that comes down from Merrow, along the back of Great Oaks Park, through Weybrook Park and the ford on Dairyman's Walk, joins the river just past Bower's Mill. It seems that the stream originated from Clandon Park and then ran through Winterhill Farm land on its way to the Wey. It has now been given the name

Car in flooded ford - 2016 (M Bass)

Merrow Common Stream. However, at times of heavy rain it becomes full and fast running, flooding gardens on its way.

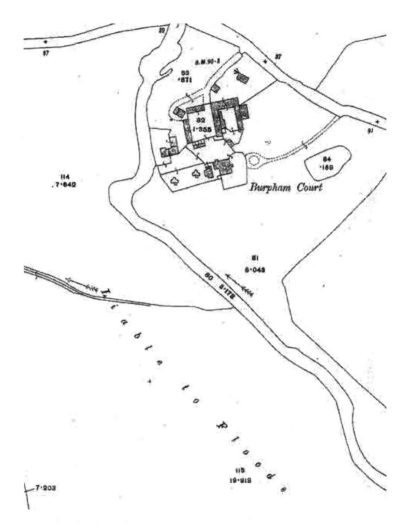

OS map 1869 clearly denotes liability to floods

The ford in Dairyman's Walk can be quite easy to drive through,
but again, at times of heavy rain, it floods and there have been
numerous incidents of vehicles being caught in the floodwater,
driven by over-optimistic drivers. There is another watercourse

221

running south of New Inn Lane, but it seems that most of that has been culverted by developments in the area. In 1997 the Surrey Advertiser reported that residents of Weybrook Park, led by Geoffrey Constantine, were saying that enough was enough and demanding that a bridge be built across the ford. He said *'Every year there are thousands of pounds of damage caused to vehicles trying to cross the ford. A couple of years ago some dinner ladies were swept downstream in their van and it cost me £2,000 to have my car engine replaced when I got stuck there.'*

Along Clay Lane it is common to see the flooded fields of Burpham Court Farm when there has been heavy rainfall, and often flooding the road as well. The Headmistress of Burpham Primary School wrote in her logbook in 1916 that *'children who came with wet feet were sent home'* and *'the school not opened as the roads were flooded'*. Flooding was one of the big problems for Bob Dearnley at Burpham Court Farm, so it was interesting to note that Surrey Wildlife Trust had to cancel their Big Wildlife Count scheduled for late June 2016 due to flooding at the farm. The question is, will this affect their partnership with Guildford Borough Council to create a nature reserve there?

The Surrey Water Management Project has recognised that there are flooding problems in Burpham. It has been proposed that a detailed watercourse walkover survey is undertaken in order to establish the source and pathway of each of the watercourses that drain towards Merrow Lane. Maintenance is required to deal with bank erosion, blocked channels in places, removing vegetation and accumulated sediment. The Burpham Neighbourhood Plan,

222

agreed by referendum in 2016, stated that *'The flood plain converted to water meadows in the early 1600s prior to the building of the Wey Navigation – the dykes and ditches built during construction have protected the surrounding area from flooding for 400 years.'* It also said *'This important area of Green Belt flood plain is critical to maintaining river levels by preventing flooding up stream and controlling water flow to the downstream section of the River Wey.'*

Pollution in the water is not a new problem. In 1895 the Surrey Mirror reported that *'At the meeting of the Guildford Rural District Council, on Saturday, a communication was read from the Thames Conservancy complaining of the pollution of streams in several parishes and stating that sewage and other offensive matters from various premises passed into channels, which ultimately flowed into the River Wey. The parishes included were Gomshall, Send, Worplesdon, Merrow, Wisley, Burpham and Ockham. The matter was left in the hands of the surveyor.'* The thought of that pollution does not sit well with the image of children playing in the river. It is to be hoped that 120 years later things are rather better and people are more conservation minded.

It is likely that there were also wells in communities, but the Tithe Maps do not show these so it is not clear where they might have been in Burpham. However, in 2016 part of the front car park of the Anchor & Horseshoes collapsed and when investigated it was found that there had been a well there.

Village pond or Traction Engine Replenishment Pond? 2016 (T Bass)

It is possible that there were various ponds around the village in past years, but it has been difficult to confirm these. According to the Tithe Maps of 1838 there was a pond next to the Anchor & Horseshoes pub on London Road, but it is thought that this was filled in and cottages were built on that site. Farms usually have ponds, so perhaps there were ponds on each of the farm sites. The only one that still exists seems to be at Burpham Court Farm, just inside the entrance gate on the left.

In 1914 The Angling Society reported that Britton's Pond, Burpham, had been stocked with Thames Dace, in deference to the wishes of many members.

However, there is a pond in the woodland between New Inn Lane and Merrow Lane. The first mention of this in BCA papers was in 1975 when there was reference to clearing the woods on Merrow Lane. As part of this project the Conservation Society from George Abbot boys school had cleared the pond area. Then in 1986 the BCA newsletter reported on a conservation project to clean and restore the pond saying that it was '*the village pond – Burpham's best kept secret'*. They were hoping to introduce plants and fish and said that it was already a habitat for newts, frogs and dragon-flies, with occasional visits by mallard ducks and deer. In about 2004 the BCA again reported that the pond was to be restored but no more has been heard of the project. This pond was unknown to the majority of Burpham residents and seems to be rather out of the way for a village pond.

It has been suggested that it was probably a traction engine water replenishment pond instead and perhaps a definitive answer will not be found. However, OS maps from the late 1800s show what was probably a pond in that area, so presumably it has been there for at least 140 years. Pete Gardner remembered that there was a good place for young people to meet up in the woods by the pond, known as Middle Oak.

With all the flooding around Guildford over the years it has to be assumed that there was similar flooding around Burpham. Two of the worst years were 1900, when wood and debris from Moon's Timber Yard smashed into the Town Bridge, destroying it; then 1968 when the John Collyer menswear shop (now Wagamama's) on the corner of High Street and Friary Street had floodwater half way up their door. Ken and Doreen Marshall remembered that in 1968 the Girl Guide camp was flooded out so the girls had to be rescued.

Skating on Shalford Meadows in 1908 (Guildford Institute)

Besides the flooding, there were also various opportunities for skating when the river and water meadows froze over. This happened in 1895 when the river at Millmead was completely frozen. No records have been found to provide evidence of anything similar in Burpham, but it is quite possible that members of the local community were out on the river or the fields skating, as they did on Shalford Meadows.

In April 1979 the BCA reported that following exceptionally heavy rain, the stream behind Great Oaks Park houses had become a raging torrent, overflowing and submerging gardens and flooding

226

houses. This caused thousands of pounds worth of damage. The Council gave £25,000 to render the stream safe.

Flooding at Burpham (J Allen)

THE RIVER WEY AND GODALMING NAVIGATIONS

Alan Crosby, in his book A History of Woking, wrote that by the late 16th century the potential growth and prosperity of Guildford, where the wool and cloth trade was in decline, was restricted because of limited access to London. Sir Richard Weston lived at Sutton Park, owning land by the River Wey. The river was largely unnavigable, with many twists and turns, making it almost impossible to use for transportation. But his idea of cutting artificial waterways over meadows and fields and constructing 12 locks provided a shortened route and all year round navigation, giving access to the River Thames from both Guildford and Godalming.

In around 1618 Sir Richard cut through his land, from Stoke Mill to Sutton Green, creating a towing path and several bridges. One of the benefits was to enable him to irrigate his fields by flooding many acres of his farmland in a controlled manner, through the creation of water-meadows. This included *cutting watercourses through the highways and wastes of the manor of Burpham*' in order to make and maintain bridges. In 1619 he agreed, with James Russell of Horsell, access *to repair the new river, its banks and a cartway adjoining, on the land of James Russell in Burpham*'. In 1621 he agreed a contract with Burleigh Cooper, yeoman of Burpham, for *access to land in order to amend the river bank and watercourse of a new river*', for a consideration of 50 shillings per annum. As a catholic and a supporter of the King, Weston's land was seized during the Civil War and he fled to

Europe, travelling mainly in the Netherlands and Belgium, where he was very impressed by the canals and locks.

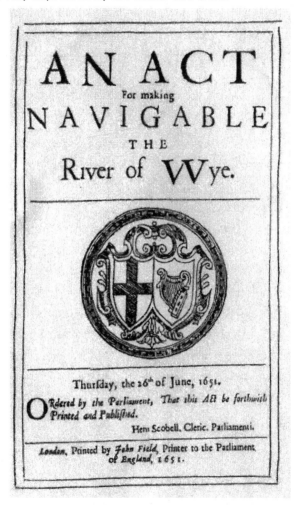

AN ACT
For making
NAVIGABLE
THE
River of Wye.

Thurſday, the 26ᵗʰ of June, 1651.

ORdered by the Parliament, That this Act be forthwith Printed and Publiſhed.

Hen: Scobell. Cleric. Parliamenti.

London, Printed by John Field, Printer to the Parliament of England, 1651.

Act of Parliament for the Wey Navigation 1651 (SIHG)

He returned in the late 1640s with ideas for controlled flooding of pastures and creating navigable channels as highways. Through

229

James Pitson, a Commissioner for Surrey, Richard Weston was acquitted and was able to present a bill to Parliament for creating a navigable stretch of the River Wey. This became an Act of Parliament in June 1651, funding provided by issuing shares, and work started two months later with around 200 men employed as 'navvies'. The toll for carrying freight on the river was set at four shillings.

Sadly, he died in May 1652 before the project was finished, but with ten of the fifteen mile route completed. His son George continued the work, enabling the waterway, from Guildford to Weybridge, to be opened officially in 1653. There were four new weirs, twelve bridges, ten new locks and a wharf at Guildford. The project had cost £15,000, which was a considerable amount of money at the time, and had bankrupted the Weston estate. His legacy, however, was the largest and first commercially viable waterway in the country, effectively preceding the so-called Canal Age by at least 100 years. In 1675 John Weston of Sutton Place agreed the lease of land belonging to William Banister of Burpham, yeoman, for an *annual rent of 33s 4d for cutting the new river through lands called Bancroft in Burpham, and for access to the watercourse and banks*.

Transporting timber for the shipbuilding yards on the Thames was a great source of income but after the Great Fire of London in 1666 there was a need for wood for rebuilding the capital. Surrey forests provided the wood and the Wey Navigation provided the transport.

There was another project in 1760 to extend the Navigation from Guildford to Godalming, with four more locks, and this opened in 1763. Peter Brandon, in his book A History of Surrey, wrote that the Navigation was one of the oldest built waterways in England. *'By short-cutting bends with lengths of canal and inserting locks, it became possible for barges from the Thames at Weybridge to reach the Town Wharf at Guildford. This brought much prosperity to the town: a levy of 1d (one penny) on every load (25 cwt) in 1794 was enough to pave the streets'.* This levy was known as the River Pence.

Below Bower's Lock c. 1900 (D Rose)

Roger Hunt, in his book Rural Britain Then and Now, wrote that barge size was constrained by the size of the locks and bridges on the waterways, but usually they were less than 70ft long by 7ft 2ins wide. Most barges were brightly painted, and there are still

231

many examples of narrow boat art around, pulled by horses, mules or donkeys, which walked along the towpath. In 1867 there was an entry in Kelly's Directory for a Carrier by water – William Stevens' barges, to and from London twice and three times a week.

Map of the Wey Navigation from Ripley to Guildford (weyriver.co.uk)

Surrey Industrial History Group's (SIHG) book 'The Wey Navigations' recorded that barge horses once crossed the river below Bower's Lock, by wading or swimming as there was no bridge for them. *'There is a story that the barge-owners protested to the Navigation authorities that the immersion of their horses, hot and sweaty from towing barges, imperilled the health of the animals. A horse bridge was built but all that can be seen of it now, to the east of the lock and below the water line, are the remains of the brick abutments.'*

The coming of the railways in the 1840s, followed by the development of road traffic in the early 1900s, brought about the decline of transportation on the canals. However, there was still work from the corn mills, although this was reducing, on the Wey up to the 1930s. The National Trust took over ownership of the River Wey Navigation from the Stevens family, who had bought up shares in the 18th century, in 1964 and acquired the Godalming Navigation in 1968. They are responsible for maintenance and improvements to the waterways, using volunteers working with the Lengthsman for each stretch of the river. The weirs are owned by the Environment Agency and the towpath is owned by various landowners, so it can be a challenge getting new ideas agreed by so many different interested parties.

Richard Cant is currently, at the time of writing, the Lengthsman for the stretch from Stoke Mill to Bower's Lock. On the Burpham Community Association's website (burphamca.weebly.com) he writes a regular news item about what is going on by the river each month. The Bower's Lock gates were replaced during the winter of 2016/17 as part of the programme of ongoing maintenance. There is also an annual meeting for River Users for the River Wey organised by the National Trust. There is a visitor centre at Dapdune Wharf where people can find out about the River Wey and Godalming Navigation as well as take part in a range of activities. From the late 1800s there has been an increase in the amount of leisure traffic on the river and in the 21ˢᵗ century it is common to see narrow boats by Bower's Lock in the summertime.

Rebuilding Bower's Lock in 1959 (R Cant, National Trust)

In October 2007 there was some excitement for the local community when a television production team descended on Burpham to film part of an episode of Lewis, the off-shoot from the Inspector Morse series, at Bower's Lock. Sutherland Memorial Park was used as a base for the catering, make-up, costumes, and other trucks. Then in 2016 the trucks were back when filming for the ITV programme 'Unforgotten', again by the river. However, it is normally a quiet place, where local residents can walk, often with their dogs, and enjoy the environment. Jan Kemp recalled that just beyond the lock was a sandy beach, which was popular for children to swim in the river, and that boys used to dive into the lock.

Filming of Lewis at Bower's Lock in 2007 (R Cant, National Trust)

On the opposite side of the river from the lock lies the land belonging to Sutton Park. In earlier years, the owners allowed local residents to walk on the land up to the tree line, but the current owner in 2017, a Russian billionaire, is not so welcoming and big notices warn that the land is private and walkers must keep to the towpath.

The river can be a dangerous place and there have been accidents over the years. In June 1909 the children of Burpham Primary School attended the funeral of their classmate Sidney Ranger, the

235

eight year old son of the miller, who drowned in the river. In 1932 The Times reported that a woman's body had been found in the River Wey at Burpham on Easter Monday. She was Mrs Lily Bunting, aged 45 years, of Aldershot Road. She had gone for an evening walk in late February and not returned. The coroner said that her death was not due to drowning.

Sutton Park lands by Bower's Lock 2015

The farmer, W L Keene, died in 1974 and was found, presumed drowned, at the water's edge - he had never learned to swim. Sylvia Laney remembered that in about 1953 a boy who worked at Bower's Farm went swimming in the river, but got caught in the reeds. Although his friend tried to save him he drowned. According to Mick Worsfold's family story, in the Burpham Will

Remember Them project, William Worsfold drowned in Bower's Lock in June 1890. His clothes were found on the river bank and it was assumed that he went to have a wash after work, before going to see his aunt Fanny Grover (nee Tickner), who lived near the Green Man. William was uncle to Walter Charles Worsfold, one of the soldiers on the War Memorial at St Luke's.

Wey Navigation by Bowers Lock (BCA)

In 1944 there was a very sad incident when a Canadian soldier was found hanged from a tree, on the Sutton Park side of the river near Bower's Lock. The newspaper report in the Surrey Times said that Sapper Magnus Brown, aged 46 years, of the Royal Canadian Engineers was found in early June. He had been a farmer in civilian life and was married with three children. He had gone missing shortly after parade and was found by a soldier of the Queen's Royal Regiment. The police attended the scene and it was reported that Sapper Brown's clothes were wet and it appeared that he had been partly drowned. This happened just a few days before D-Day so perhaps he couldn't face being part of the invasion. The inquest entered a verdict of suicide while the balance of mind was disturbed.

EDUCATION THROUGH THE AGES

Until 1908, there was no local school in Burpham, so children had to travel some distance for their schooling. Derek Gillard, on his website Education England, wrote that the Education Act of 1880 made elementary education compulsory for children between the ages of five and ten years, then by 1899 further legislation had raised the age for school attendance to 12 years. Children in Burpham had to walk to Merrow, Worplesdon Perry Hill, Sandfield, Stoke Hill or Charlotteville schools. Secondary school education was not available to many children, who were often expected to work from a very young age – and even with the legislation many would miss school days in order to help with the harvest. The public school system was in place for those parents who were able to pay for education, but in 1868 there were only nine of these schools across the country. The Taunton Report of 1868 looked at education in secondary schools as a whole and investigated 782 grammar and other schools, but they found that provision was poor and unevenly distributed.

Guildford was one of the lucky towns in having the Royal Grammar School, founded in 1509 when Robert Beckingham left money in his will to '*make a free scole at the Towne of Guldford*'. In 1572 Henry Atfeilde alias Ripley of Burpham, yeoman, left ten shillings in his will '*to building and finishing the Free Grammar School in Guildford*' – perhaps he or others in his family had attended the school. The Royal Grammar School houses a very rare chained library. Although it was deemed to be a free school, fees were charged from 1608 until 1944, when it became a voluntary controlled school. However, when grammar schools were abolished in 1977 it converted to the private sector and is now a very successful independent school.

The Taunton Report envisaged three grades of secondary education:
- first-grade schools with a leaving age of 18 or 19, preparing upper and upper-middle class boys for universities and the older professions;
- second-grade schools with a leaving age of 16 or 17, preparing middle class boys for the army, newer professions and the Civil Service; and
- third-grade schools with a leaving age of 14 or 15, for lower middle class boys who would become small tenant farmers, tradesmen and superior artisans.

Clearly girls were not expected to benefit from school education beyond primary stages as they were not included. It seems that any notion of social mobility was also discouraged.

In 1915 the Surrey Advertiser reported that the Surrey Education Committee had debated the employment of children in agriculture because many schools were affected by absences. It was agreed that no children under the age of 13 years should be allowed to work, but the report admitted that *Farmers would take on anyone they could get*.

The evidence of education in Burpham seemed to have started when the new elementary school opened in 1908, to become

Burpham Primary School, aimed at the children of Burpham and Jacob's Well. In 1939 the Surrey Advertiser ran adverts for the Westwing Kindergarten School, London Road, Burpham. It catered for girls aged 5-9 years and boys aged 5-8 years. The adverts stated that there were percussion band classes, music and dancing. The Kelly's Directory of 1944/5 showed the Westwing Kindergarten & Prep School as situated on London Road, between Orchard Road and Winterhill Way. Then in 1945 another advert ran saying '*Owing to lack of accommodation at Burpham, Westwing School is being transferred to 15 Rosemary Crescent, Guildford. Miss Wyatt will have vacancies this term.*' Maybe their lease had run out and they needed to relocate, or they ran out of space?

Burpham Primary School

Burpham Primary School - artist's impression of the school building in
1908 (K Raymond)

In June 1905 the Surrey Mirror published a notice by Surrey
County Council Local Education Authority saying that it would
provide a new public elementary school for 100 children in
Worplesdon, Burpham, for the parishes of Worplesdon and

242

Merrow.   The school opened on 31st August 1908, with 28 children and two teachers - Miss Lancaster was the Headmistress. The children (and often the teachers as well) suffered in the early years from a wide range of childhood illnesses, common at that time, including measles, mumps, chickenpox, whooping cough, scarlet fever and diphtheria.   In 1912 little Harry Bennett died from diphtheria and he was buried at St Luke's. The school was closed for several weeks and scrubbed clean throughout with disinfectant before the doctor announced that it could re-open.

Interestingly, there was almost no mention in any of the school archive documents of the First World War, but presumably morning assemblies included prayers for the local families and also remembered those who lost their lives. A school inspector's report in 1924 said that the school was improving but in 1925 the School Managers discussed a possible closure because it was so small.

It must have been a difficult time for Miss Lancaster and she decided to retire in 1927. Discussions about closure continued over the next few years and in 1930 the Managers' Meeting minutes said '...there is no indication of any material increase in the school population in the District served by Burpham School, such developments as appear to be likely to cater for people who send their children to public elementary schools.' With the benefit of hindsight this seems to have been very short-sighted as the village has grown enormously since 1945, after Burpham joined Guildford with the boundary changes of 1933.   The new

243

education authority clearly thought that Burpham needed a school so life continued much as before.

Whole school photo 1937

The Second World War and Operation Pied Piper brought evacuees from London schools, along with a small number of teachers, doubling the size of Burpham School. A report in the Surrey Advertiser from August 1939 showed what arrangements for air raid shelters were to be made at schools in the Guildford area. There were some concrete shelters to be built, but many schools, including Burpham, were to have concrete-lined trenches. The report said the cost of this, for 30 Burpham children, would be £70. These were not an unmitigated success as bad weather led to the trenches filling with water – surely an outcome to be expected after the experiences of the Great War?

Many ex-pupils remember the three Burpham teachers from the post war period – Miss Chesterfield (Headmistress), Miss Lugsden (with purple hair) and Miss Pratt (who taught drama). They ruled the school from the 1940s through to the 1970s, and are generally remembered with affection. They saw building developments as the school grew after the war, providing new classrooms, a hall, kitchen and a staffroom. It has always been the case that there are more female teachers at primary schools and Burpham has been no exception to this. There have been a few male teachers for Burpham children, including Mr Hart, Mr Hornsby, Mr Bunker, Mr Dalby, Mr Trinder, Mr Holmes and Mr Drummond, as well as Mr Goddard, who was Headteacher from 2003-2014.

Classroom late 1920s/early 1930s (P Hudson)

Jean Menzies was a pupil from 1937-1942 and remembered '*The building consisted of two classrooms divided by a folding*

245

partition, which was opened up for special occasions, a small hall and a cloakroom area with pegs for coats and washbasins. The toilets were across the playground next to the churchyard. They were eventually demolished in recent years - I think they should have been listed buildings! There was no office or admin staff and only two teachers: the Headmistress Miss Apling who took the top class, and Miss Hartley who taught the younger class. Classes were divided into standards based on age and ability. Desks were double seated and arranged in rows. Books were stored at the back of the classroom on shelves behind gingham curtains and had to be kept tidy. There were no felt tips or ball point pens, just pencils and then we progressed to a dip-pen, which was a nib on a stick. There were ceramic inkwells in the desks and monitors had the job of cleaning these in the cloakroom and removing the blotting paper which had been scrunched into them.'

Burpham Primary School children 1952 (Surrey Advertiser)

Vincent Tickner, 1954-59, remembered *'I was frustrated that there were no boys' sports in the school (completely run by* women), particularly of football, which we were not even permitted to play in the playground during the breaks, presumably because of limited playground space. Accordingly, I got into trouble at one point through running round and round the school in one lunch break with a friend shouting "We want football".' Also, remembering school dinners 'There seemed to be a government plot to feed us lots of cabbage, which palled after a time. One day, the meat was so gristly that I refused to eat mine. This was a crime. I was taken to the headmistress's office, where I was told that I could not leave until I had eaten it. At the end of the school day, I had still not eaten it, but I think the headmistress had seen how horrible it was, and I was summarily dismissed.'

District Sports, mid to late 1940s (J Menzies)

Christopher Harris, at the school 1963-69, remembered 'Miss Pratt was famous for shaking pupils by their ears and Mr Bunker

247

who had three rulers held together by elastic bands to hit you with. Wouldn't get away with that today.'

Mary Fry, 1960-66, remembered '*The vicarage opposite the school stood by itself, and once we were in our classrooms we could look out at cows grazing in the fields. I remember being out in the playground one day, when a noisy group of pigs rushed past, making their escape up Burpham Lane.'*

Morriss Kemp remembered that when he went to the school as a parent in the 1960s his wife Jan was astonished when he greeted Miss Chesterfield as Joyce. It turned out that they knew each other from playing badminton. Jan's father was the school caretaker after he gave up market gardening and her mother was a dinner lady.

Pete Gardner remembered that in the early 1960s his class was given '*what must have been the latest bit of techno kit in the form of a wonderful mechanical adding/subtracting/multiplying machine. You had to move levers to choose numbers and wind a handle to get the result. I loved it!'*

In 1976, having previously had well over 300 children on roll, the school converted to become an Infants' School, with only 90 children on roll and Miss Doxford as Headteacher. For the next 17 years most of the children of Burpham had to move to Bushy Hill School in Merrow at age 11 years. Then in 1992 a new Headteacher, Gayle Mawson, started the process of expanding back to full primary status and in 1995 the school gained Grant

Maintained Status, allowing it a great deal of autonomy. However, with the Labour Government of 1997 came the return of schools to the Local Authority fold and Burpham Primary School converted to Foundation Status.

Dinner ladies 1960s (J Beck)

From 28 children in 1908, the Centenary Celebrations in 2008 found 220 children experiencing an Edwardian school day, including a teacher with a cane and a bona fide school lunch of hot pot with bread rolls, followed by jam roly poly pudding, using Edwardian recipes. At the Open Day many ex-pupils joined the children and staff in celebrating 100 years of history, sharing their memories and stories. The Juniors' annual production for Centenary year was performed to sell-out audiences at the Electric Theatre in Guildford - the version of Alice Through the Looking Glass was written by an ex-parent. Parents and staff enjoyed a

Dinner Dance, there was a special Centenary Summer Fair and the year finished with a lovely Carol Service held at Holy Trinity Church in Guildford.

Burpham Primary School Centenary 2008 - whole school in Edwardian costume (M Hall)

From its opening in 1908, when it was intended for the children of Burpham and Jacob's Well, to the post war years, the school catered for the local community, but, with the developments of housing estates from the 1980s onwards, it became increasingly difficult for local children get a place. Admission criteria decreed that siblings took priority over those that lived nearest to the school. Derek Oliver remembered that when his family moved to one of the police houses in Burpham in the early 1950s, his father was told that Derek could not join the school. It seemed that Miss Chesterfield would not allow police families to be part of the school community – quite different to later years. With increasing popularity and success, by 2011 there were only three places available for children who didn't have an older sibling already in the school.

250

In 2012, in order to meet the demands for additional primary school places, the school started a programme of expansion to double in size. Each year, from 2012 to 2018, an extra year group class would be added so that by September 2018 there should be 430 children in the school. The new buildings were completed in 2015, so all the classrooms are ready for the new classes over the coming years. Burpham Primary School has for many years had a very good reputation in the local community. In recent years the school considered the possibility of becoming an academy or joining an academy trust, and in February 2017 the Governing Body decided to go ahead with becoming an academy as part of the local Multi-Academy Trust, Guildford Education Partnership, from September 2017. Following a visit by Ofsted Inspectors in March 2017 the school has been rated as Outstanding in all areas – a wonderful achievement.

Burpham Primary School's new junior block, opened 2015 (J White, Burpham Primary School)

Secondary Education

Secondary education in Guildford in the 20ᵗʰ century was offered by a range of schools. In the past, children who passed the 11+ examination were able to go to grammar schools, such as the Guildford County School, or for those less successful in this test then the Central School in Guildford (now the Adult Education Centre on Sydenham Road) was the likely destination. The Guildford Junior Technical School opened in 1912 as a trade school for boys aged 13-16 to receive the necessary training for employment. The Central School opened in 1928 - a mixed selective school for children over 11 years - but after the war it converted to a bilateral school, with elements of both grammar and secondary modern education. The name changed to Pewley County Secondary School in 1945 and the Headmaster, who went with the boys to Burpham later on, was Mr Raynham.

In 2013 the Guildford Dragon website reported on a reunion of ex-pupils from 1954. One described the old school as '...*built on three levels and looks like terraced gardens but for one thing – no flowers! Except for a solitary plot that is on its own. At the lowest level stands the hall. Its friendly old beams, high windows and creaky stage all add to the flavour of age. The classrooms are lofty, large and draughty. Most of them are separated by wood and glass partitions which are considered soundproof, but many a time two adjacent classes have both shared the same joke.*'

Since the late 1950s, most of the Burpham children have moved on to George Abbot for secondary education, but some go to other local schools, including the independent sector.

George Abbot School

In 1955 it was proposed to create two new schools for girls and boys in Burpham, and these were named the George Abbot County Secondary Schools in 1958. The boys' school brought pupils from the Junior Technical School (part of Guildford Technical College) and Pewley County Secondary School, whilst the girls' school brought pupils from the Commercial School (also part of the College) and Pewley County. The boys' buildings were mostly completed and classes taking place in 1957. These were known as the Burpham Annexe. In 1960 the school officially opened as a mixed school until the girls' school buildings were ready, then they operated as two single-sex schools until 1975, when they merged. The first Headteachers were Mr Raynham for the boys' school, who had moved from Pewley County, and Miss Elmslie for the girls'. They have been remembered through using their names for buildings on the current school site.

Pamela Patten remembered being there on the very first day the school was opened. For the first two days, the pupils had to take off their shoes before going into the hall. Only one classroom wing was ready as the rest was still being built. They had to go round the outside to get to the dining hall as the connecting corridor wasn't finished. She lived in Great Goodwin Drive but as the subway had not been built at that time she either walked to school or caught a bus into Guildford and then another one back out to Burpham.

Prince Philip visiting George Abbot School c. 1963 (P Servian)

Chris Fairs remembered that when he joined George Abbot School in 1959 it was a tri-lateral school, with secondary modern, technical and a grammar stream, in which Latin was taught. '*The school was very strict, with ties worn at all times and blazers only removed during hot summer days in class, with special permission.*' He also remembered the Headmaster, Mr Edward Gaston Raynham (nicknamed The Gut due to his large stomach), who almost always wore a brown suit with an academic gown. Pupils came from as far as Aldershot, Farnham, Kingston and Richmond, as well as from Woking, though most of the pupils were from Burpham and Merrow and some from Bellfields. '*When the girls' school was built the playing fields were shared, but an imaginary line existed over which the sexes were forbidden to cross during break times. One boy in my year smuggled a large*

254

placard into the school in his cricket bag and paraded along the line – the placard read 'This is Burpham, not Berlin!'".

Jenny Jones also remembered the imaginary line, but said that it depended on who was on patrol at lunchtime as to whether or not it was enforced. She thought that it was a very modern school for its time, with the language lab and wonderful domestic science and needlework rooms. There was a lovely dining hall and school dinners were excellent for five shillings a week, payable on a Monday. She also remembered getting caught in town by the Head Girl when she and her friend were not wearing their uniform hats. The resulting punishment was writing out lines, which had to be taken in the following day.

Chris Fairs also remembered the school secretary, Mrs MacDonald, who lived in Woodruff Avenue. *'Prefects, who happened to be passing the secretary's office at an opportune moment on a Monday, could be asked to take the week's school 'dinner money' to the bank in Burpham. It was handed over in a big canvas cash bag, put inside one's school case and taken, on foot, unaccompanied, to the bank. It never went astray. It must have been the equivalent of several thousand pounds in today's money but no thought was given to security. It would and could not happen today, with the school's biometric lunch and refreshments payment system.'*

John Boon remembered that George Abbot School had a tuck-shop, which sold iced buns and that Mr Raynham was a Headmaster to be feared. Mr Potts taught French. Ray Mitchell remembered that Mr Rose was the teacher who used the cane for punishment. One of the pupils had a sheepskin pad that others could hire from him to put down their trousers.

In line with government changes in 1976 the school reorganised to provide 12-18 year olds with comprehensive education. Then in 1993 this was extended to 11-18 year olds when the age of transfer changes took effect. The sixth form has around 400 students, most of whom have come through the school. George Abbot has for many years been one of the most successful secondary schools in Surrey and is often over-subscribed.

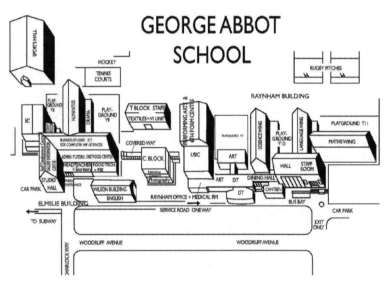

Site Plan of George Abbot School (P Stubbs)

Named after the Guildford man and Archbishop of Canterbury, George Abbot, the school holds a commemorative service in Holy

256

Trinity Church on, or as close as possible to, the anniversary of his birth date of October 29th. The school runs a house system, which used to be named after eight notable Britons. However, these have been changed over the years and now there are five houses named after mythical creatures.

George Abbot School, C Block (P Stubbs)

The school has a achieved a number of awards, including Investor in People, Artsmark, Sport England, International School and Healthy School. It has been an accredited provider for Initial Teacher Training and is also a National Support School, offering training for teaching assistants and administrative staff. Sports facilities include an all weather pitch for football, lacrosse and hockey. Surrey County Cricket Club's Cricket Academy is based in the school grounds, which houses a sports hall that is used by school pupils. Facilities include dedicated space for photography,

257

performance arts, textiles, science laboratories, computers, and construction amongst others.

George Abbot School converted to academy status in 2011, then in 2013 it formed a Multi Academy Trust with Boxgrove Primary School, which has now become Guildford Education Partnership. Since then four other schools, both primary and secondary, have joined the trust, which believes that all schools are more effective when they work in partnership than when they stand alone. The last Ofsted inspection rated the school as Outstanding.

George Abbot Sixth Form 1979 (K Newman)

Ex-pupils from the 1970s Facebook group (George Abbot School pupils aged 40) remembered using plastic dinner tokens to pay for the school lunches, which apparently were a bit of a challenge for aspiring vegetarians. What would those youngsters think of the biometric fingerprints used in the present day? One of the favourite puddings was butterscotch tart, but semolina was very unpopular. Would the children of 2017 know what Spam fritters were?

Pre-school and nursery education

Opportunities for children under five years of age to start their early education are a more recent addition to Burpham. There are several organisations working with these youngest members of the community.

Burpham Pre-School opened in 1967 as Burpham Playgroup and is found at the Church of the Holy Spirit hall. Its first Supervisor was Mrs Yvonne Smith and she ran the playgroup until she retired, when Mrs Gwen Ravenhill took over. In 1996 Mrs Jenny Philpot became the next Supervisor and she was instrumental in creating a garden area alongside the side of the church, where the children could play and learn about the natural world. In 2011 Lyn Baxter and Hazel Arnold took over the leadership of the Pre-School. Dedicated parents make up the committee that runs the Pre-School on a voluntary basis. It is good to know that Burpham Pre-School has maintained its place as one of the leading children's nurseries in the area.

Christopher Robin Day Nursery opened in 1990 in the old Rectory on Burpham Lane, opposite Burpham Primary School. The vicar deemed the house to be too big for his needs, so it was bought by the nursery group. It follows the Montessori principles and provides nursery education for 44 children.

Prior to 1994, there was a toddler group in Sutherland Memorial Park Pavilion, where health visitors did weigh-ins and mums could chat to each other. Then the Sunshine Nursery opened in 1994 and is open every morning each week in the Cricket Pavilion. It aims to provide high quality care and education for the children by working in partnership with their parents. It follows the Curriculum for the Early Years Foundation Stage (EYFS) and is linked with George Abbot School, welcoming students to observe the children as part of various subjects, such as sociology, art and childcare.

Christopher Robin Day Nursery 2016

The Tom Thumb Nursery originally opened in 1998, in the New Pavilion, and was then registered under new ownership in 2006, but closed down in 2016. In its place, the Peter Rabbit Nursery opened in September 2016 at The New Pavilion at Sutherland Memorial Park. It also follows the Curriculum for Early Years Foundation Stage.

Other educational opportunities

Surrey Adult Education used to base some of their evening classes at George Abbot School, which was very convenient for Burpham residents. However, in recent years they have concentrated all the Guildford classes at the Sydenham Road site (which used to be Pewley County Secondary School). Adults wanting to learn new skills, or just explore new interests, can join classes through the Adult Education programme; at Guildford College (which used to be the Technical College); or the Guildford Institute. It is also possible to find courses at the University of Surrey or Merrist Wood College. However, for those who are retired or partly retired, there is another option – the University of the Third Age, or U3A as it is normally known. Offering a wide range of groups, covering many different subjects, U3A is the biggest user of the Burpham Village Hall and thus provides very cost effective educational opportunities for the older residents of Burpham and Guildford.

From nothing in 1907, Burpham in the 21st century offers a great range of education for its residents, whether it be compulsory education in one of the two very successful schools or a chance to pursue skills and interests later on in life.

DEVELOPING THE RETAIL EXPERIENCE

Last vegetable market, North Street 1896 (Guildford Institute – Box 3C - 3113)

Up until the end of the 19th century shops were mainly to be found in Guildford, supplemented by the markets in the town, held variously in the High Street, North Street, Woodbridge Road and Slyfield. Although primarily for buying and selling livestock, these were also a place to buy materials for the home. Farms would sell milk, eggs and some meat to the local community. Tinkers travelled around the country selling ribbons, fabric, buttons, as well as pots and pans.

The first mention of a shop in Burpham was in Kelly's Directory for 1895. The entry recorded that Alfred Clark was a shopkeeper on London Road. However, there was no mention of him in either the 1891 or 1901 census records so it is not known exactly where he was a shopkeeper. The next mention was in Kelly's Directory for 1905, when William Edwin Turner was recorded as Shopkeeper at 54 Burpham Lane. Born in New Haw in about 1874, William had been living in Pimm's

Gate to the site of the Turner's shop

Row in 1901, when he was recorded as a Foreman Brickmaker, probably working at the brickfield behind Pimm's Row.

Mrs Emma "Granny" Turner, Surrey Advertiser 1960 (J Menzies)

By 1905 he and his wife, Emma, had moved over the road to what is now known as the Olde Post-House. Although William was officially recorded as the shopkeeper, it seems that he continued working in the brickfield, while Emma ran the little shop from the front room of their house. Norman Hamilton noted that a wide range of

'Snowy' Turner c. 1950 (T Howard photo, Surrey History Centre)

products was available to buy in the shop, '*from parsnips to paraffin*'. By 1915 they had added Sub-Postmaster to their list of responsibilities and they continued to provide this important service to the community until about 1938. They had a son called William Arthur, born in 1899, who married Ellen Mary Cripps in 1927 at St Luke's. He and Ellen had a daughter called Pam, later Pam Bartlett, who worked in one of the London Road shops. In later years Jan Kemp remembered calling the younger William 'Snowy' because of his shock of white hair and his mother, Emma, was known as 'Granny Turner'.

In the early 20th century the Kingpost was built on the corner of London Road and New Inn Lane. Apparently it incorporated some old beams in the building, but no records have been found to confirm this or say where they might have come from. Norman Hamilton recorded that the building started off as the Astolat garden shop, but again no further information has been found about this. The name Kingpost comes from the architectural term, being a *'central vertical post...to support a beam below from a truss apex above'*. It became a Restaurant in the early 1930s and a swimming pool was added. There was also a café, which provided refreshments for coach passengers and cyclists. Norman Hamilton recorded that in the summer of 1939 there were plans to make the buildings and site into a 'sports Atheneum', but the idea was shelved when war broke out. In 1953 the Restaurant was recorded in Kelly's Directories for the last time and later that year the building was loaned to the Catholic Church to provide somewhere to hold Mass.

From 1927, the Kelly's Directories recorded a number of market gardeners and smallholders in Burpham, who would also be selling their produce to the community. Farms continued to sell milk and eggs, some of them moving into the idea of small farm shops. Lymposs & Sons concentrated on dairy produce when they took over Winterhill Farm in around 1913 and they had a dairy in Guildford, which sold milk from several of their farms. Hugh Lancelot Robson, who was a fruit grower in Orchard Cottage from 1911, may have sold his fruit around the village too. From about 1924 to 1953 there was a laundry in Burpham Lane, owned and run by Arthur Love and his wife. Then, it was taken over by P Howard & Sons Ltd, a local building firm.

The next mention in Kelly's Directories for shops in Burpham came in 1938, recording the first four shops in the parade on London Road. However, since the postbox there is an Edward VIII box, it is likely that the shops were there in at least 1936.

London Road shops c. 1962 (postcard)

Arthur Manfield & Co were the newsagent and post office shop; Harold Kimber & Sons were grocers; Mrs W Ryall ran the General Drapery; and, last but not least, Marianne, Ladies' Hairdresser (later changing to Irene). There was also a Kimber's shop in Merrow, and Harold Kimber was Mayor of Guildford in the 1950s, as well as being Chairman of Governors for Burpham Primary School for 15 years. Barbara Stone remembered buying Neville's bread at Kimber's, which cost 7½d for a loaf – before the days of sliced bread.

For about 12 years, these were the only shops for the community, but by 1955 they were joined by Purkiss of Burpham, Ironmongers; W Charles Ltd, Butchers; Percy Pettitt, Fishmonger, Fruiterer & Greengrocer; Sid Sidey, Confectioner; Burpham Pharmacy Ltd. From 1957 to 1966 J Hartley established his antiques business from Lilac Cottage, next to New Inn Farmhouse. These were the days before supermarkets, so pretty much everything that was needed could be bought locally. Tony Mallard remembered that when the shops were first built all the shop signs had to be bronze coloured with the same style of writing. Allen Mead remembered that Sid Sidey had been a dairyman, who was reported for selling perishable goods on a Sunday and was fined. Joyce and Stephen Tate remembered Tom at Purkiss wore a brown overall, rather like Arkwright in the BBC series Open All Hours. Pete Gardner remembered that there was a paraffin machine outside the shop. Also, the Tates remembered that the butcher had a big model lamb in the window of the shop and sawdust on the floor.

Les and Vera Glew outside London Road shops, late 1950s/early 1960s
(T Howard photo, Surrey History Centre)

Burpham residents were lucky that so much was available to them without having to travel into town. Jan Kemp remembered that

Mr Evenden was the manager at Kimbers and he lived upstairs in the flat above the shop. He would travel round to collect orders from the houses and then the goods would be delivered.

By 1961, the second part of the development of Burpham shops, called Kingpost Parade, was built, providing Carlos & Thrale Ltd, Wine & Spirit Merchants (soon to change to Arthur Cooper); Midland Bank; Coombes Bakery; S Frost & Co, Grocers (later to become Home & Colonial Stores); Mussell & Co Ltd, Confectioners (later to become Fentons); G Connor, Greengrocer (later to become Quality Corner); Walton Electrics, Radio Dealers (later to become Burpham Electrics); and finally Elizabethan Cleaners, Dry Cleaners (later to become Polyclean and then Burpham Launderette).

Kingpost Parade shops, postcard 1960s

Ken and Doreen Marshall remembered that Sid Sidey and his sister ran their shop; Tom, in Purkiss's, always found bargains for customers; Muellers kept good quality food and their deli produce

268

was lovely; the drapers was where one bought school badges and uniform as well as wool. Mr Mueller was German and had two shops in the parade. Pete Gardner remembered working there on Saturdays, stocking shelves, for 2/6p per hour.

Arthur Manfield 1952 (Surrey Advertiser)

In the 1977 Silver Jubilee programme there were adverts from Phase Television Trade Servicing, Nimble Fingers (haberdashery & handicrafts), Cliffs of Burpham (greengrocer) as well as some of the other shops. At some point Mad Jak, selling ladies' clothing and accessories were in the parade, but they are now located in Shere village. By the 1980s the shopping parade included Penny's Hardware, in the spot where the Raj Doot Indian Restaurant now stands; Howzat sports and school uniform, now Guildford School and Sports; the Dutch Flower Shop; the video hire shop, which also sold lovely hand-made cards; and the Tile Shop.

In the late 1980s, competition from the new Sainsbury's meant that the chemist moved into the supermarket a few years after it opened. In 2017 there is still a newsagent and post office, McColl's; and a hairdressers, The Strand. The bank has gone, along with most of the food shops (apart from the convenience foods in McColl's and the bakery). There are three takeaway food options – the Raj Doot, Seafare Fish & Chips and Shangri-La Chinese takeaway. Also an estate agent, cycle shop, wine shop, carpet & flooring, bakery and dry cleaning. Peggie from the Drop-In Club remembered that the van for Cheeseman's, the greengrocers, used to go up to Covent Garden to collect produce for selling each day. However, they would set off at 2.00 am, often disturbing the neighbours as the van started up.

Sainsbury's delivery van, shown at the Burpham 2000 fete (BCA)

Burpham has offered a number of eating out opportunities over the years. Both the Green Man and the Anchor & Horseshoes pubs offered food – indeed, the latter still does. The Kingpost Restaurant was an option from the mid 1930s to the mid 1950s and in 2017 the Raj Doot is a very popular restaurant.

Kingpost Parade was named after The Kingpost Restaurant, now MJA Car Sales, on the corner of New Inn Lane and London Road.

270

The restaurant was closed by 1955 and the site was then used by PSG Coachworks Ltd, then Wilcox Coachworks, then Technical Designs and by 1969 it turned into Mid-Surrey Caravans, which many people still living in Burpham will remember. On the other side of New Inn Lane stood the petrol station. When this first opened, back in about 1927, it was called Super Service Stations Ltd, but by 1944 it was Pantiles Service Garage, which many people have remembered. In the 1980s it became a Mobil petrol station and more recently, BP. Pete Gardner remembered that his father bought their first car from Pantiles – a Ford Popular for £450.

Pantiles Garage on Coronation Day, 1953

Pantiles Service Garage 1953 (postcard)

Just past the Anchor & Horseshoes are two more businesses. Tyre City, previously called Chessington Tyres, occupies a building that has been used for motor related businesses and builders since 1915. At one point Binsted Bros, Builders, were next door to Joseph Binsted, Motor Engineer. The latter turned into Burpham Motor Works, then was at various times PSG Coachworks, Pantiles Service Garage, W G Skew & Son, car hire, and Burpham Motor Co. Guildford Signs, with Rose Cottage next door, occupies the building that used to be the Blacksmith's forge. In the late 1950s it was home to Peter Scarfe, Special Occasion Catering and Bakery for a few years. Many people have remembered looking at the delicious cakes through the windows.

Bakery on London Road (Surrey History Centre)

In 1963 a planning application for residential development on Bower's Farm was refused but by the early 1980s Sainsbury's had applied to build there. This was the time when supermarkets were growing and sites were sought to build more of them out of the town centre. According to records held at the Surrey History Centre, in 1982 Waitrose applied to build on the site next to the Green Man and Asda applied to build on Bower's Farm. The BCA wrote to the Planning Officer saying that '*most people in Burpham are against a superstore on Bower's Farm, but would welcome the proposed Waitrose supermarket next to the Green Man public house, to improve local shopping facilities*'.

Chessington Tyres (now Tyre City) 2015

The Guildford Society wrote to Guildford Borough Council expressing concerns about traffic congestion and destroying the viability of local shopping facilities in Burpham and Merrow. At around the same time both Tesco and RACS (Royal Arsenal Co-operative Society) were looking to build on the Ladymead site, but both were turned down. Apparently the Co-operative Society supported Burpham's opposition to the Sainsbury's proposal and the Planning Committee were split 50:50, so the Chairman's vote was the decider.

Sainsbury's won the day and opened in 1985. However, it was not an easy process as the proposals aroused strong emotions within the community. The original plan was to build on the Sutherland Memorial Field, whose facilities would then move to the other side of Clay Lane. Roger Marjoribanks noted that '*the issue was debated at a crowded and highly emotional meeting of the Burpham Community Association, where residents voiced their opposition not only to the location of the store but to the traffic problems that could be expected to ensue and (a matter always of vital interest when such major developments are considered) the effect on house prices in the area. The point was made that even though the Borough owned the field it held it in trust for the people of Burpham and could not morally, and perhaps not in law, surrender it without Burpham's consent.*'

As a result Sainsbury's re-thought their proposals with a new plan to move to the north of Clay Lane on land that had already been earmarked for development. They also felt able to donate the land that they had bought previously to become an extension to the playing fields. The company had to amend the original plan to build a supermarket with garden centre and Home Base store, to one providing just the J Sainsbury store. The impact on traffic has not been as bad as anticipated, apart from very busy times such as Christmas, and the building itself is quite discreetly hidden by trees and shrubbery. Sainsbury's helped to provide the

274

village sign, which was erected in 1991, and has given very welcome support to the local schools, especially through the Active Kids vouchers, which buy equipment and other resources.

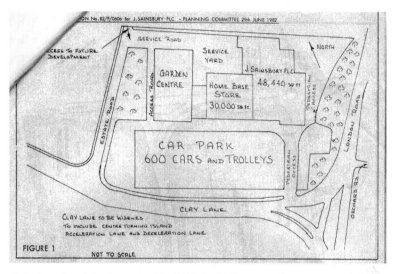

FIGURE 1   NOT TO SCALE

Sainsbury's original proposal in 1982, including a garden centre and Home Base store (BCA)

There will always be changes as life moves on and by 1992 the company was asking for restrictions on Sunday opening to be lifted. Tony Mallard, then Chairman of the BCA, wrote to the Surrey Advertiser saying he was not surprised in view of the general trend towards more Sunday trading. He did not expect much opposition from Burpham residents, but the Association would be canvassing opinion. 'The trading at Sainsbury's doesn't cause any inconvenience to the residents of Burpham, as everyone feared when it was first built. My initial reaction is that it won't cause much of a problem in terms of traffic or noise, as long as *there won't be too many big lorries making deliveries.'* However, some residents were appalled by the proposal, blaming Sainsbury's for the traffic problems in Burpham. In 1997, despite more local opposition, Sainsbury's added a petrol station to the site. However, on the whole Sainsbury's seems to have brought positive results to the community.

Sainsbury's Supermarket (BCA)

For many years it appeared to be that the Burpham parade of shops and Sainsbury's were enough, even for the ever-growing community. However, in 2006 Aldi bought the Green Man site, when it was sold by the Harvester Group, with plans to develop a store there in competition with Sainsbury's. There were several planning applications over the next eight years, with objections from residents as well as the BCA and Merrow Residents' Association. During this time, the pub building was allowed to deteriorate to the point where it was demolished for health & safety reasons. The Planning Committee finally gave the go ahead in February 2014 and the store opened in November 2015. Feelings across the community are mixed, with some people still strongly against having the store here and some people who think that it is good for local residents. Certainly it is very

276

convenient for those who live in West Court, next door. On the opening day there was traffic chaos as cars queued along London Road to get into the store's car park off Burpham Lane.

By early 2017 Aldi had successfully won appeals against planning decisions relating to opening hours and HGV deliveries.

Aldi store 2015

In 2017 Burpham has two supermarkets (including a pharmacy), one estate agent, five food outlets (including Starbucks in Sainsbury's), one pub, no bank, one hairdresser and one barber, a carpet/flooring shop, a cycle shop, a wine shop, a sports/school uniform shop, one newsagent/post-office/general store, two petrol stations, and, new in 2017, a sun-tanning shop and a funeral director. Recent changes in Sainsbury's have included the pharmacy becoming Lloyds Pharmacy, Argos opening a small branch and Timpsons providing key cutting and other services.

London Road shops 2015

CLUBS, SOCIETIES AND ORGANISATIONS

Before the late 1800s there is no evidence of clubs or societies in Burpham. But a membership card found in a violin case in the

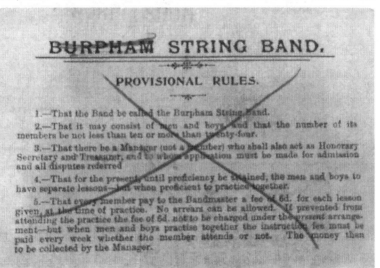

Burpham String Band membership card 1905 (Surrey History Centre)

late 1960s, showed that in 1905 the Burpham String Band had been re-named the Worplesdon String Band. The pre-printed card had a date starting 189_, so it can be assumed that the band was a going concern in the 1890s. Apparently the band was a popular activity with a subscription of 3d p.w. when the membership was 20 or more, though if membership fell to 10-14 members then the fee rose to 6d. Sadly, it is not known what happened to this band.

Burpham has three community halls for groups to hire – Burpham Village Hall, Church of the Holy Spirit Hall and Sutherland

Memorial Park Hall, as well as halls at the two schools. Norman Hamilton recorded that Burpham Village Hall *'was built in*

Village Hall 1980s (BCA)

1922 from surplus war materials auctioned at Thursley Camp. It was put up at a cost of £180 on land leased from the Duke of Sutherland at a peppercorn rent. Electricity was installed in 1935, and the Women's Institute held a jumble sale to help pay for it.' The village hall was used by the children of Burpham Primary School during and shortly after the second World War. After being renovated and extended, there is now a large hall and a small hall, as well kitchen facilities.

In 1976 T G Loweth wrote an article for the BCA about the hall. He recorded that *'...word reached the then Vicar of Burpham that a building, suitable for use as a village hall, was to come up for sale at an auction at Thursley Camp.'* He explained that it had been a wooden hospital ward, with a dispensary attached, which had been imported to take Canadian casualties, but had never been used. The Vicar and Mr George Gatley arranged for the building to be transported to Burpham and to erect it as an addition to the Church Room, which had been on the site for some time. However, on the day it was raining heavily and the lorry bringing the building got stuck in the muddy grass by Burpham Lane. For several months the pieces of building lay on the grass before it could be put together. When this eventually happened, with the addition of two tortoise stoves for heating the premises, it was ready to be used for community activities.

The land was leased from the Duke of Sutherland for one shilling a year and Mrs Marshman was engaged as caretaker, at a wage of nine shillings a week. Minor repairs were made by members of the Committee, and contractors were brought in for large scale changes.

Morriss Kemp said that the Trustees for the Village Hall in 1923 were Mr C H Binsted, Mr H C Binsted, Mr H Kerr, Revd A Theodosius, Mr A Berry, Mr J Archer and Mr P Gatley. Others who had either left or died included Mr G Gatley, Mr P Collins, Revd E C Storr and Mr H L Robson. Mr Bidwell was Honorary Secretary and Mrs Bidwell ran the scouts group. In 1940 the lease agreed for the hall was for a further 99 years, and the rent was kept at one shilling per annum. The minute books for the early years were hand written, but unfortunately these were thrown away as valueless by Mr Gatley's executors, though apparently they made fascinating reading.

In the early days, the hall was used for the Friday Whist Drive, which was very popular before the advent of television, and also for the Women's Institute, Mothers' Union, wedding parties, etc.

281

There was a convention that strong drink should not be consumed in the hall, though this was lifted temporarily to allow wedding parties to enjoy sherry and champagne. The premises were never licensed for the sale of drinks. During the Second World War the hall was used for a mothers and babies clinic under the aegis of Mrs Stock, and pupils from Burpham Primary School walked to the hall for their lunches.

Burpham Village Hall 2015

Mr Loweth recorded that improvements were made after the war, including a new stove, new floor and lining for the roof. When Mrs Marshman gave up being caretaker her daughter, Mrs Joyce Tanner, took over, followed by Mrs Pam Bartlett. For some years there was a lack of interest, which hampered the running of the hall as no-one wanted to help. Then a public meeting was well attended, possibly due to a belief that the hall was to be pulled down and the land sold, with a possible distribution of monies to those persons interested enough to turn up. When these dreams were dispelled a Hall Management Committee was set up, formed by representatives from the various users of the hall.

The Sutherland Memorial Park Hall was built after Sainsbury's donated extra land in 1985 and there is a small hall overlooking the cricket and football pitches with bar facilities. The Church of the Holy Spirit hall on New Inn Lane was built in 1961 and has provided facilities for many local activities, including the pre-school group as well as brownies, guides and the ever popular Drop-In Club for pensioners.

Burpham Women's Institute

The Women's Institute (WI) was started in 1897 in Canada, but in 1915 the movement moved to Britain. *'During the First World War it was formed to encourage countrywomen to get involved in growing and preserving food to help increase the supply of food to the war-torn nation.'* The object of the women's organisation was to raise the standard of homemaking with the motto 'For Home and Country'. The first WI was in Anglesey, North Wales, and the first in England was at Singleton, Sussex. 40 WIs had opened by the end of 1916, by 1917 there were 137, and by the end of the war there were 199 across the country.

The women of Burpham opened their own WI in 1931 as an afternoon group. Sadly, the early records were lost when there was a fire in the Village Hall; however, Mamie Grover wrote down some of her memories to fill this gap, and these are kept at the Surrey History Centre. The founder members included The Hon. Mrs Hopewell, Mrs Bidwell (who was Treasurer for many years),

Mrs Berry, Mrs H Marshall and Mrs K Grover (Mamie's mother-in-law). Other members included Mrs Andrews, Mrs Binsted, Miss Gatley, Mrs Sturgess and Mrs Sheppard.

The Yorkshire Evening Post reported in November 1936 that *'Burpham Surrey Women's Institute decided, after a debate, that married women have a better time than single women.'* It seems that they were talking about a report of a woman at Tottenham court who said *'My husband threatened me. I just looked at him – and he ran out of the house'*. In 1937, it was proposed that microphones be installed in the village hall as some members found it difficult to hear speakers.

In 1939, a report in the Surrey Advertiser said that at their monthly meeting *'the choir gave a very spirited performance of old songs, which were much enjoyed'*. It also reported that Mrs Braybrooke was the winner in the potato competition with one of 26 lbs. During the war members would make swabs for the local hospital at their meetings as well as making marmalade. Members brought their various skills to the group – Miss Gatley was very good at butter making for local shows, Mrs Warder organised wonderful Christmas parties for the village, Mrs Collins taught leather work and Mrs Sheppard was the entertainer. The ladies ran jumble sales and outings to the Houses of Parliament amongst other activities. A coach trip to Worthing cost 4 shillings (20p) and this included tea.

Minutes of meetings from 1939 recorded that the outbreak of war disrupted the programme of classes and activities. Instead they

284

collected baby clothes and prams for the evacuated mothers staying at Gosden House and spare clothes went to the evacuated mothers in the village. They also collected toys for children who had been evacuated to Burpham. They knitted comforts for the troops and still made jam. Social activities continued to be organised but often had to be postponed due to air raids.

In the days before the National Health Service, Women's Institute members collected eggs and potatoes for the local hospitals, and vegetables were also sent to St Mary's Hospital in London.

In 1947 the Surrey Advertiser reported on the Surrey Womens' Institutes County Rally, which was held at Clandon Park. It was very well attended, attended by crowds of about 15,000, with local dignitaries including the Guildford Mayor, Earl of Onslow and representatives from the WI Federation.

After the war, meetings returned to normality. Records show that they would begin with singing the WI song – Jerusalem – and often ended with the Chairlady saying *and so ended another interesting and happy meeting.'* In 1952 there was a minute's silence in memory of the late King George VI, followed by singing of the National Anthem. That year also saw the celebration of 21 years of the Burpham WI, with a special event attended by 150 past and present members and a photo in the Surrey Advertiser.

In 1953, the Surrey Executive asked for Burpham's assistance in the Coronation Procession, but no further information was recorded about how this progressed. However, there was a coach trip to London to see the coronation illuminations. WI members were asked if they would make flowers for the coronation for the Civic Restaurant. In 1946 these had taken over from British Restaurants, set up in 1941 to combat the severity of rationing, selling basic meals at reasonable prices, off ration, run by volunteers, often members of the WVS. Members were also invited to the coronation celebrations at Sutton Green. At the meeting on 1st June 1953 the notes reported that '*The village hall was beautifully decorated with flags and flowers for our coronation and birthday meeting on June 1st. Sang national anthem and Jerusalem.*'

The Burpham War Memorial Committee asked the WI for help to provide a playing field as a war memorial after the second world war. They raised money at social events and at the opening of the Sutherland Memorial Playing Field in 1956 they ran a stall as part of the fete.

The WI had a drama group, which put on plays in the village hall. In 1959 this included a one-act play called 'Red Wax', which was a feature of the Good Companions' club birthday party for lonely people over 60 years in Burpham.

1964 saw the 33rd birthday celebration of the Burpham WI and money was raised for Burpham Homes and the Betatron Appeal for St Luke's Hospital. Later that year there was a Grand Fete at the Burpham War Memorial Playing Fields and the WI provided refreshments. Other entertainments included a children's art exhibition, the sea cadets' band, children's novelty races, a keep fit display by the Surrey Evening Institute, as well as games such as hoopla, bingo and a coconut shy. In 1965 the National Federation of Women's Institutes celebrated the Golden Jubilee and Mrs Joan Petry was invited to represent Burpham at a Royal Garden Party at Buckingham Palace.

A Women's Institute banner was made by Miss Draper and Mrs Willcox, but sadly this was lost in the fire at the village hall, along with early records. There was an arrangement with the Crusoe Club for the Blind in London, who visited Burpham each August and had lunch with WI members in the village hall. In 1987 they celebrated the 25th anniversary of this friendship. The Burpham afternoon WI closed down in 1991 because they were unable to enlist a new Treasurer.

Joan Petry, President in the final years of the afternoon group, wrote that after the war '*We were coming to the age of speed and labour saving devices – perhaps it is because of the modern appliances that we find time to take part in the Women's Institute or maybe the facilities that are offered to us are a challenge to the women of today. Yes, the WI is definitely "with it" – we still make jam, enjoy cookery demonstrations and education talks, run drama groups, etc. For further education we can attend Denman College in Berkshire for dressmaking, painting for pleasure, maintenance of cars and public speaking (to name a few subjects.) Much voluntary work is carried on by our members at St Luke's out-patient canteen, visiting the Burpham Homes and collecting stamps for Cancer Research.*'

Members of Burpham Evening WI (Mary Pearce) and Burpham
Afternoon WI (Mrs Joan Petry) celebrating the 75th Anniversary of the
Women's Institute at a garden party with residents at Burpham Homes
1990 (G Grainge)

Since October 1989 Burpham has had a second WI group, which
celebrated its 25th birthday in 2014. Reflecting the changes of
modern life, where more women are out of work during the day,
this group meets in the evenings – thus allowing more women to
join and participate in events. The first committee consisted of
Mary Pearce as President, with Valerie Boon as Vice President,
Diane Kett as Secretary and Sue Marjoribanks as Treasurer. These
were joined by Gill Allgar, Gill Hopkins, Alison Melville, Maggie
Hamilton, Jackie Ring and Donna Armstrong. The first meeting,
in October 1989, included a talk about Concorde. Gill Grainge
remembered that '*there were just ten of us at that first meeting,*

when a British Airways engineer gave us a talk about Concorde. Most of us were then in our 30s or 40s. During the next few months our membership grew, we held a successful jumble sale to raise funds and in addition to the monthly meetings, we held a medieval banquet, which was a great success. Over the years we have entered WI competitions, started several special interest groups (book clubs, walking, theatre, craft) and our membership has gone up and down. We currently have about 60 members.'

WI Medieval Banquet 1989 (G Grainge)

The WI has always been one of the major users of Burpham Village Hall. The group has a wide range of subjects for their monthly talks, including in 2016 cheese tasting, Guildford Cathedral, crop cycle mystery and Antarctica. They also arrange visits out and about, such as a boat trip with cream tea, Brookwood Cemetery and Loseley Park. There is an annual meeting in November and social events for the summer and Christmas. It is a lively group, which provides for a range of interests for the ladies of Burpham.

289

Burpham Ladies Club

When the afternoon WI closed down in 1991 some of the members decided to carry on meeting and this group became the Burpham Ladies Club. This provides an opportunity for the members to get together for tea and a chat, as well as having occasional speakers. Some of the talks have focussed on helping the elderly.

Burpham Women's Guild

In 1957 a group of ladies came together to form the Burpham Women's Guild, also meeting in the Village Hall. This was a non-denominational group, which offered evening meetings for ladies who went out to work during the day.

Burpham Gardening Club

Started in about 1960, the club originally met in a garage in Marlyn's Drive. Two shows were held in the village hall each year, one in the summer and one in the winter. Trophies were awarded including the best-kept summer front garden – Edgar Hunt used to grow pompom dahlias and won prizes for them, and his wife showed dahlias at the Royal Horticultural Society professionally. Edgar used to travel to a nursery in Somerset to buy bulbs. The club meets six times a year and runs a trading hut behind the hall from mid-February to mid-October (except in August, from which members can buy compost, bean sticks, etc). The club used to have about 450 households participating but this has reduced over the years to about 200 in 2016. Perhaps the pace of life in the 21st century has led to a winding down of interest?

Guildford Photographic Society

This club, which originally was founded in 1892 *'with the object of advancing the art and craft of amateur photography'*, meets regularly in Burpham Village Hall.

Guiding and Scouting

The girls of Burpham have been able to join Brownie and Guide groups for many years. Valerie Boon ran the Brownies in the church hall until Jean Menzies took over. Valerie remembered that they had to write to the vicar for permission to do anything and he would write back. No picking up the phone for convenience in those days. Apparently Revd D Bryant wanted to have a Cub pack in Burpham, but didn't get permission, so the boys had to go to Merrow instead. Although Morriss Kemp remembered that Mrs Bidwell had run a Scout group at the village hall at one time.

Mary Fry remembered being one of the 1st Burpham St Luke's Brownies in the early 1960s. Mrs Maguire was Brown Owl and the weekly meetings were held in the church hall, with church parade once a month. *'At St Luke's church I remember several of us were whispering during the service, and we were sent outside to the porch by the vicar (the Revd Douglas Bryant). Some of our Brownie subs might still lie buried under the 'new' church because once again my friends and I were talking too much, and we were sent to wait outside the church hall this time. The church was being built, so we decided to bury the coins on the building site, to prevent our mothers finding out! We had several Brownie outings, including ones to Chessington Zoo and Hampton Court...I also remember going to Brownie Revels, held in the grounds of Sir Humphrey and Lady Mynor's house. I think this was in Sutton Green and that other Brownie packs were also there. I know that I loved this event and that their garden seemed massive.'*

Burpham Community Association (BCA)

Set up in 1973, the Association is committed to representing the community of Burpham. A committee of ten people, chaired by Donald Simmonds set up a programme of meetings and some social occasions. The main issues addressed at that time included the A3, Weylea Farm, Bowers Farm and the stream under the A3. Within four months the membership grew to 430 families in the area and by 1979 this had risen to 800. Newsletters would be produced three or four times a year, informing members of local news. The BCA provides a forum where people can bring their concerns for the community and know they will be listened to, and, where appropriate, it represents Burpham in matters of general concern. It also brings local issues to public attention and explains the implications to the community. It is a member of the Campaign to Protect Rural England (CPRE) and the Open Spaces Society. It is affiliated to both the East Guildford Residents Association (EGRA) and the Guildford Residents Association (GRA).

The BCA liaises with the local Member of Parliament, local borough and county councillors on a variety of local issues, such as planning, road and traffic problems, flooding and drainage problems and the protection of amenities. Meetings, formerly held in Burpham Village Hall, are now bi-monthly events in

Sutherland Memorial Hall and usually include a speaker who has insight into local concerns and interests. A double page spread in Burpham Pages informs residents about topical issues and forthcoming meetings.

The BCA website includes information about the history of Burpham, reports from the Wey Navigation Lengthsman, reports on meetings as well as information on joining the Association. In the last few years the BCA has fought planning applications from Aldi and Martin Grant Homes (for housing developments on Gosden Hill Farm), as well as the Clay Lane Link Road, the Slyfield Area Regeneration Project, and numerous others. Working with EGRA, the BCA has put local views forward about developments at Wisley and Newlands Corner, both of which would affect residents of Burpham. The Guildford Local Plan for 2016 includes many of these developments, putting more strain on the already stressed infrastructure for the community.

In the 1970s newsletters told of the travelling library coming to the Burpham shops; the reorganisation of primary schools; Red Litter Day in 1974; proposals to move County Hall to Stoke Park; and the need locally for additional medical services; the loss of elm trees around the village; unpleasant fumes coming from the pig farm on London Road; plans for the Silver Jubilee; Operation Daffodil to refurbish the village hall; and flooding problems. In the 1980s issues included the preservation of the Burpham Lane bridge; Gosden Hill Farm development proposals, new roundabout by Woodruff Avenue; Sainsbury's proposals; village sign competition; minibus service to Guildford; improvements to

Sutherland Memorial Park; and traffic volume problems. By 1986 membership had risen to 1,000 households, including Ganghill and Abbotswood.

The new Millennium brought the worrying prospect of an incinerator being built on Slyfield, which would have affected the Burpham community. GAIN, the Guildford Anti Incinerator Network, led by Revd Colin Matthews and his team and working closely with the BCA, successfully persuaded the Council to turn this down after a prolonged fight.

Youth Initiative
The first mentions of a youth club were in the 1950/60s, when they met at the new cricket pavilion on the Sutherland Memorial Park. Michael Hunt remembered a Mr Nuttall running the youth club and John Pidgeon remembered that Mr & Mrs Cooper from Peaslake were involved with the Burpham Youth Club. They met every Monday night, playing table tennis or having discos, until the Guildford music scene developed and then local groups came to play. In the late 1990s the youth sub-group of the BCA worked with the Guildford Borough Council to get some facilities for teenagers in Burpham and the result was the basketball court by the children's recreation ground. Tony Higgs, a parent governor at Burpham Primary School, was a key mover in getting this agreed. They also started up a 'meet & greet' area in the park, with a shelter so that youngsters would stop sitting in bus shelters.

The BCA Youth Sub-Group opening the basketball court 1999 (Surrey Advertiser)

Then in 2003/4, Dr Sandra Domizio, appalled by the vandalism and litter in the park, as well as the abuse suffered by the ice cream vendor, set up a meeting with local organisations. These included the local police, the Safer Guildford Partnership, the Parks Department, both school headteachers and the BCA. She also went jogging in the park in the evenings and talked to the youths who were there. Most of them were bored and vandalism was something to do, though some of them were drunk and caused a lot of trouble.

They liked her suggestion of a youth club with activities and as a result they came to a meeting to discuss what to do. Sandra, along with Maggie Spinks and Cheryl Humphrey, set up a committee, found a venue, applied for grants, went to see other youth clubs, got parent volunteers to run it and advertised the club. Sandra said *'We had a huge turnout every week at the Village Hall and it was very successful. We did a huge range of activities every week, including park games and educational*

295

speakers.' The project also extended the basketball and goal area for kick-abouts in the park. Initially the vandals came along to the club every week and the vandalism stopped, but eventually they stopped coming. However, the club was still full and the vandalism did not restart, so as a community venture it was a great success. After about 18 months Sandra, Maggie and Cheryl handed the running of the club over to a new committee, but sadly after another year it stopped due to a lack of community volunteers.

Church Groups

In 2016 there are a range of youth activities organised through Burpham Church for both 11-14 year olds and 15-18 year olds. However, there have been groups, such as Sunday School running in the community for many years. In the late 1940s Ann Keane remembered that the older children went to Sunday School at the church, while the younger children went to the village hall. Afterwards they would have tea at the Kingpost – though she didn't say if everyone went there or just her family. Jan Kemp remembered that Miss Marshall was the Sunday School teacher - she never married but led quite a solitary life in Paddock Road. Mary Fry remembered a Sunday School party in the Village Hall and an outing to Frensham Ponds. The teacher was Miss Bentley. Pete Gardner remembered the St Luke's Church Youth Club, held at the Church of the Holy Spirit hall, run by Mrs Shale. *'It was good for meeting young ladies, listening to music, playing table tennis and badminton.'*

Drop-In Club

Run by the Burpham Church, the Drop-In Club provides a weekly opportunity for the older members of the community to meet up. They come to the Church of the Holy Spirit Hall on New Inn Lane where they can chat to friends over a cup of tea and a piece of cake.

Drop-In Club Christmas get-together (Burpham Church)

Other Organisations

In 1914 the Surrey Advertiser reported that a meeting of the Worplesdon & District Conservative and Liberal Unionist Association was held in a room over the stables at The Paddocks. Mr A R Birks, who had lent the room, was in the chair. The topics included the Home Rule Bill, comparing Ireland with New Zealand Home Rule. Attendance was only moderate due to the weather and local flooding. Proceedings closed with singing the National Anthem and afterwards a number of those present signed the British Covenant (a protest against the Home Rule Bill).

Sports in Burpham

Jan Kemp remembered that when the Duke of Sutherland owned Sutton Place there was a polo ground opposite Burpham Court Farm, off Clay Lane and the Duke of Edinburgh played there on occasion. Mrs June Eliott remembered that Mr Bollins, who lived on Bower's Lane, used to look after the polo ponies for the Duke. In the 21st century there are lots of opportunities for sports in Burpham. However, it was not always so until the opening of the Sutherland Memorial Playing Fields in 1956 brought the chance for football and cricket to be played locally. Since then there have been many improvements made to facilities at the park, enabling other sports to be played there. As well as the various clubs that use facilities in the Park there are also facilities for Burpham residents to use, including the children's recreation area and the Basketball court for the Youth Initiative.

Burpham Football Club

Established in 1956, there was only one football pitch on the original playing field and for about a year football was the only club that played there. Percy Howard, the local builder, built the small pavilion that was used for a changing room and the club got an alcohol licence, so that they could have a barrel of beer for after training or matches. The footballers played on Saturdays so that the cricketers could play on Sundays. The Green Man also had a football team that played on Sundays during the winter and they used the pub as a meeting place. Brian Wheeler, the publican, even gave them a football.

**Burpham Football Club 1978 - players and officials received annual awards
at special celebration dinner (E Voller / Daily Advertiser)**

Burpham Football Club (E Voller)

In the early days the mainstays of the Football Club were Percy Howard, John Cresswell, Les Glew, Charlie Eyre, Eric Voller and Neville Clayton. Allen Mead remembered that Les Glew ran the youth football and cricket teams in the 1950s/60s, which were based at the youth club in the village hall. Eric and Mervyn Tremeer ran a boys' football team in the 1970s. The club continued through the next 25 years until great changes came about in 1996.

Guildford City Football Club had started out as an amateur club in 1877, becoming a professional club at the end of 1920. They played at Joseph Road and were accepted into the Southern League. However, in 1974 the club merged with Dorking, to play at Meadowbank, and the Joseph's Road ground was closed prior to becoming a site for housing development. For the next 25 years there was no Guildford club, until in 1996 Bill Bellerby, Mayor of Guildford and President of the old Guildford City F.C. approached Burpham F.C. asking if they would be willing to move to the Spectrum Leisure Centre and represent Guildford. The first and second Burpham teams moved to become A.F.C. Guildford and the remaining teams were promoted within Burpham F.C. The new A.F.C. Guildford changed its name to Guildford United in 2005, but soon after changed again to Guildford City (despite the fact that Guildford has not got city status).

Burpham F.C. plays in the Surrey County Intermediate League (Western) Division One, while the Reserve and 'A' teams both play in the Guildford & Woking Alliance Football League, divisions 3 & 4 respectively. There are three teams at the time of writing in

300

2016 and matches are played at the Sutherland Memorial Playing Field.

Burpham Boys Football Club 1970 (E Voller)

Burpham Juniors F.C.

This was founded in 2000 by a group of Burpham fathers, including Nick Uwins, Martin Bradley, Peter Gissell and Andy Penson. There was one team, but the League allows mixed teams up to age 13/14 years. Membership is around 200, from Under 7 to Under 18 groups. It is a friendly, social environment providing a club for all abilities. There are about 15 teams now, playing in the Surrey Primary League, which is affiliated to Surrey FA. The youngest children play 5-a-side, 9-10 year olds play 7-a-side, 11-12 year olds play 9-a-side and the older members play 11-a-side. They play at Sutherland Memorial Park and the club is mainly run by parents on a voluntary basis.

Burpham Cricket Club

Burpham Cricket Club c. 1980 (T Roberts)

Established in 1957, this was one of the earliest clubs to use the new War Memorial Playing Field. In 1999 there was a merger of Burpham and Worplesdon Cricket Clubs – the first clubs in Surrey to consolidate the strengths of two clubs, but a number of others have gone on to do the same. The facilities at Burpham in the early days were very limited, with a small 'pavilion' being not much more than a shed. A new pavilion was opened in 1965, which included changing rooms and other facilities for both football and cricket teams. After the merger a proportion of the club's games were played at Burpham, but since 2011 the new club play all their games at Worplesdon, where a new pavilion, built in 2008, now provides a bar and kitchen – essential for the cricket teas.

Burpham Tennis Club

The Burpham Tennis Club was started in May 1990 by Jane Hill. When Sutherland Memorial Park was extended in the 1980s, as a result of land being donated by Sainsbury's, the new facilities included tennis courts. Jane noticed that they were not being used much and approached Guildford Borough Council about starting up a club. An introductory meeting was held at Burpham Village Hall, and subsequently 40 people joined up, a committee was formed and the club started its mission to be a *'friendly group of players with a wide range of abilities who enjoy the opportunity to play tennis'*.

Burpham Tennis Club (Burpham 2000)

It has been a fantastic success. Coaching sessions have been arranged and for several years there was also a junior section of the club. In the early days Jane remembered organising a dinner for 65 people, all cooked on hired portable cookers and bringing in all the necessary furniture and equipment to the pavilion. The

303

club operates all year round, come rain or shine, on the three all-weather courts at Sutherland Memorial Park. They play occasional Round Robin competitions, with prizes for the winners and also meet up socially two or three times a year. The club welcomes new members.

Burpham Bowling Club

Burpham Bowling Club Committee, early 1990s (E Voller)

Established in 1990 as a mixed club, it is one of the largest bowling clubs in the Guildford area and welcomes new members of all ages and experience. Major Keith Crossman was a founding member of the club and served as secretary for several years, he was also club president and club captain. There is a clubhouse, with licensed bar, and access to the various amenities in the pavilion of Sutherland Memorial Park. The season runs from April to September and there are competitions at regional, county and national levels. There are also programmes of mens', ladies' and mixed matches. When the weather changes in the autumn there is a very active social programme.

Burpham Bowling Club (Burpham 2000)

Other Sports

Table tennis was played at the Burpham Youth Club. Derek Oliver's father taught youngsters, and both Derek and his father were excellent tennis players. Derek remembered his father running a table tennis club for young people in an outbuilding behind the Kingpost. Derek was also a coach at Merrow Bowls. The Guildford Table Tennis Association Celebration of 75 Years, by Ted Simpkin and John Diggens, recorded that Gerald and Eric Lillywhite played exhibition matches at The Kingpost before the second World War. In 1938/9 there was a team from the Kingpost playing in the League. In 1974/5 the team from Burpham won the Premier Division, the Percy Lawes Cup and the Handicap Cup. Clearly there were some very good table tennis players in the community.

Mr Oliver teaching table tennis (D Oliver)

Burpham Neighbourhood Forum

In 2014 the Guildford Dragon website reported that concerned Burpham residents were submitting their own development plan to Guildford Borough Council. Burpham Neighbourhood Forum was set up two years earlier by people who were passionate about their community and wanted to ensure that future development in Burpham would be appropriate and of a high standard. Ros Pollock, Chairman of the Forum, said '*Input into the plan by local people has been extensive and, subject to a local referendum, I look forward to the plan becoming part of the development plan for Burpham and therefore a material consideration in the determination of planning applications in the ward.*'

Burpham was the first community in Guildford to designate a forum and prepare a neighbourhood plan. This was a flagship government policy, designed to empower local communities. Following a local referendum and Council consultation the

306

Burpham plan was adopted in April 2016 as part of the development plan for the Borough.

The plan covers a wide range of issues for the community, including public open spaces and green spaces; natural features; historic environment; parking, cycle routes and footpaths; support for younger people; improvements to infrastructure; water and flooding; housing density; public transport, shopping; improvements to A3, schools; and access to natural leisure facilities.

HOUSES AND FAMILIES

The majority of information that is available about Burpham is from the 1841 census onwards, though there are some details about life in earlier centuries, mainly through wills and deeds. The British Listed Buildings website gives some information about the Grade II listed properties in the village: St Luke's Church is 19th century; Sutton Place Lodge Gates are 16th century with later remodelling; Lilac Cottage / New Inn Farmhouse are 17th century with later additions; and Pimm's Row is 18th century with later alterations.

Tudor Cottages - 1,3,5,7 Burpham Lane (Surrey History Centre)

The Tudor Cottages, numbers 1, 3, 5 & 7 Burpham Lane, thought to be the buildings of Green Man Farm on Burpham Lane, were

308

Grade II listed and owned by Courage, Barclay & Simmonds Brewery. Brian and Sylvia Wheeler remembered that when they were at the Green Man the cottages were behind the pub's ladies' toilets and that chickens were kept there. Ken Marshall remembered that Mr Carpenter, an old soldier, had lived in one of the cottages. There was a lot of debate from the late 1950s onwards about what to do with them, but due to their dilapidated state the Historic Buildings and Antiquities Office eventually made no objection to them being demolished as it would have cost too much money to restore them. They were pulled down in the early 1970s in order to provide additional parking space for the Green Man and later West Court. Pete Gardner remembered sneaking into one of the cottages in the early 1960s, going upstairs and catching stag beetles there.

At the end of the 19th century Lord Onslow decided to sell various properties from his large Surrey estate. In 1905 many of the Burpham properties were auctioned, but few of them sold, resulting in further auctions over the next few years. Many of the sales particulars stated that the properties would be good for development. In 1920 Lord Onslow agreed to sell the remainder of New Inn Farm and Ganghill, apart from 'No Man's Land' at the top of New Inn Lane, on the right before the railway bridge. Michael Hunt remembered that the woodlands from the bridge down to the road used to belong to Lord Onslow but were given to the people of Burpham. Perhaps this was the same patch of land? Michael also remembered that Surrey County Council had wanted to widen New Inn Lane, taking some front gardens to provide a footpath. The land in front of Church of the Holy Spirit and down towards the roundabout was left unused, ready for a widening project at a later date. However, with the restricted width of the road going under the railway bridge, and no plans to widen that, there was no further progress with this project.

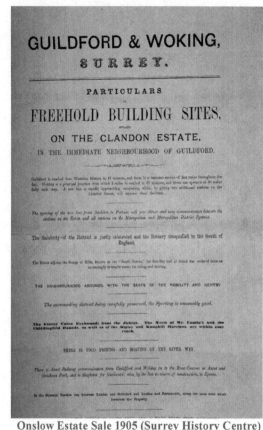

In 1900 Burpham was still mainly a two road hamlet, with farms along either side of the London Road.

Onslow Estate Sale 1905 (Surrey History Centre)

Along the road, building of the two estates of Abbotswood and Ganghill had been started. The next housing estates came with the sale of Winterhill Farm in the late 1920s – Kelly's Directories showed Lymposs & Smee to be the last occupiers of the farm in 1927. A letter from a surveyor to Guildford Rural District Council in 1929 complained that the density of proposed houses was too high and outside the

Council's policy. The planning proposals at the time were for 357 plots across 67.23 acres of land, but on 31 acres there would be 169 houses, giving a density of 5.4 houses per acre, which was higher than the accepted 5.3 houses per acre.

Delay not, or you may be too late!

The charming

Winterhill Estate

On LONDON ROAD, at Burpham (200 yds. beyond The Green Man)

has developed so rapidly that 31 houses are sold or let, and only a few more plots are available

YOU can select from Seven Designs, or we will build to satisfy your requirements. Plans can be drawn by the Estate Architect to conform to your desires. It will pay you to visit the Estate to see the charming homes which we have erected. Let us build one for you!

Popular Mansard Design

PRICES
£700
TO
£950

EASY TERMS
ARRANGED
IF DESIRED

All Winterhill Estate Houses, which are brick built, are designed by an eminent architect to suit individual plots and to catch the maximum sunlight

Apply

ARMSTRONGS ESTATES Ltd.
REDROOFS, WINTERHILL ESTATE

Advert in Guildford City Outlook 1934 (D Rose)

David Rose recorded that houses on the Winterhill Estate were on sale in 1934. '*Delay not, or you may be too late!*' said the advert in the Guildford City Outlook magazine, noting that the houses on the Winterhill Estate were more expensive than other places, but, had been '*designed by an eminent architect to suit individual plots and to catch maximum sunlight*'.

Prices ranged from £700 to £950 (rather different values to those seen in 2017) and easy terms could be arranged if desired. There were seven designs to choose from, or the developers would build to satisfy a new owner's requirements. By the time the advert appeared, 31 houses had already sold. The estate seems to have included Orchard Road, Winterhill Way, Briar Way and Hawthorne Way only, and the old farmhouse remained until about the 1960s. Great Oaks Park was built later on, linking Gosden Hill Road with the London Road. Michael Hunt remembered that council houses were built on the site of the brickfield on New Inn Lane. Barbara Stone remembered that when the contractors were clearing the woodland area for Gosden Hill they were throwing bricks at the rabbits as they were all being disturbed.

In about 1935 the particulars for a new housing estate in Burpham advised prospective owners to *'Turn left at Kingpost Café on London Road and proceed along New Inn Lane.'* It went on to say that *'The Glendale Estate occupies what must undoubtedly be regarded as one of the most attractive positions in the district. Settled back, just off the main London Road and approached by a pleasant country road, the Estate enjoys most delightful surroundings amidst a background of fine trees.'*

'Within a few minutes' stroll is the popular 18 hole golf course on Merrow Downs. Also within close walking distance the public grounds of Stoke Park, with its splendid bathing pool and tennis courts. Other facilities in the town for sport include the public swimming baths, the municipal sports ground in Woodbridge Road, public tennis courts, bowling club in Woodbridge Road and a number of recreation grounds for children.'

The nearest cinema to the Estate is the newest one in the town, the Odeon, which is situated at the junction of Epsom and London

Roads. There are three other cinemas in the town, also a first-class Repertory Company, and an Amateur Operatic Society.'

The houses varied from three bedrooms / two receptions / semi-detached at £600, to £825 for a detached house. The properties were described as a *'superior type of detached residence'*. All had ample garage space and excellent gardens, while all windows were *'Crittall's famous all-steel casements. These windows are storm and draught proof and carry with them a maker's guarantee'*, though they would not provide the double glazing or triple glazing deemed to be essential in the 21st century.

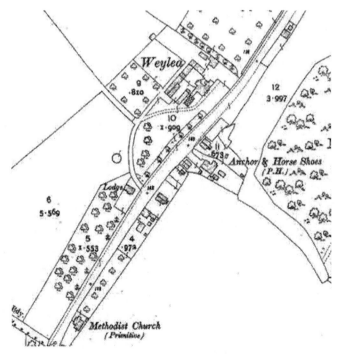

London Road cottages 1912 OS map

The London Road has developed over the last hundred years, with more cottages being built before the war, then houses after the war. In 1912 there was no sign of the two semi-detached cottages set back from the road behind the Smithy. By 1934 they were clearly on the map, as was the motor engineers, belonging to Joseph Binsted (but now Tyre City, recently Chessington Tyres), which first appeared in Kelly's Directories in 1915. Houses from New Inn Lane down to the turn to Merrow Lane seemed to have been built after the war, though there were 18 houses recorded there on the 1939 Register.

In 1939 Percy Gatley was still farming at Winterhill Farm, Leo Keene was at Gosden Hill Farm, Frank Eve was at Weylea Farm, William Winzer was at New Inn Farm and there was a farm manager called Daniel O'Brien at Bower's Farm. The 1939 Register recorded people living on London Road, Burpham Lane, and the Winterhill Estate, New Inn Lane, Merrow Lane and Meadway, Pimms Row, and a small number of houses on the 'Paddicks Estate'. These latter dwellings appeared in Kelly's Directory as 1, 2, 5 & 6 Burpham Lane – the Tudor cottages.

In 1934, Burpham Lane, or Jacobs Well Road as it was then known, still had almost no houses along the road between the Tudor Cottages and the track that would become Marlyn's Drive. However, the plans for the Paddocks Estate were being finalised as early as 1930. A prospective purchaser, name unknown, wanted to have both residential and business use for part of the estate, including woodworking shops, yard and offices, from

314

Burpham Lane up to the end of the cul-de-sac. The residential plots included land where The Cloisters development is now, as well as two plots in Paddock Road. In the Kelly's Directory for 1938 William Chambers, builder, lived in one of the houses on Meadow Road – possibly he was the unknown purchaser in 1930? The Paddocks Estate, including Paddock Road and Meadow Road off Burpham Lane, were built on land from the Marlyn's estate, and some of these were started at around the same time as the Winterhill development, but in 1934 it was still a work in progress. By 1945, there were 18 houses on Paddock Road and 11 on Meadow Road. On the right, next to the village hall, were the Council Cottages, built in the 1920s. Anne Marshall remembered that they had long front gardens. These were demolished in the late 20th century and a gated development of flats took their place.

Council houses behind New Inn Farm 1952 (Surrey Advertiser)

It was after the Second World War that development began in earnest, with demand for housing increasing as people returned

315

from war service and wanted to settle down. Glendale Drive had 30 houses in 1945 but by 1955 it had grown to 77 houses, and near by Coltsfoot Drive had 43 houses. Gosden Hill Road was built over the next few years and by 1959 there were about 72, mainly council, houses there.

The New Inn Farm estate, which included Coltsfoot, Woodruff, Burnet, Charlock – collectively known by some as the 'herb estate' - was started by local builders, Holfords, then developed in the 1950s by Ideal Homes, but work had started shortly after the war ended – a Council plan showed drainage being put in but no houses were built at that time. A plan of part of the estate from 1952 showed that 3 houses were occupied on Burnet Avenue, 24 on Coltsfoot, 27 on Woodruff, but none on Charlock Way. Mary Fry remembered '*The houses were not luxurious by today's standards – no central heating, and only one bathroom, but as my mother often pointed out, they'd moved from a house with an outside toilet and no bathroom.*' A Guildford Borough Council plan from 1955 showed the site for the police houses off New Inn Lane, as well as the site for the homes for the aged and a secondary school. Many of the houses were built for police staff and their families, though most of these have now converted to private ownership. The Great Oaks estate had been built by 1960. Peggie at the Drop-in club remembered that the rent for a council house in 1951 was £5.

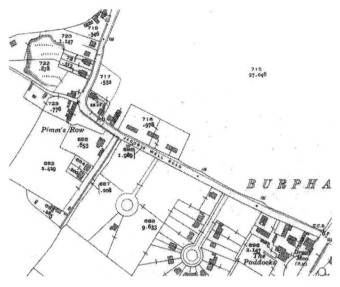

Burpham Lane - 1934 OS map

Thomas Howard moved to Glendale Drive in 1939 while working for Vickers-Armstrong (Aircraft) Ltd at Weybridge. Thomas had taken up photography before the war and he took many snapshots of local Burpham people going about their daily business. He then worked for Surrey County Council as Clerk of Works and took photos of workmen putting together the prefabs and housing that was so badly needed to house the growing population. His son said that the area had not been properly developed when they first moved to Burpham, but was heavily populated by many evacuees. '*The community surrounding his family on Glendale Drive in Burpham, a country village two miles from Guildford, was made up almost entirely of evacuees from London, housed under requisition by the government on an unfinished suburban housing estate of semi- and detached houses*

317

not yet connected to the main drainage system. It was this community that he began to photograph in his spare time.'

Thomas Howard photo of two men drinking in the car park of the Green Man, with Kingpost Restaurant in the background (Surrey History Centre)

Allen Mead remembered that Glendale Drive was built for people moving out from London and other places. It was partly council houses and partly private houses, but a fantastic place to live for young families. Upfolds Green was a great meeting place for children and teenagers, who played games there – putting jumpers on the ground for goal posts. They also made trolleys and raced down the green.

The Marlyn's Estate development came in the early 1950s and was built by G T Crouch, builders. The style of houses were shown at the Ideal Homes Exhibition. Phil and Anita Branson bought one of the first houses on the estate. Phil remembered that one day he saw a man laying out the plots across the field

318

and asked him what he was doing. The man told him about the new estate and said that one particular plot would be a good one, so Phil contacted the Council and bought it and has lived there ever since. By 1956, when Doreen and Ken Marshall moved in, the pavements still hadn't been made up on the estate.

Council houses at Upfolds Green 1952 (Surrey Advertiser)

In 1961 Weylea Farm was owned by Messrs E & R Thomas Ltd and the next big development came in 1975 when six planning applications were submitted to Guildford Borough Council to build on the land, varying from 405-618 dwellings. One of the developers was planning to build 35 houses per hectare (the whole estate totalled 19.9 hectares), but the application was refused. Clearly not deterred by this, the developers continued to submit more applications over the next few years. In 1979 the

Guildford Society expressed their concerns that building 500 units on the estate would cause significant problems for both Burpham and Merrow as the population grew but the infrastructure did not improve – some things never change.

In 1980 there was an application '*to erect 91 detached two-storey dwellings and garages with construction of new roads and footpaths at Weylea Farm, London Road'*. Again concerns were expressed, this time about the potential for '*the estate being used as a rat run from London Road to the improved A3 to London*' – a very realistic concern. The BCA responded to another application saying that 400 dwellings was excessive on a 47.5 acre site; that a rat run would be created; and there was a potential issue of access to the village hall during construction. A meeting was held in the Paddock Rooms at the Green Man in April 1980 between Focus 21, the developers who owned Weylea Farm, and residents in the roads immediately adjoining the estate. The plans were eventually approved and the estate was built. Those who expressed concerns about a rat run were proved right as drivers seek to cut off the mini roundabouts between Aldi and Sainsbury's. The estate has been extended over the years. There are a number of warden-assisted bungalows on the estate, run by Anchor Housing.

The Sutton Place Lodge houses on the A3 are included in the Burpham boundaries. John Pidgeon remembered that an Irish family called Burke lived there. Mrs Burke worked as housekeeper for Paul Getty when he owned Sutton Place.

There are blocks of flats in Abbot's House and West Court on Burpham Lane, Grosvenor Court on New Inn Lane and The Cloisters on London Road, as well as next to and above the London Road and Kingpost Parade shops. It was reported that a number of flats in The Cloisters were bought by Russian investors and the developer's sales & marketing team had to include a Russian speaker. There are also flats included in the main housing estates.

Entrance to Weybrook Park Estate from Great Oaks Park roundabout, c. late 1980s (BCA)

The last big estate to be developed in Burpham was Weybrook Park, on the old Bower's Farm land. In 1982, the Surrey Advertiser reported that an American property Company, Anglo Texan Property Ltd, owned the land, having bought it from the Getty estate in 1980, after Paul Getty's death. There was a proposal to build more than 500 upmarket, executive-style homes over 58 acres. Three large developers were negotiating with Anglo Texan's London agents, New Ideal Homes Ltd, Miller Group Ltd, and one other, name unknown.

321

In 1984 there was an agreement setting out the ownership and usage of the land between Guildford Borough Council, J Sainsbury plc and New Ideal Homes Ltd. Sainsbury's appeared to own the land and the property developers were to purchase those parts of the farm that were not designated for the supermarket development, including the copse beside Sainsbury's, land that would later become the extension of the Sutherland Memorial Park, land that would become Churchfields and a plot of land on the far side of the river. The Council retained ownership of various parcels of land. In the document Sainsbury's agreed '*not to use the New Ideal Land for any purpose other than for the purpose of agriculture ... the provisions of this sub-clause shall not prevent the New Ideal Land being developed for open space and/or recreational use and/or for residential purposes whether with or without a library sports facilities and/or a doctors and/or dentists surgery and/or an hotel...*' It is an interesting thought that perhaps at some point someone had ideas about building a hotel in the village.

Two years later the Council granted outline planning permission to Ideal Homes for mixed residential development, to include roads, services and open spaces; and to the Miller Group Ltd for the erection of 66 dwelling houses and garages.

One of the concerns about the estate was proximity to the A3, which would become highly used and noisy by the 21st century. A big mound was created between the A3 and the estate as a noise bund, known as the 'Giant Slug', now mostly disguised by trees.

Gosden Hill Farm

For over 35 years the BCA has been challenging proposals to develop housing on the Gosden Hill Farm estate by Martin Grant Homes. However, the Guildford Borough Council Local Plan 2016 proposes that the development goes ahead, including 1,700 (reduced from 2,000) new homes, shopping, new schools, a railway station, offices and traveller pitches, as well as a Park and Ride for up to 1,000 vehicles. The BCA's response to the Council expressed many concerns about the impact of such a development on the local community, saying that Burpham would *'cease to be a definable village and diminish to just the name of an area within the urban sprawl of Guildford.'*

Pimm's Row

Pimm's Row, 1952 (Surrey Advertiser)

The 1905 sale of Onslow properties in Burpham included eight cottages known as Pimm's Row. The description said that they were built of brick and tile roofed, each containing four rooms with garden, arable and pastureland. The lot included not only the eight cottages, but also a brickfield, a sandpit, part of the towpath and fishing rights (shooting rights could be bought for an additional £10 p.a.). The lot was offered for sale at £2,200 but didn't sell. It was offered again in 1909 for £1,490 and it is thought that Surrey County Council bought the cottages. Norman Hamilton recorded that the bricks used in the buildings were hand-made from the local brickyard.

In 1979 sales particulars for a house in Pimm's Row said 'Formerly two cottages in a row of eight, the property now comprises one unit, affording the following accommodation: Three bedrooms, bathroom on the first floor, lounge, dining room, extensive kitchen / utility room, outside WC on ground floor.' There were stone floors throughout the ground floor, though some were covered with linoleum. The particulars also mentioned outbuildings *'existing barn is to be demolished and removed'*, but there was space for a possible garage at the rear. The cost at the time was £18,000.

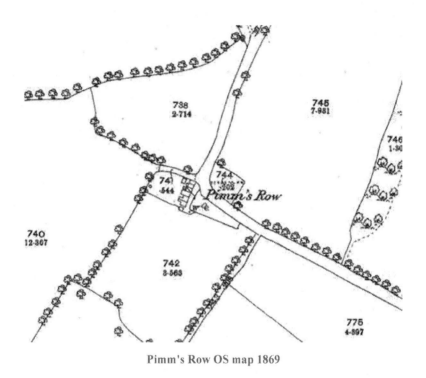

Pimm's Row OS map 1869

The British Listed Buildings website described the properties as a *'row of six cottages, now three. Mid C18, altered. Red brick in Flemish bond, plain tile roof. Two storeys, six bays. Cottages formerly one bay each set in handed pairs with doors to outside. Segmental header-brick arches to openings, the doorways with modern frames and board doors...'* The website said that one of the cottages had older timbers reused as beams inside. The site went on to say that *'Reference is made in an indenture of 1909 to*

325

a late C16 indenture concerning this property, but from the architectural evidence, although earlier materials are incorporated, the row as it now exists was built in the C18. It is thought to have been built for a local brick works.' Other sources suggest that the cottages were for farm workers or mill workers.

Karen Robinson found a copy of the 1909 document, which was between Lord Onslow as vendor and Surrey County Council (or as it was known then the Administrative County of Surrey) and related to a plot of land behind Burpham Primary School, St Luke's Church, the cottages along Burpham Lane past Pimm's Row and back to the river. It stated that Lord Onslow was the Lord of the Manor of Burpham and confirmed that he owned the property. The indenture referred to a one thousand year *'indenture of lease dated the thirtieth day of June in the Thirty fourth year of the reign of Queen Elizabeth and made between Edmund Windesor of the one part and Thomas Atfeld otherwise Ripley of the other part...'* - this would have been in 1592. It went on to refer to an Indenture of Assignment dated 1876 as well as Letters Patent granted by King Charles the First and King Charles the Second.

Interestingly the document goes on to describe *'those eight messuages hereditaments and premises firstly hereinbefore described and formerly known as Streters otherwise Stretery's but now called Pimms Row.'* Although it has not been possible to confirm any other history of buildings on the site before the existing cottages, this document does seem to imply that there were buildings there before the 18th century. The document also mentions that the land was part of Burpham Farm, now known as Burpham Court Farm.

1909 indenture relating to Pimm's Row / Streeters (K Robinson)

Thomas Attfeilde alias Ripley's will in 1626 referred to '*my messuage and land for life which I have of the demise of Edmund Windsor, late of Hillesden Bucks for one thousand years at 10s 8d per annum*'. Then George Garment of Burgham's will in 1710 referred to land that he bequeathed to his son '*also the messuage called Streeters alias Streeters, three acres in Burpham, and two closes Cursie Crofts, four closes Cottesfurlong and Cottersland in Burpham and meadow adjoining all in my occupation; demised by Edward Windsore of Hillesden Bucks by indenture of 30th January*

327

1581 at 10s 8d per annum to Thomas Atfeild alias Ripley of Burpham for one thousand years and now by divers conveyances mine.' Presumably both Thomas and George owned the land that later became known as Pimm's Row.

In the Tithe Maps of 1838 the eight cottages were part of a large piece of land owned by William Francis Pimm, including Green Man Farm and Marlyn's, where he and his family lived. William also leased land from Lord Onslow, including Burpham Court Farm, Bower's Mill and this land stretched across the northern boundary of Burpham above Burpham Lane and as far as London Road. The name Pimm's Row was first used in the 1861 census, but in the 1841 census the cottages were just denoted as eight houses in Burgham.

One was occupied by Ann Collis, a widowed laundress, her daughter Laurey and her son William, who was a farm labourer. Others were occupied by:
- Richard Stiles, with his wife and five children.
- George and Sarah Cook;
- John and Sarah May, with four children;
- William and Elizabeth Searle;
- James and Sarah Dean;
- John and Mather Golden with four children;
- John and Mary Chapman with eight children, which must have been rather cramped.

Most of the men and older boys were farm labourers, but John Chapman was a sawyer and James Dean was a miller.

Pimm's Row Cottages c. 1969 (Surrey History Centre)

Ten years later, the census enumerator called the road Green Man
Lane and Ann Collis was still there with her son William, along
with John Chapman, Richard Stiles and William Searle. One
cottage was uninhabited but others were occupied by William and
Louisa Keale; James and Frances Waltham; and Lousia Grover. By
1861 Ann Collis and John Chapman had died, but their sons
continued to live there with their families, along with Richard
Stiles, James Waltham and William Keel. Almost all of the
cottages had new families in 1871, apart from William Collis with
his wife and sons. The others were Henry Pullen, William Jelley,
William Trigg, Henry Woods, Frederick Hooke, Susan Woods and
Henry Alexander. Three of them worked at Bower's Mill and one
at the brickfield.

By 1891 William Collis was still there with his wife Christine, but
by this time he was a road labourer. Henry Woods still lived in an
adjoining cottage, while other occupants were Charlotte Faithful,

329

Charlotte Cowley, Thomas Tigg, John Hoar, William Grantham and Henry Sop. Sadly Charlotte Faithful died in the Guildford Union Workhouse in 1902. By 1901, William Collis was living with his son George's family in Merrow but later that year he died in the Guildford Union Workhouse as well. William was interesting as he was married twice, first to Mary and and then his second wife, Christine, was Danish but naturalised British. In the 1881 census a Jane Collis from Worplesdon was recorded as William's wife, but by 1891 it was Christine again. Was this just a transcription error by the census enumerator or did he lead a complicated love life?

One question that remains is whether or not this William Collis was any relation to the William Frederick Collis on the war memorial? The latter had lived in Buryfields but his wife, Mary Stone came from Worplesdon and their daughter Dorothy was baptised at St Luke's in 1916, so presumably there was some connection with Burpham.

In 1901 the other occupants of Pimm's Row were Albert Tidy, Alfred Woods, Henry Sopp, Henry Woods, William Turner, James Usher, Thomas Elliot and Charles Grey (father to one of the men on the war memorial). By 1911 some of the alterations had been made to enlarge the cottages and there were five family dwellings in the row. John Howlett, Frederick Simpson and Alfred Marshall all had cottages with six rooms, whilst Charles Grover and George Henry Sopp had cottages with only three rooms.

Lord Onslow had been a careful landlord, insuring his properties against fire through the Hand in Hand Fire & Life Insurance

Society. The record for Pimm's Row noted that the property was *'within 15 feet of a brickyard but no kiln within 66 feet'* and went on to note that there were eight cottages with woodhouses.

Silas Kilby (J Kemp)

Information gathered as part of the Burpham Will Remember Them project included a fairly detailed description of the Durrant's home in Pimm's Row. *'The cottages had been built as farm workers' cottages for workers at Burpham Court Farm. Two up, two down, very narrow, so a squash for the large Durrant family, even with two cottages. There was no connecting door between the cottages and to go to the privy in the garden you had to go from the scullery into the coal shed, through the adjoining coal shed into the garden. Later they had a connecting door inside. Thomas kept a pig and some chickens at the end of the long garden and grew lots of vegetables to feed the family. Pimms Row was a close knit community and Tom and other neighbours had allotments beyond the gate. Thomas' horse, Sharper, grazed in the meadow and had his own stable. There was a lean-to shed for the cart. Nothing was wasted – Agatha boiled nettles to use as vegetables. The older members of the family living at home lent a hand with the chores and sold produce, as well as working full or part-time.'* Another source recorded *'A family called Howlett lived at no. 1 – they owned an open backed lorry and sold and delivered vegetables produced by the Pimm's Row families'.*

Kelly's Directories did record some dwellings on Pimm's Row from 1930, including Silas Kilby and Albert Russell as market gardeners, but they were just noted as Burpham Lane. The next official record of house occupants was the 1939 Register and this showed that there were four cottages lived in by John, Elizabeth and Arthur Howlett; George, Florence and Edward Isard; Agatha and Ruth Durrant; and Silas Kilby. The Howletts, George and Silas were market gardeners. After the war Kelly's Directories provided information about the occupants at all addresses in Burpham. In 1944/45 there was no change from 1939, but in 1950, by which time the cottages were recorded as numbers 43, 45, 47 and 49 Burpham Lane, there was an additional person at Silas Kilby's cottage, W A Tickner, for a short while, perhaps a lodger? Silas died in 1955 and Geoffrey Mace took over the house; Agatha Durrant died the same year, but her daughter Ruth continued to live in the cottage. Ruth had been a pupil at Burpham Primary School from 1911 and then worked at the school as a dinner lady during the second world war.

Pimm's Row Cottages 2016

The land in front of and behind the cottages was used for market gardening and smallholdings.   Between 1926-1963 there were much correspondence with the Council about purchasing the land and its subsequent management.   As said in previous chapters, the cottages and adjoining land has been at risk several times. From the route for the A3, which would have demolished all the buildings, to playing fields for the school, which took land to the rear of the cottages.

In 2014 the Surrey Advertiser published a piece about the Durrant family history as part of their coverage of the Great War.   The following photographs were shared by the family.

Agatha Durrant with some of her children (Surrey Advertiser)

Thomas Durrant with two of his children (Surrey Advertiser)

Marlyn's

It is not clear exactly when the house Marlyn's and its neighbour Marlyn's Cottage were built, but they both appeared in the Tithe Maps of 1838 and the 1841 census. On the Tithe Maps the Marlyn's Estate included land from the house and down to Pimm's Row on Burpham Lane, totalling over 37 acres. The land between Marlyn's and Shagden (Weylea) Farm was a large orchard and much of the land between Marlyn's and Burpham Lane was for paddocks. The house included a chapel at the back.

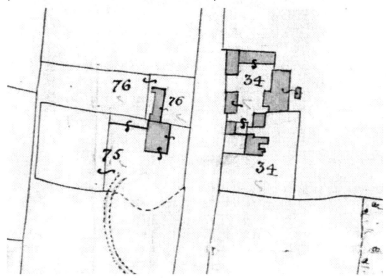

Marlyn's and Marlyn's Cottage (nos 75, 76) 1838 Tithe Map

It is unlikely that the current houses were built earlier than around 1800, but there is evidence that there was a property with the same name almost 200 years earlier. The Court Baron minutes of the mid-1660s recorded that '*William Cooper and his wife Grace, late Symonds, had a parcel of Marlyns with Henry Attfield*' and '*Grace Underwood had a parcel of Marlyn's with*

336

Henry Attfield'. Unfortunately there is nothing to explain exactly what this meant, but at least it does show that there was either land or property with the name at that time. So who or what was Marlyn? The first mention of anyone in the Worplesdon parish records with the name was in 1573 when John Cooper alias Marlyn was baptised – his father was Richard. There were four other legitimate children and one bastard son, William in 1576.

In 1615 Thomas Marline alias Cooper died and in his will left his house and land at Burpham to his son, Thomas Marline alias Cooper. The younger Thomas died in 1635 and by that time had changed the spelling of his name to Marlyn. He left to his wife, Alice, *'my messuage in which I live and 14½ acres of arable land in Burpham for 11 years, and then to my eldest daughter Alice Marlyn alias Cooper when she is 21 years old. My wife to bring her and my other daughter Joyce up and after her daughter is 21 to have £4 per annum for life'*.

A Rent Roll document dated 1800 recorded that Joseph Pickstone, who was the Steward for the Manor of Burgham, had a leasehold of Marlyns. In 1855 a Rate Book for Worplesdon recorded that £20 0s 0d was due for Marlyn's House and garden, but doesn't say who was responsible for payment.

From the early 1800s William Francis Pimm owned Marlyns and all the land from Shagden Farm down to Burpham Lane, apart from the Green Man. He also leased land from Lord Onslow, from Burpham Court Farm, past Bower's Mill and over to the London Road, where Bower's Farm would be in later years.

Marlyn's, c. 1977 (N Hamilton)

William was born in Send in 1782, married Mary Winkworth in 1820 and they had four children. He appeared in the Electoral Registers from 1832, living at Marlyn's, but the first record of him was the Land Tax records of 1826 where he was shown as the occupier of a house and land owned by John Pimm. Unfortunately, these records did not usually name the houses, but perhaps it was Marlyn's and John might have been William's father? By 1829 William was both owner and occupier. After his death in 1844 his widow, Mary, was recorded as head of the house on the 1851 census, with 370 acres of land. William's will was long and complex as his estate included land, buildings, farms, stocks and shares. He left it all in trust to his wife (as long as she didn't remarry) until their youngest child was 21 years old. Then after her death in 1854 their son, Arthur, aged around 30 years, was recorded as the owner. However, by the 1861 census Arthur had moved up the road, past Marlyn's Cottage, and he only had 18 acres, having presumably sold off the rest of the estate.

The next owner of Marlyn's was William Robert Alchin, who lived there from the mid-1850s for over 20 years. He was only 30 years old at the time of the 1861 census and was described as a Merchant and Farmer, but no records have been found to explain what sort of merchant he was. He was born in 1829 in Kent, where his father was a wealthy farmer, and in 1852 he married Mary Anne Prior.

Roger Marjoribanks recorded in his history of the village that the Alchin family were prime movers for the establishment of a

Methodist chapel for the community. He said that *'the blacksmith's shop, leased to Charles Puttock, on part of whose land the chapel was built after the Alchins' retirement to Sussex, had been bought by Mary Ann Alchin, his wife, in 1876 and was now sold on for £60 to the trustees of the Guildford Circuit of the Primitive Methodist Church'*. In the 1881

Stained glass windows of the chapel at Marlyn's

census record William described himself as a Protestant Trinitarian Minister at Marlyn's Chapel, Marlyn's House, so perhaps he built on the chapel at the back of the house.

339

William was a keen gardener. His produce would be exhibited at the Send & Ripley Society's Horticultural Exhibition held at Ripley Court. In 1870 the newspaper stated he was an '...*honorary contributor with four brace of cucumbers grown by his gardener at Marlyn's House. Two cucumbers called Marlyn's Challenge and Marlyn's Surprise. All were over 30 inches in length, thick in proportion and covered in beautiful bloom. Grown by perfect process of forcing in ten days. A finer flavoured cucumber than one of Marlyn's Challenge we have never tasted.*'

William and Mary Ann had retired to Hastings by 1891, where they were recorded as 'living on their own means'. Mary Ann died in 1901 and the following year William married again, to Elizabeth Gibbs in East Grinstead. William died in Ticehurst, Sussex, in 1906.

By 1891, William Henry Burbidge had bought Marlyn's, but at the time of the census he was staying at the Royal Hotel in Ventnor, on the Isle of Wight, presumably on holiday. However, his servants Harriet and Alice Hodgskin were at the house so it is clear that he was the owner. William was born in 1837 in Camberwell, where his father was a distiller. He was married in 1864 to Clara Eliza and they were together for 56 years.

In the 1871 census he was living with Clara in Camberwell, where he was a tea merchant, but he could not be found in the 1881 census records, so it is not known where he was living – perhaps he was working abroad? The 1901 and 1911 censuses recorded him as a retired tea merchant living at Marlyn's with Clara, and

340

his servants. They don't seem to have had any children. William died at home in 1920 and was buried at St Luke's. Clara continued to live at Marlyn's until her death in 1937, aged 94 years, and she was also buried at St Luke's.

Stained glass window in Marlyn's with initials WHB

There is a stained glass window on the staircase in the house, which seems to have the letters WHB, possibly for William Henry Burbidge. He was an avid analyst of weather and rainfall, contributing to a local newspaper's monthly column on this subject. In 1914 the paper reported that, owing to indisposition, William had to give up taking his records and therefore his monthly letters would cease. The 1911 census stated that there were ten rooms in the house, not including bathroom, lobby and scullery. Behind the house are buildings, now houses, but were probably stables originally.

There were no updates for Kelly's Directory during the second world war, but according to the one for 1944/5 the house seems to have been used as offices for the company Borax & Chemical at the end of the war. From 1950 to 1959 William Henry Bullen lived at Marlyn's and, according to Norman Hamilton, he sold the house to Abbeyfield Properties (Guildford) Ltd to be converted into flats for retired ladies. The room at the back with the stained glass window, which originally went from floor to roof, had to be divided horizontally. In 1965 the electoral register recorded that the eight occupants were Jane Sheppard, Esto Marshall, Muriel Bane, Blanche Moore, Edith Smith, Margaret Williams, Josephine Reynard and Jessie Sully. Over the years ownership changed but 25 years later three of the ladies were still there – Muriel Bane, Blanche Moore and Edith Smith. By 1985 men were allowed in and there was one married couple living there. At some point there seems to have been some alterations to create fewer, but perhaps larger, flats as the 1990 register showed six flats.

In 1979 the BCA reported that there had been a planning application to erect a block of five terraced houses with garages and parking spaces at Marlyn's, but this was rejected due to the development of the A3 diversion from Burpham to Ladymead.

Front of Marlyn's 2015

Christopher Harris lived in one of the flats in the early 1980s and remembered that they were mainly occupied by old ladies, who were very deaf and played their radios and televisions very loud. There is a big basement in the house, which could have been a wine cellar in previous years. It has been suggested that the ghost of a woman walks along the hallway.

Although part of the same building as the main Marlyn's house, Marlyn's Lodge appears to have been a separate property. It is the rooms on the London Road side of the building and comprises a two-storey dwelling. The name Marlyn's Lodge first appeared in the census record of 1871 when James Mills lived there with his wife and six children. James was a domestic gardener, perhaps working for William Alchin in the main house? In 1881 Edmond Robinson, with his wife and son, were the occupants, in 1891 William Lemon, a brickmaker, was there with his wife and five children, but by 1901 George Thomas Howlett had moved in. George was a brickmaker, probably working at one of the two brickfields in Burpham, and he lived with his wife and six children at Marlyn's Lodge in 1901 and 1911. The census record stated that there were five rooms in the house. The only other records found for Marlyn's Lodge were: in 1944/5 when James Smith was living there; in 1965 it was Dawn and Leonard Chuter; in 1975 Robert and Gladys McGee were there; in 1980 it was Susan Thomas; in 1985 it was Peter and Evelyn Lally; and in 1990 Marilyn and Steven Mochrie.

Census records in 1851 showed a dwelling called Marlyn's Farm, where Richard Steven, Thomas Smallpiece and Job Grover, all farm labourers, lived with their families. It is possible that this was the Lodge or the Cottage, but it is equally possible that there were other farm buildings used for labourers on the site.

Marlyn's Cottage lies next door to Marlyn's House on the London Road. In 1861 George Wright, a retired draper, was living there with his wife and son. In 1871 Fanny Greening was the occupant, with her two daughters and a servant – she was described as an annuitant's wife, so her husband received an annuity or benefit to live on. In 1881 Daniel Beazley, a farm labourer, lived there with his wife and son, but there were four others recorded at the same address. William Cornish, an Inspector of Agents and ex-Baptist Minister, was with his wife, three daughters (one of whom was a minister's wife) and two granddaughters. William Searle Snr, a wheelwright, lived with his wife and two nieces; William Searle Jnr, a brickmaker, lived with a housekeeper; and George Grover, a gardener, lived with his wife and four children.

In 1891 there was an artist and painter called Edmund Coldwell living at the Cottage with his American wife, Celestia. Then in 1899 two sisters, called Sarah and Margaret Hodgson, moved in, with their servant Ellen Sparrowhawk. They were ladies of independent means who had come from Kent, but were recorded as living in the house at least until 1915. Their father was the Vicar of Croydon and their mother's family came to England from the island of St Helena. There were nine children and the family was clearly wealthy as in 1871 there were six servants living with them. Sarah and Margaret never married and it seems that three other sisters did not marry either. Margaret died in 1915 and was

344

buried at St Luke's. It is not known what happened to Sarah, but maybe she moved back to Kent as there are some deaths recorded there after 1918. It is possible that perhaps Hodgson Gardens is named after these sisters?

Marlyn's Cottage

For several years after Sarah Hodgson left Marlyn's Cottage it was rented to be used for the curate, Revd. J W Clarke, and then the vicar, Revd. E C Storr. In 1930 Kelly's Directory recorded Captain Piers Edgcumbe as the occupant, then by 1939 Allan D Coward had bought the property. He was born in Wandsworth in around 1889 and in the 1939 Register was recorded as living at Marlyn's Cottage with Mary H Coward, possibly his wife. He seems to have married Agnes Ross in 1951 so perhaps she was his second wife as she was living there in 1965. Allan died in 1967, however, by 1975 the electoral register showed a Jean Coward living at the Cottage and remaining there until at least 1985. Was she another wife, a daughter or a sister? Unfortunately that information has

345

not been found. There was a suggestion that the Cowards were related to the actor and playwright Noel Coward, but no evidence has been found at this time to support this. In 1990 the Cottage was occupied by John Pursley.

In recent years the current owners were doing some work in the back garden and took down a lean-to shed. Behind it they found what are believed to be several bread ovens, presumably from the days when Marlyn's was a working farm and there were lots of farm labourers living in the various buildings.

Bread ovens discovered at rear of Marlyn's Cottage

The Paddocks

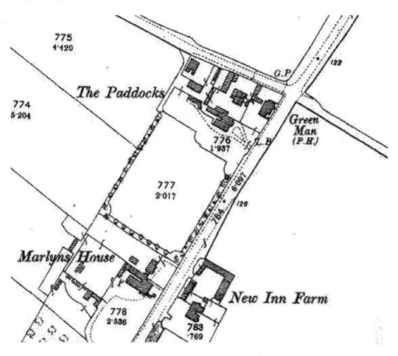

The Paddocks, London Road, OS map 1895

This house first appeared in census records in 1871, so was probably built shortly before that, on land that used to belong to the Marlyn's estate. The census of 1871 recorded Mrs Anne M Williams, a widow who was born in Liverpool in about 1807, as Head of the household. She was recorded as being a landowner, but no information has been found to confirm where she might have owned land. By 1881 the house was owned by John Mitchell, who owned one of the brickfields in Burpham, probably the one on Burpham Lane. He lived there with his wife Fanny and their

347

little daughter Minnie. He was only 33 years old at the time, so presumably had been successful with his business in order to afford this big house. Fanny died in 1890, aged only 30 years, and was buried at St Luke's. Perhaps John decided to move away after his wife's death as by 1891 the house was owned by John Soutter. He was born in Sussex in 1828, and was recorded as a widower living on his own means, with his sons John, an architect, Ernest, a surveyor, and his daughter Jane, a landowner. John, the father, died in 1899, leaving a substantial estate of over £17,000, confirming that they were a fairly wealthy family. John, the son, took over as head of the house and in 1901 was living there with his brother Ernest and his wife Louisa, who was a professor of music.

The Paddocks (on the left), used as a function room for the Green Man, about 1964 (D Rose)

348

By 1903, they had moved away and the 1911 census recorded Arthur Rawson Birks, a retired Judge, as living there. In 1873 he had worked for the Indian Civil Service, at the Chief Court of Lower Burma until 1900. He was born in 1850 to the Vicar of Kelshall in Hertfordshire. He married Jane Kent Durrant in 1876 and two of their children were born in Burma. He died in 1923 at The Priory, Roehampton and was buried at St Luke's. The last mention in Kelly's Directory of him living at The Paddocks was in 1915, and when Jane died in 1930 the burial register for St Luke's recorded her address as Mount Esk on London Road. Arthur Birks would lend the room above the stables at The Paddocks for meetings of the Worplesdon & District Conservative and Liberal Unionist Association, for which he would be Chairman.

Coach House for The Paddocks (W Lawrence)

In 1919, according to the Electoral Register, William Bramwell Gates, of the Cow & Gate Dairy Company, was living at The Paddocks. However, he only lived there for a short while. The house was bought by Hodgson Kingston Brewery in 1930 to be used as a function room for the Green Man. The Coach House for The Paddocks is thought to have been off Burpham Lane.

PARKS, PLAYING FIELDS AND OTHER

GREEN SPACES

From being a small corner of the vast Windsor Forest in the 12th century, Burpham developed into an agricultural community and

OS map 1869

it is only in the last 100 years that the green spaces have started to be replaced by housing. First to go was Winterhill Farm, when the Winterhill Estate was built in the early 1930s. Then New Inn Farm was sold to developers between the wars, with buildings going up from the 1930s onwards. Weylea Farm continued as a farm until the 1970s but then was sold to developers for housing. Lastly, Bower's Farm was sold to developers to create the Weybrook Park estate with Sainsbury's supermarket.

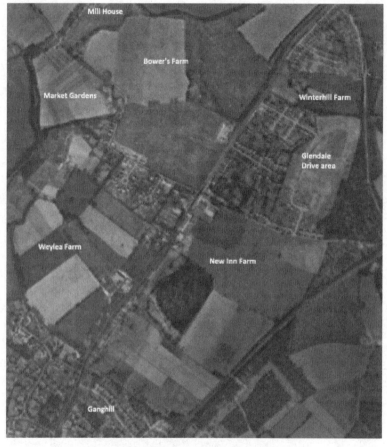

Aerial photo of Burpham 1945 (Google Earth)

352

thousand nine hundred and fifty four B E T W E E N THE MOST NOBLE GEORGE GRANVILLE DUKE AND EARL OF SUTHERLAND K.T., P.C., of Sutton Place Guildford in the County of Surrey (hereinafter called "the Settlor") of the one part and THE MAYOR ALDERMEN AND BURGESSES of the Borough of Guildford (hereinafter called "the Trustees") of the other part _____

W H E R E A S :-

(1) Under a Vesting Deed dated the Twentieth day of August One thousand nine hundred and thirty and made between The Most Noble Niall Diarmid Duke of Argyll and The Right Honourable Eric Viscount Chapli of the one part and the Settlor of the other part the property herei after described and hereby conveyed (being part of the Settled Lands comprised in the said Vesting Deed) is vested in the Settlor in fee simple free from incumbrances _____

(2) In order to provide a Public Recreation Ground and Playing Field as a War Memorial to the residents of Burpham near Guildford in the County of Surrey who were killed on active service during the late W the Settlor is desirous of granting the property hereinafter describ to the intent that the same shall be held for the purposes authorise by the Recreation Grounds Act 1859 and the Trustees have agreed to a as such Trustees as aforesaid _____

(3) The expression "residents of Burpham" shall mean and include the persons from time to time residing within the boundary for the time being of the ecclesiastical parish of Burpham-cum-Sutton which is situated at the date hereof partly within the Borough of Guildford a partly within the Rural District of Guildford _____

(4) Under a Settlement dated the Thirteenth day of September One thousand nine hundred and nine and made between The Most Noble Cromartie Duke and Earl of Sutherland K.G., of the one part and the said The Most Noble Niall Diarmid Duke of Argyll and The Right Honourable Eric Viscount Chaplin (therein called "Niall Diarmid Campbell" and "Eric Chaplin" respectively) of the other part the Settlor as tenant for life of the said Settlement has power to grant

Deed of Conveyance of land by Duke of Sutherland to the residents of Burpham 1954

The first sign of an outdoor community facility was when the Duke of Sutherland gave land as a War Memorial gift to the

353

village, to provide a playing field. However, this was not without its problems. The Times newspaper published a piece in May 1956 headed 'Defence of Village Playing Field'. This reported the dismay of Burpham villagers to the news that the Trustees of the playing field had been approached by a petrol station concern to sell a strip of the land. At a village meeting, attended by about 200 people, it was declared that residents had a right to be heard before such a sale was agreed. As a result, it was decided that this piece of land would be excluded from the Royal opening the following month by having a length of rope cordon off the area.

The Deed stated that the Mayor, Aldermen and Burgesses of the Borough of Guildford would be the Trustees of the playing field but that local people would be the Manager, through the Burpham War Memorial Committee. These included the vicar, Revd Arthur W H Theodosius, Councillor Kenneth R Velde, Mrs Vida B C Collins, Mr Arthur Manfield, Mr Robert Dickie, Mr Oliver E Garside, Mr Maurice T Edgeley and Dr Derek F Parkin. Alderman H Norris was the Honorary Solicitor.

In 1975 a piece was written by John Saxton for the BCA called 'Burpham's Greener Side – A Potted History', which proffered a lot of details about the Sutherland Memorial Playing Field. John was the Chairman of the SMPF Management Committee and included some dry humour.

SUTHERLAND PLAYING FIELD

(Burpham War Memorial Committee).

GRAND FETE

WEDNESDAY, 27th JUNE, 1956.

Programme of the Afternoon Events

Music by the W.R.A.C. Staff Band

(by kind permission of the Director and Officers of the Corps).

P.M.
2. 0. Fancy Dress Parade and Judging.
2.30. Police Dog Demonstration.
3. 0. Races for Under 5's. 20 yards.
       Races for 5—7's. 30 yards.
3.30. W.R.A.C. Band Counter Marching and Marching.
4. 0. Decorated Bicycle Parade and Judging.
4.30. Races for 7—9's. 50 yards.
       Races for 9—11's. 80 yards.
5. 0. Prize-giving for Competitors successful in above events.
5.30. Races for Over 11's. 100 yards, etc.
6. 0. Dog Show.
       Classes to be announced on Village Notice Board.
7. 0. Prize-giving for Over 11's events.

DANCING until 10 o'clock will conclude the day.
REFRESHMENTS AVAILABLE.

SIDESHOWS including:
BOWLING FOR PIG (Pig presented by R. Dickie, Esq.)
HOOP-LA.   PENNY ON THE BOARD.
DARTBOARD.   AEROPLANE.   COKERNUT SHIES.
STALLS.
WOMEN'S INSTITUTE.   MOTHERS' UNION.

Grand Opening of Sutherland Memorial Playing Fields, Programme of
Events 1956 (C Ridsdale Smith)

355

'Why so called? In the early years after the war the Duke of Sutherland, then owner of Sutton Place, probably like so many landed gentry looked to the periphery of his domain for development, probably to help maintain and run the remainder. Guildford Corporation, either in their infinite wisdom or perhaps because they had an eye on it for themselves, did not agree to any such development. The Duke, with equal cunning, promptly decreed that if he could not build, no one would, and by common and cordial consent of all, bequeathed the freehold by deed to the Borough of Guildford provided it was held in perpetuity and in memory of the people of Burpham and Jacobs Well who gave their lives during the preceding world conflicts. This same deed provided for permanent trustees in the Mayor of Guildford, the

Prince Philip opening Sutherland Memorial Playing Fields 1956 (BCA)

Vicar of Burpham and Sutton Green and the Duke's representative and not more than five representatives of the community.
This august body so formed, duly levelled and seeded our field and prepared for the grand opening, performed by HRH the Duke of Edinburgh, after descending in his whirlybird to be greeted and

356

feted by civic dignitaries and local personages alike. He duly planted a commemorative tree! This was in 1956. A further

Prince Philip meeting Burpham Primary School children, with Miss Pratt, at Sutherland Memorial Playing Fields Opening 1956 (Burpham Primary School)

feature to be recalled at this time were the worthy personages of the Mens Fellowship working steadfastly as men of the soil, not reaping and sowing, but collecting flints and stones by the sackful to ensure that the footballers and local schoolchildren continued residence on the field rather than at the County Hospital with cuts and bruises.

Hard work in fundraising by Esmond Ellis' committee and in particular aided by the Guild, W.I. and the then formed football and cricket clubs with annual fetes etc was the order of the day into the early '60s, a cricket square had been laid, swings provided and Douglas Bryant, then Vicar, had found a shed

357

surplus to requirement left by his predecessor, that was acting as a pavilion.

The football club were, by this time, establishing themselves as formidable opposition in the Guildford League, and with much hard work the cricket square was playing truly. An added feature of interest was the catering arrangements for cricketers' teas, where Pam Loweth boiled water in an open vat over a sawdust burner, converted successfully to send out smoke signals every time a wicket fell.

Such were the pioneering days. By the mid '60s with cricket club assistance we had planted 30 trees, affixed seats and added to the children's play area. Alas in a short time a large number of trees suffered the fate of the Duke's tree, by then replanted at least four times, i.e. that of canine and junior over zealousness.

The Management by now were realising that the size of the field was somewhat limited, especially with a planning restriction imposed pending possible widening of the A3, approach through the Duke's Secretary for further land was however receiving favourable reaction when alas the Duke's death came. A more permanent building in place of the shed was also a necessity, this indeed was hastened when the latter received superficial damage in the wee small hours, whilst the adjoining cricket club store shed, also in timber, was razed to the ground by fire.

Meanwhile the Borough, who throughout had always been of considerable assistance, were approaching the Duke's successor for more land, alas the value applied by the District Valuer in no way arrived at that assessed by the new owner, whose price was obviously based upon oil being struck at any time.

WELCOME. Child- ren waving Union Jacks to greet the Duke of Edinburgh as he prepared to land his helicopter at B u r p h a m, near Guildford, Surrey, yesterday. The Duke, who had flown from the grounds at Buck- ingham P a l a c e, opened the Suther- land Playing Field, and he is seen below with some of the schoolchildren.

Newspaper report of Prince Philip's helicopter arriving for the opening of Sutherland Memorial Playing Fields 1956 (C Ridsdale Smith)

We were however in better luck with regard to the pavilion. The sleuth like instinct and patience of the Chairman, Arthur Gavins, unearthed an unpaid claim for loss of development upon the field and with assistance of the Duke's executor, this was transferred into management funds and also a Government Grant awarded, thus provided us with funds to construct our present pavilion, (despite cries of skulduggery from one later to become one of

Guildford's most popular Mayors and indeed a very good friend and ally to our field!!).

Finally on the wettest day at least of 1965 the then Mayor, Barry Nicklin, opened the pavilion, having first kicked off in a football match with the pitch at least 3" under water.

From then on things went a little more quietly for some time, the pavilion receiving good usage not only from footballers and cricketers but by a newly formed table-tennis club, the W.I., etc. who held coffee mornings from time to time and the Civic Youth Club (since defunct) who, having no permanent building of its own, used the building as one of its three venues.

Approach was made during this period for tennis courts (badly needed in this part of Guildford until this day) enlargement of the children's playground etc., but the aforementioned restriction for possible road widening and a new Local Authority Act passed through Parliament designating an area of open space for Car Parking prevented further development. Soon further trouble was to brew with renewed activity on the A3 front. Imagine our concern when in 1969 the line of a revised Burpham Lane not only went through the middle of the football pitch but also the middle of our pavilion, the position of which had been dictated to us by the planners only those few years earlier. Many hours were spent both outside of and finally at the public enquiry ensuring that the powers that be knew the views not only of the Management but also that of the community represented by all groups within the parish. Fortune was on our side, the road construction unit, sympathetic, resulting in these recommendations not being implemented.

Only two years later the same problem again arose, this time the loss of land was to be on the side of the existing A3 and a new road planted parallel to Burpham Lane on the opposite boundary, thus preventing any possible further extension, demolishing the swings, etc. and eliminating privacy and the view enjoyed by all, etc. etc. This time the Borough were more clearly on our side and gave strength to our continued objection. It would appear that again, through the understanding of the Planners and recommendation of the Ministry Inspector, that the field will be maintained and who knows, even extended.

Well, thus ends my potted history spanning 20 years, I hope it may have been of interest to newcomers to our community.

To all those unnamed here that have helped so much in the past, not least the Borough of Guildford Council, the grateful thanks of the Management.

Finally a thought for the future – come and stand in our field and take in the peacefulness and pleasantness of the view behind that bushy hedgerow – even if marginally extended to provide much needed extra facilities, the rural aspect could well be lost for future generations. The Planner is at work again – did you know, that if the road schemes go ahead, the farm land beyond our field is sadly scheduled upon the Town Map for development with bricks and mortar? – such a tragedy that the once rural aspect of a once village atmosphere may be finally lost for ever.'

What would John Saxton think of the Burpham of 2017, with all the housing developments that have happened since he wrote his history?

Sutherland Memorial Park 2016

Eric Voller remembered that Percy Howard had built the pavilion in the 1960s and it was used by the table tennis club as well as the football and cricket clubs. In order to get better use of the pitch it was decided to put floodlights in. These were only a couple of telegraph poles, sourced by Percy Howard, and the electrics were sorted by an electrician who was a member of the football club. One of the big advantages of the pitch was that it drained very well. Even if it poured with rain in the morning, it was ready for play in the afternoon due to the sandy soil there.

In 1963 new Byelaws were published relating to The Burpham War Memorial Playing Field and these included:

'A person shall not
    (a) *Carelessly or negligently deface, injure, or destroy any wall or fence in or enclosing the ground, or any building, barrier, railing, post or seat or any erection or ornament on the ground.*
    (b) *Wilfully, carelessly or negligently soil or defile any wall or fence in or enclosing the ground, or any building, barrier or railing.*

(c) A person shall not except in pursuance of a lawful agreement with the Council...bring any beast of draught or burden or any cattle, sheep, pigs or goats.

(d) Bring any barrow, truck, machine or vehicle other than a wheeled bicycle or tricycle; a wheelchair, perambulator or chaise...conveyance of child or invalid.

(e) Ride any bicycle, tricycle on any part of the ground.

(f) Remove, cut or displace any gravel, soil, turf or plant.

(g) Erect any post, rail, fence, pole, tent, booth, stand, building or other structure on the ground.

(h) Beat, shake, sweep, brush or cleanse any carpet, drugget, rug or mat, or any other fabric retaining dust or dirt.

(i) Hang, spread or deposit any linen or other fabric for drying or bleaching.

(j) Wilfully obstruct, disturb, interrupt or annoy any other person in the proper use of the ground.

Every person who shall offend against any of the foregoing byelaws shall be liable on summary conviction to a fine not exceeding two pounds.'

Will Lawrence remembered that a glider landed in Sutherland Memorial Park sometime in the 1970s, with about three feet to spare. It approached from the petrol station end and finished up a few feet from the fence of the first house on that side of the lane. The pilot was an instructor, who told Will that someone with less experience wouldn't have made it.

In 1989 the National Playing Fields became involved in the running of Sutherland Memorial Park. They provide grants for enabling and protecting open spaces. There is a standard of six acres of open spaces per 1,000 population, with heathland such as Whitmoor Common being a special protection area - Suitable Alternative Natural Green Space (SANGS) funding helped to upgrade Riverside Park. During the 1980s the playing field was renovated and a new pavilion was built. The project was managed by Mike Beckwith, who worked for Guildford Borough Council's Parks Department. Mike worked with the four main sports clubs that used the park's facilities to ensure that the pavilion met the needs of all users, setting up an Amenities Club. However, the Cricket Club still used the old pavilion as well as the new one, and the Bowls Club raised further funds to build an extension with windows overlooking their green. The courts are multi-use, which allows the Tennis Club to use the facilities as well as 5-a-side football to play there.

Sutherland Memorial Park information notice

The children's playground was created in the 1980s, although there had been some swings and slide in the corner of the field opposite the Green Man. The new playground has been upgraded over the years and now provides an excellent play area for the younger children of the community. Mike remembered that the car park had been a bit of a challenge. There had to be enough parking space for the users of the sports clubs using the facilities, but inevitably there are times when demand is far greater than availability, such as school drop-off and pick-up times, a wedding or funeral at St Luke's, or when the village hall users cannot get into their car park. In 2007 and 2016, when film crews were in Burpham, they used the car park for their catering, costume and make-up vans - taking up quite a lot of space for a few days each time.

Entrance to Sutherland Memorial Park from Burpham Lane

Sometimes coaches would park up overnight and eventually the Council decided to have locked gates to prevent this. However, this caused problems on more than one occasion when the children of Burpham Primary School were doing one of their annual productions. Parents would leave their cars in the park while they watched the children, but when they returned to their cars they couldn't get out of the car park. The outcome was the eventual installation of crocodile teeth in the ground of the 'out' lane, so that people couldn't get in but could get out after a certain time. For much of the year, when the weather is good, there is an ice-cream vendor in the car park. Agreement for this had to go out to tender, but for many years it was Mr Tony.

Sutherland Memorial Park has attracted groups of young people over the years. Some of the secondary school end of year celebrations took place there, with the inevitable problems of under-age drinking and litter left on the site, and there was also some bullying. The Youth Initiative was begun as a way to avoid unwanted use of the park, but to provide a place where teenagers could meet safely, with some facilities for them to use. In talking to the teenagers about what they wanted, it became clear that some wanted a place to meet, but it should be near to local houses in case help was needed.

In his Honorary Remembrancer's Report to the Council for 2005/06 Roger Marjoribanks said that 'Sutherland Memorial Park received the national Green Flag Award from the Civic Trust in July 2005 as being welcoming, safe and well-maintained. Since it was first expanded from a relatively small playing field some 15 years earlier, at the time when the Sainsbury's Superstore was in the planning stage, it has been developed into a community

366

facility with attractive planting, a variety of sporting facilities, a playground for toddlers and another for slightly older children. Further facilities are planned, targeted at young people.'

Upfolds Green

Upfolds Green was created at a time when it was thought to be important to have open spaces within housing developments. On the Tithe Maps of 1838 it was part of Winter Hill Farm and there was one field called Upfolds, one called Upper Upfolds and a wood called Upfields Row. It is nice to see that the old names have been retained in the more modern developments. Pete Gardner remembered also a small recreation area near the Glendale Drive council houses.

From an idea in the late 1970s, Riverside Park, a Local Nature Reserve, was developed from the mid 1980s and has grown as additional parcels of land have been acquired. Some was bought from the developer of the Weylea Farm estate and the National

Trust owns a small triangle of land between the lake and the river. The site extends between the River Wey and the A3, from Burpham, past the back of the Spectrum Leisure Complex, to Ladymead and the Woking Road.

Riverside Park (T Bass)

The park is owned, managed and funded by Guildford Borough Council. '*The lake and meadow were by-products of gravel extraction during the construction of the new A3 Guildford by-pass. At this time conservation work was carried out to preserve the wetland habitat to the north of the A3 and the boardwalk was constructed to allow public access to this area.*' (description from the www.lnr.naturalengland.org.uk website). It goes on to say that '*these low lying areas are permanently marshy with occasional flooding in the winter months.*' The company doing

368

the gravel extraction went into liquidation, leaving Guildford Borough Council to prove that there was no value to the land so that it was not included in the administration. The lake is filled from the Merrow Common Stream, which flows via culverts under the A3.

Deer in Riverside Park (M Cox)

The majority of open water in the park is in the man-made lake in the centre of the site. The park is a wonderful facility for Burpham residents and other visitors, who can walk dogs, picnic, bird watch and jog through the area. Fishing is prohibited, as is kite flying, due to overhead cables. The site has won several Green Flag Awards. Mike Beckwith produced the master plan for Riverside Park in the 1980s, including a few ornamental trees around the site. One of the objectives in designing the park was to reduce noise from the A3. The field running along the back of Manston Road down to Burpham Lane belongs to Riverside Park. The original deeds for the land included rights for snipe shooting in season around the lake.

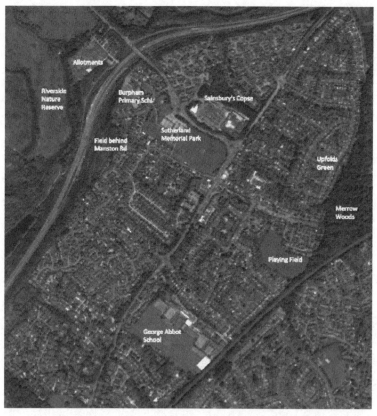

Aerial photo of Burpham's green spaces 2015 (Google Earth)

JACOBS WELL

The name of Jacobs Well only started to appear on maps in the early 1800s and before that it was deemed to be part of the wider Burpham tything. Why was the area called Jacobs Well? Despite extensive searching, Jim Miller admitted that they were none the wiser. He said that originally it seemed to have referred only to a small area of just one field and two buildings by the crossroads.

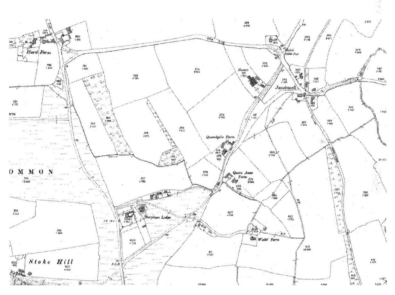

Jacobswell 1895 OS map

Early maps from 1816 to 1841 seem to place Jacobs Well near to the crossroads of Clay Lane and Blanchards Hill. Jim Miller wrote that in 1963 the Surrey Advertiser ran a question about how the village got its name and Mr H Farris wrote '*In my boyhood days, there was, in the bank on the other side of the road, opposite to Willow Grange, an ancient brick well. Owing to its age and the fact that it was a roadside well, everybody knew it as Jacob's Well. In the area around there were only a very few houses and it was to this area that the old well gave its name. I know that it was still there in the late 1890s.'* Matthew Alexander, who was curator at Guildford Museum, suggested that perhaps the well was named after the village rather than the other way round. The Tithe Maps of 1841 marked a field approximately where Mr Farris had described, calling it Well Field. In a map from 1686 there is a small, unexplained symbol in the same place – could it have been the well?

The village itself developed almost one hundred years later, though there are some very old buildings in the community, such as Queen Anne Farm, where part of the house was originally a timber-framed medieval house probably dating from the late 15th century; Jacobs Well Farm, now known as Jacobs Well Cottage, was originally an open hall medieval house built about 1500; Queen Hythe, once known as Queen Hive Farm, appears to be late 17th century; Watts Cottage was probably built in the late 16th century. Willow Grange and Burpham Court House, which used to form Hurst Farm, built in the 16th century, though references to Hurst go back to 1290; and finally, Burpham Lodge, now The White House on the Woking Road, thought to have been built in the 18th century.

As part of Burpham Manor, Jacobs Well was a small, rural community, and even now has no school, church or public house. By the time of the 2011 census there was a total population of 1,123, of which a large number were of retirement age. It is a thriving little area, with lots of activities centred around the village hall. Jacobs Well was included when Burpham separated from the parish of Worplesdon to create firstly the new ecclesiastical parish of Burpham-with-Sutton in 1920, then the parish of Burpham in 1954. However, in 1960 it became part of the Conventional District of St Peter's, Hazel Avenue.

Burpham Court House, known as Hurst Cottages, c. 1900 (J Osler)

The Crosse family commissioned a map of the estate in 1686, which is now held at the Surrey History Centre. This shows that the area now known as Stringers Common was then known as Burgham Green. The family lived in the house now known as Burpham Court House, but previously known as Hurst, on the corner of the Woking Road and Clay Lane. The house seems to be mainly early 17th century, but with earlier parts dating back to 1500. Sale particulars from 1934 say, rather grandly, that the

373

earliest portion of the house dates from the reign of King John, but as that was in the 13th century the statement is questionable, though the current owners do have a document that talks about a medieval hall. Perhaps that was demolished at some time and the current house built in its place.

Burpham Court House 2015

However, the sale particulars described the house as a XVIth century residence, with two reception, eight bedrooms, a boudoir, two bathrooms and modern domestic offices – these include kitchen, scullery, larder, pantry and servants' sitting room. There were also a cottage, a bungalow, stabling, various sheds and tennis court included in the three acre property for sale.

The Russell family lived across the road from the Crosse family (to whom they were related by marriage), in what is now Willow Grange – the Bishop of Guildford's residence. Apparently, the property was owned by Samuel Ayling in the late 1700s, but as he and his wife lived in Petworth they leased Hurst to Worplesdon farmers. These included William Wells, Joseph Cobbett and James

Willow Grange (J Miller)

Smallpeice. The Aylings sold the farm to Richard Sparkes, who owned land adjacent to Burpham Court Farm, and he let the farm to George Burt. At some point, probably about 1856, the farm ownership changed again, when William Bovill QC, Member of Parliament for Guildford from 1857 – 1866, bought the property.

When Major Henry Treeby returned from the South African Wars in 1898 he bought Hurst Farm, extended the old farmhouse to its present dimensions, and renamed it Willow Grange. He bought several other properties in the area at the same time. Henry Treeby was a Justice of the Peace and Brigade Major of the East Surrey Volunteer Infantry Brigade. After he died in 1935 the house was occupied by a Mrs Willett. When the Church

Commissioners first rented Willow Grange it was from the Willett Estates. Mrs Willett's husband, William, had been a builder of some substance, but he is chiefly remembered for introducing 'daylight saving' into Britain after the First World War.

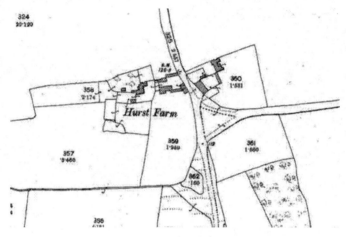

Hurst Farm on both sides of Woking Road, OS map 1895

Jim Miller recorded that Hurst was included in the 1877 auction sale of farms and other buildings in the area. Lot 1, described as part of Hurst Farm, consisted of the house west of the Woking Road (Willow Grange) and just over 35 acres of land. The house was described as '*A comfortable old-fashioned farm house built of brick and tile and containing five bedrooms, two parlours, kitchen, pantry, brewhouse, dairy, etc.*' The adjacent homestead comprised '*A barn, two cow sheds for 13 cows, another cow house for six cows, cart horse stable for four horses, chaff house, meal house, pigsty, with farm yards and productive gardens.*' By the late 19th century the house had been converted into

376

tenements, or apartments, for the farm labourers. Lot 2, comprised the house east of the road (Burpham Court House), divided into five tenements of three rooms each, together with a stable for four horses, a shed, a farmyard, a large garden and two fields, totalling over 34 acres in all. Neither of these lots reached their reserve prices.

Farm workers at rear of Hurst Cottages (now Burpham Court House) c. 1900 (J Osler)

In the late 1920s Hurst Farm Cottages were converted back to one house, which was modernised and then lived in by Mr & Mrs Phillip Benson. For some reason the name of the house changed to Burpham Court House. Apparently in 1897 a local historian had noted that 'the old saying is that it was the old manor house and that the courts of the parish used to be held there', but no evidence has been found to support this. It is more likely that Burpham Court Farm, at one time known as Burgham House, was the old Manor House. In 1927 the Surrey Mirror reported that the Bishop of Guildford had taken Burpham Court House as a temporary residence until a permanent official residence could be found. In 1942 the paper reported that Mrs Eileen Leach of Burpham Court House had been appointed a Justice of the Peace for Guildford.

Burpham Lodge on Woking Road, OS map 1895

The third house on the Woking Road is The White House, on the corner of White House Lane. This property was described by estate agents Savills as 'a period house, in Georgian style', and this is confirmed by the John Rocque map of 1754, which seems to show the house for the first time. By 1871 the name Burpham Lodge appeared and was on OS maps for the next 50 years. In around 1930 the new owner, Major Archibald Boyle, renamed it White Lodge, presumably due to the white building.

Although most of the available information about properties in Jacobs Well relate to these older farms and cottages, there were also many other, smaller, cottages in the area. In the 19th and 20th centuries new housing developments have extended the village to its present day size. The first village shop was set up in 1921 in Coachhouse Cottage, then gradually over the years more shops have come to add some retail opportunities for the village.

The White House, formerly Burpham Lodge (Savilles)

At the crossroads in Jacobs Well there used to be the village pound. This was used to hold stray animals until their owners recovered them on payment of a fine or fee. The pound was guarded night and day because local gypsies resented having to pay to reclaim livestock that they had allowed to roam free.

In addition to Major Treeby and Sir William Bovill there was another distinguished person who lived in Jacobs Well. After 1945, The Honourable Sir Bede Clifford bought Queen Anne Farm when he had to retire from the Colonial Service, where he had been Governor of the Bahamas, Mauritius and finally Trinidad. He was a friend of the Duke and Duchess of Sutherland, which may have been the reason for moving to the village.

In 1953 the Surrey Advertiser reported that Jacobs Well would have 155 new houses. Guildford Rural Council had approved in principle a plan for developing the hamlet, which would increase the population from 440 to about 1,000, providing shops, a school, church and village inn. The plan was based on four main assumptions: *'That the village will maintain its existing character; that, because the village is surrounded by agricultural land, no further expansion should be allowed; that the plan will provide for all facilities usual for a normal village community; and that adequate playing fields are provided on the existing common.'* The Worplesdon Parish Council accepted the plan in principle but presumably changes were made later on as Jacobs Well still does not have a school, church or inn.

Heather Kidman has lived in Jacobs Well since 1956. She remembered that the road from Burpham used to be just a clay soil track, presumably why it is now called Clay Lane, and the houses on Queenhythe Road were called Clay Lane Estate. The milkman stopped at the end of Jacobs Well Road to sell milk, and Mr Coleman from the shop in Sutton Green would take orders, then deliver the goods to his customers. Mr Lee, with his horse called Sheila, sold fruit and vegetables from his cart and the road Holly Lee is named after him. The coalman delivered coal for heating the houses. The village doesn't have a pub, but perhaps this is no loss as instead they have the Jacobs Well Social Club, which puts on entertainments, such as quizzes, luncheons, bingo, etc. The Scout Hall, by the Village Hall, was used to put on little shows by The US Group, and the profits from these were used to build the Village Hall.

Watts Farm (J Miller)

The first Village Hall for Jacob's Well was an old Nissan Hut, which was moved from Almond Close (off the Woking Road) in about the mid 1950s. The new Village Hall was opened in 1969. The Scouts and Guides used this until their new hall was built, to replace their old headquarters, in about 1984. Ian and Di Craigie remembered helping to take down the old building and painting the new one.

Ellen Hart was born and brought up at Clare's Cottage, at Burpham Court Farm, in the 1950s. She remembered that Mrs Saxby ran the local village shop. It was an idyllic life on the farm, where her father drove the tractor. There were pigs, dairy cows and chickens, the dairy was up by St Edward's church on the Sutton Place estate. The children played in the hay loft or in the water down at Bower's Lock. There was a library in the village hall. The Duke of Sutherland kept polo ponies and some of the local girls would help to exercise them. She remembered the family doctor was in Burpham – Dr Parkin always had a lollipop for the children.

ABBOTSWOOD AND GANGHILL

Until the early 1900s, the Abbotswood estate was part of Stoke Park Farm, while Ganghill was a common and wooded area, which extended from London Road up to what is now Bushy Hill in Merrow. According to Michael Drakeford's book 'A History of Abbotswood', Stoke Park Farm was originally called Alden Farm and Ganghill was Granghill Farm. All of this farmland belonged to the Earl of Onslow until he sold off most of the area in the early 1900s.

Stoke Park Farm, London Road, OS map 1912

Stoke Park Farm was sold to A G Taylor, a surveyor, in 1909 for development into housing. He bought land, acquired planning permission, put down roads and services, then sold plots to builders and prospective house owners. The roundabout, still known to many as the Old AA Roundabout, was built in the late

383

1920s in order to improve traffic problems and give access to the new by-pass, now called Parkway, in 1934. However, the majority of traffic still had to come through Burpham on the London Road to get to the by-pass and it continued to be a very busy road indeed. Michael Drakeford said '*I can recall living in digs at Rose Cottage, 178 London Road between 1965 and 1970, not far from the Anchor and Horseshoe pub. The traffic noise was continuous. I could tell the time on waking in the morning, be it 7 a.m., 7.30 a.m. or 8 a.m., by the amount of traffic droning past the house. During my stay, vehicle and pedestrian accidents occurred numerous times between that house and the AA roundabout. On one occasion I arrived home to find a bus in the front garden; the driver had tried to avoid a car in which that driver had suffered a heart attack and died.'*

Much of Abbotswood is still in the Stoke Parish, but some was in Worplesdon Parish. When brickmaking became more widespread in the late 19th century, two brickfields being located in Burpham, it was important to Alfred Taylor that no-one tried to set up any form of brickworks in Abbotswood. In order to do this he included a covenant in the deeds to the houses stating that '*No bricks or tiles shall at any time be burnt or made nor any clay or lime burnt on the land*' and these have continued into the deeds for subsequent purchasers.

The Abbotswood estate was designed and built between 1909 and 1925, and the first residents moved into their houses in 1913. The idea was to build houses to reflect a countryside ideal; for the middle-class man who wanted to have space and facilities in his home. This was also the thinking behind the Arts and Crafts Movement, promoted by William Morris; using the methods of craftsmen rather than machine-made features. Alfred Taylor and Claude Burlingham were ready to create houses that met these ideals. The first Abbotswood houses were large, showing off the wealth of the new owners. They had modern conveniences including running water, mains sewerage, gas and electricity. Some even had telephones.

Development after 1913 slowed due to the Great War, ceasing in 1916 and no new planning applications were made until 1920. After that, economic uncertainty had its effect as plots of land were smaller and some bungalows were built. By the time of the General Strike in 1926, Burlingham had moved his attention to other parts of Guildford, such as Orchard Road, Ganghill, Merrow Downs Estate and finally the Boxgrove Estate. Many of the early houses in Abbotswood had at least one servant's bedroom, bell pushes for calling staff and usually a tradesman's entrance gate. Later houses reflected the changes in the way people lived, more manageable with less need for servants.

In the early 1900s house ownership was less common than in the 21st century, with only about 10% of the population owning their homes. The deeds for the first 14 houses in Abbotswood showed that initially few were sold, but instead many were rented out by the developers. After the First World War, there was a great need for more housing in and around Guildford. Onslow Village was developed in the 1920s and 1930s, mainly consisting of houses for rent and eventual ownership by residents. The first council houses had been built in Charlotteville in 1906, but Burpham had to wait for another 20 years before it had any of these.

The entrance to Abbotswood is a distinctive, purpose-built, brick and stone gateway, designed by Burlingham, with pedestrian archways on either side. The word Abbotswood is carved in stone on the pillar on both sides of the road, surrounded by a wreath. It leads into a tree-lined avenue, with raised flowerbeds alongside parts of the road.

Entrance to Abbotswood 2015

Stoke Park Farmhouse is still there in Abbotswood, providing a link back to the original farm. The British Listed Buildings website describes the house as 17th century, extended and altered in the 19th century. Michael Drakeford reported that a survey carried out in 1988/9 by the Domestic Building Research Group concluded that '*This house contains one reconstructed bay and short remnants of two other bays of a medieval hall. A large chimney (late 16th / early 17th century) stands on the site of one demolished bay linking it to a timber-framed cross wing which was probably contemporary with the chimney.'* At the sale of Onslow land in 1909 the farm and estate was described as having five bedrooms, a bathroom, two sitting rooms, kitchen, scullery, dairy, farm buildings and a pair of cottages, all in 145 acres. The price was £7,500.

Claude Burlingham was a newly qualified architect in 1910 when Alfred Taylor was planning the new estate of Abbotswood. It has been suggested that the houses he designed reflected his growing confidence and abilities as he became more skilled. In Abbotswood he was responsible for 35 houses and seven bungalows, including 21 individual designs. The number of bedrooms varied, although all except one of the bungalows had three. He ensured that the external designs of the houses were different, thus he was able to record that he had created the greatest number of designs for his institute's records. The 12 houses he designed in Burpham were all referred to as 'small' houses.

It might be expected that the houses would have been built starting at London Road and then moving along into the estate, but in fact the first two houses, built in 1912, were a little further in. The next five were built in 1913, including The Gate House, which for many years was home to the Guildford Chiropractic Centre. Three more in 1914 and four in 1915, but there was then a gap as the effects of the First World War hit the building industry, until 1920 when 11 houses were built, followed by five in 1921, two in 1922, eight in 1923 and then one in 1925.

When Taylor and Burlingham began the Abbotswood estate, cars were very new and therefore garages were not included in the first designs. However, one of the houses built in 1914 did have a garage, known at the time as a motor house, separate to the main house. By 1923 the first integral garage was built into a lower ground floor of a house, which was still in place in 2008. According to Michael Drakeford, Burlingham did little about garden design, although the deeds included a covenant to the effect that the owner had to maintain a hedge to the border fronting the road, enclosing the gardens. This was different to Ganghill where the gardens were more open plan.

Before 1914 houses mainly used fireplaces as the method for heating rooms. However, the larger of Burlinghams's houses also had radiators powered by coal-fired boilers as well as a hot water system, although these were probably fairly inefficient. Another area of early trend-setting was for the Abbotswood houses to have bathrooms, although they were shared by all the bedrooms. The houses also had internal toilets – a great improvement on the Victorian houses with outside facilities. Again, this would be shared by all the bedrooms, but the use of a chamber pot in the bedroom continued well into the 20th century, as will be recalled by many people even in the 21st century.

Kitchens included a cast-iron range, heated by coke or coal, very similar to the modern ranges that have returned to popularity. They also included a built-in dresser, though most of those have now been replaced. Sculleries, pantries and larders were common in larger houses for many years into the 20th century, but modern houses rarely have room for these as everything is crammed into the kitchen or utility room.

House prices have varied tremendously over the years, with 21st century houses at the highest values ever known. In 1925 one of the Abbotswood houses sold for £3,825, compared to the houses on the Guildown estate that were priced at a minimum of £1,000. In 1934 the Winterhill estate houses for priced at £700-£950 but around the same time The Gate House was sold for £4,200.

Abbotswood, OS map 1934

It might be thought that The Gate House name referred to its location in the estate, but it was also the home of Bramwell Gates, of Cow & Gate. In 1954 it was bought by Donald Harry Bennett who used it as the surgery for his chiropractic practice, followed by his son Russell, who in 2006 moved the surgery to New Inn Farm and the house returned to being a private residence. In 1922 Mr Elliott Kitchener bought one of the houses and he was cousin to Lord Kitchener of Great War fame. Another was owned by Thomas Thorp, who had the antiquarian book shop at the top of Guildford High Street.

The Church of Jesus Christ of Latter-Day Saints owned one of the houses for four years, from 1996. The Mormons were looking for a plot to erect a church and there was a risk that the largest and most imposing house in Abbotswood would fall to the bulldozer. The residents got a protection order placed on the trees and then enlisted the help of local councillors. The church leaders, realising that demolishing the house was not going to be allowed, proposed altering the existing building instead and called a public meeting so that they could persuade residents that their church would be acceptable. However, a committee of estate residents approached English Heritage, resulting in listing the building for its high architectural qualities reflecting the later style of the Arts and Crafts Movement in Surrey. The Mormon Church, resigned to the opposition, sold the house to a local builder, who carried out a superb restoration.

After 1926, Abbotswood continued to develop with new architects and builders, many of them following the Modern Movement of house design, which some claimed was influenced by the Arts and Crafts style. Three houses were built between 1926 and 1939. The Second World War interrupted house building, then after the war came a surge in demand for cheaper accommodation. Three new, smaller roads were created in the estate, often using part of the gardens of older houses, to provide more properties. 11 houses were built in Abbotswood Close; 29 in Westward Ho; and four on the site of number 11 Abbotswood.

Local developments in and around Stoke Park may have affected the residents over the years. In the late 1960s there was a proposal to move County Hall from Kingston, which is now outside the county boundary, to a site on Stoke Park, where the Spectrum Leisure Centre is now located. This was not approved, and several years later the proposal to move County Hall to Woking was not approved either, so it remains in Kingston. The Spectrum was opened in 1993, providing a wide range of sports facilities, including swimming, ice skating and ten pin bowling.

When it was proposed in the late 1980s there were many protest groups objecting to a development that would spoil their beautiful Stoke Park. One of the protestors was Miss Phyllis Powell, who lived in Burpham and before retiring had been Deputy Head at George Abbot School and then English teacher at the Grammar School. She challenged the comment that it was 'an unused piece of land and should be built on', explaining that she and many others had used the land for years as somewhere to walk and enjoy the air. Michael Drakeford wrote that she made the poignant remark that she used its beauty each time she went past on the way to Guildford, but '*Sadly, shortly after she had sat down, she collapsed and died later in hospital.*'

In 2005 there was a proposal to build an 8,000 spectator football stadium on the Spectrum side of Stoke Park, but this was rejected by Guildford Borough Council. Hopefully any further such ideas will also be turned down, leaving the park as the 'green lung' of Guildford. With the modern penchant for 'garden grabbing' in order to find more land for housing there is still a possibility that more houses will be built in Abbotswood, but perhaps the ambience of the estate will be retained. It is the only estate to include two listed properties in Guildford.

There are three residents associations in Abbotswood, originally needed because the local authority did not adopt the entire road and therefore residents were responsible for road repairs. One of the earlier residents, Peter Doresa, recalled to Michael Drakeford that when he lived there 'there was a general agreement that a call would go out on Friday afternoon for anyone who wished to go to Guildford or Burpham, that they should do so before 4 p.m. It was recognised that after that time it would be almost impossible to get out onto the London Road. At the best of times, the traffic was such that to turn right was nigh impossible, and the only way was to turn left and go around the roundabout at the Green Man, the nearest available roundabout at the time.' In 2016 there are still times when it is almost impossible to turn right out of the estate towards Guildford, as the traffic from the old AA roundabout races towards Burpham rather faster than the 30 m.p.h. limit should allow.

Ganghill Copse was bought from Earl Onslow in 1929 by Onyx Country Estates, together with Claude Burlingham. Apparently, he obtained permission to build a bridge over the railway track that dissected Ganghill Copse, in order to extend the road onto the other side, but this never happened. Shortly afterwards he put in an application to extend the road to the left at the T-junction, rather than over the railway track. The entrance to Ganghill, built in 1929, also has pedestrian archways on either side of the road, made of Bargate stone. Unlike the enclosed front gardens in Abbotswood, those in Ganghill have an open plan design, which means that anyone walking or driving along the road can see the houses clearly.

In the ten years up to the start of the Second World War Claude Burlingham designed 12 houses in Ganghill. He applied to build five more houses at the entrance to the road in 1939 but was told that approval was subject to a proposed road improvement scheme to provide a service road, and this was never built. Other architects designed the rest of the houses in Ganghill, taking the total to 43.

Entrance to Ganghill 2015

393

One of the Onslow Estate properties in the sale of 1912 was Ganghill Copse, fronting London Road, including a Keeper's cottage. Joseph Blake, a pensioned Keeper, was allowed to remain as tenant rent free during his lifetime. The sporting rights for this property were let to Colonel E.T. Browell up until the end of February 1913 at a rent of £75.

THE MILITARY AND REMEMBRANCE

Military history information for Burpham residents is rare before the 20th century. Way back at the time of the Battle of Hastings it is likely that the county furnished a contingent to King Harold's army as his brother, Leofwine, held an earldom that included Surrey. It is quite possible that Burpham men could have served at Agincourt, against the Armada, in the Civil War or any of the 19th century conflicts such as the Napoleonic, Crimean, Zulu or Boer Wars. However, very few details are available before World War One for Burpham and most were recorded by parish, so it is hard to ascertain who was from where.

The Surrey Advertiser & County Times in February 1900 reported in their Extracts from the diary of a Surrey Officer '*The new glasses Herbert sent me are pounds better than the old ones. I could see the Boers in their trenches at 4,000 yards quite plainly when last on outpost duty...I hear they are sending us out some subaltern officers, who will be most useful; every company ought to have at least three officers with the present extension...slept a bit in the afternoon to make up for last night. We played football at 5.30 this afternoon against the Naval Brigade, and beat them by two goals to one; it was a very good match. The Naval Brigade officers dined with us tonight.*' Another item in the same year was a request for more Surrey volunteers for 'The Lord Mayor's Own'. Also '*All marksmen and first class shots in the 2nd VB 'The Queens Royal West Surrey Regiment calling for volunteers to join a company for services with the territorial regiments now with Sir Redvers Buller's force in Natal'*.

Return of Second Service Company, Queen's RWS Regiment, 30th May 1902, from Boer Wars (Guildford Institute – Box 3A - 4008)

The Surrey Advertiser in February 1942 reported that *'Military honours were accorded at the funeral at Stoughton Cemetery on Wednesday of Mr George Howard, aged 70, of Anchor Cottage, Burpham, who was formerly in The Queen's Royal Regiment'.* George was born in about 1872 and enlisted in the Medical Staff Corps when he was 19 years old and completed 27 years in the RAMC. He served in the Sudan, Egypt, South Africa Boer Wars and India. He was made Sergeant in 1908. He was also a member of the Royal Antediluvian Order of the Buffaloes, a charitable organisation, for 21 years. He was survived by his wife Eliza. Perhaps he was one of the men in the photo above.

396

There are certain to be many more but, apart from those who appear on the Burpham War Memorial and their families, the following are some of those found so far.

- **Joseph Bentley**, born in 1881 in Wisborough Green, in 1915 he lived at Collingbourne Cottages. He was an engine driver for the Queen's Royal West Surrey Regiment, but only stayed in the army for a short time before being discharged on medical grounds. He died in 1964 and was buried at St Luke's.

- **Frank Bicknell** was born in 1886, he lived at Bower's Lodge, was a labourer and he enlisted with the MMS Corps in 1902. His father, Thomas was caretaker of Bower's Mill in 1911 and was buried at St Luke's. After the war Frank and his wife, Florence, lived in Peasmarsh and then Wanborough.

- **Arthur William Christmas** was born in 1883 and was living in Collingbourne Cottages when he enlisted in the Queen's RWS Regiment in 1915. He transferred to the Labour Corps and was demobbed in 1919.

- **Percy Thomas Elliott** was born in 1909, was baptised at St Luke's in 1910 and lived in Pimm's Row. Before joining the army he was a nurseryman. He enlisted with the Royal Tank Corps in 1927 and was discharged in 1938.

- **Edward Alexander Grey** was born in 1900, lived in Pimm's Row and was baptised at St Luke's. In 1911 his parents were at Jacob's Well Farm and Edward was a cowman there. He enlisted with the 5th East Surrey Regiment in 1918 and then transferred to the Machine Gun Corps. His older brother,

Charles, was wounded on the Western Front and died in 1917.

- **Charles George Grover** was recorded as born in 1883 in Burpham but in 1891 he and his family were living in Merrow and in 1901 he was a bricklayer's labourer. He enlisted with the Royal Engineers in 1902, went onto the Army Reserve List in 1911, but was re-engaged in 1914. In 1916 he was appointed to the 5th Airline Section.

- **Leonard Longhurst** was born in 1889 at 4 New Cottages. He enlisted in the Army Service Corps in 1914 and served in Egypt. Discharged in 1919, his army records stated that he was a sober, reliable and intelligent man.

- **George William Marshall** was born in 1880 in Pimm's Row, where his father Alfred was a smallholder. Before the war he was a courier. He enlisted in the Grenadier Guards in 1914 and transferred to the 1st Battalion of Welsh Guards.

- **Cyril Apsley Ranger** was born in 1897 at Bower's Mill, where his father Robert was the miller for many years. He enlisted with the Queen's RWS Regiment in 1914 and was recorded as having been an engineer's apprentice for Dickinson & Burne in Guildford prior to the war.

- **John Standage** was born in 1888, lived in Burpham Church Cottages and his father was a brickmaker. He enlisted with the RAMC in 1906.

- **George Victor Stinning** was born in 1887 in Burpham, but his family had moved to Sussex by 1891. He enlisted with the Royal Navy in 1917 and served on two ships, the Victory I and the Hercules. However, he caught pneumonia in March

1918 and died. He was buried in Aldingbourne Churchyard, near Chichester.

- **Harvey George Vinall** was born in 1885 in Burpham but his family had moved to Stoke parish by 1891. In 1911 he and his wife Florence were living in Chobham, where he worked as a gardener. He enlisted at Stoughton Barracks in 1917 with the Royal Army Service Corps, saw service in France and was discharged in 1919 before being transferred to the Army Reserve.

- **John Woods** was born in 1878 in Rydes Hill. He was married to Florence, living in Horseshoe Cottages on London Road and working as a labourer when he enlisted in 1915 with the Royal Garrison Artillery. He was a Bombadier in the Siege Battery and served in France. The Surrey Advertiser & County Times reported in 1918 that John had been awarded the Croix de Guerre.

The War Memorial - World War One

In August 1920 a local newspaper reported that a '*very peaceful, very solemn, and exceedingly beautiful service in the churchyard of St Luke's Church, Burpham, on Sunday afternoon, a cross, which has been erected by the people of Burpham in memory of their fellow-villagers who fell in the war, was unveiled and dedicated. The cross, of granite, stands on a rough block of granite and bears the inscription: "To the glory of God, and in honoured memory of the men of this parish who fell in the Great War 1914-18". Below are the names: - Frederick Adams, William Collis, Harry Durrant, Tom Durrant, Percy Gunner, Edward Gunner, John Gunner, Samson Albert Gunner, Charles Grey,*

399

*James Knight, Robert Charles Knight, Norman Arthur Phillips,
John Albert Russell, Thomas Albert Searle, George Frederick
Stilwell, Henry Ernest Williams, Robert Worsfold.*

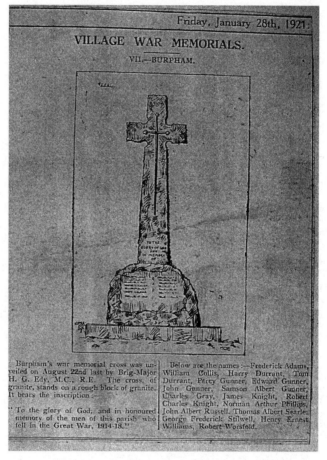

Newspaper report of unveiling of the War Memorial in 1921 – without
Walter Wisdom's name (Guildford Institute)

*Around the cross on Sunday afternoon assembled a large number
of people, including a body of ex-Service men and the Burpham*

400

Company of Girl Guides and Brownies, in charge of Miss Willmott. The Bishop of Guildford, who dedicated the memorial, was accompanied by the Rev. G Collingwood Bruce, Rector of Worplesdon, Bishop's Chaplain and the Rev. J W Clarke, priest-in-charge, who conducted the service...'. Hymns and psalms were sung and the cross was unveiled by Brig. Major Harold Griffin Eady, M.C., R.E., Croix de Guerre with Palms, who said that he was proud to unveil the memorial, which had been erected in a spirit of pride in the loyalty and patriotism of the men who had died. The Bishop said that the men, some of them hardly knowing the cause of the war, went, without any brag or fuss, at the first call of their country's need, and met death and suffering in its most monstrous forms cheerfully. The service concluded with the Last Post, sounded by buglers of the Queen's Regiment. A large wreath of white and mauve flowers was placed at the foot of the cross. It had attached to it a card on which was written: *'In proud and affectionate memory from the parishioners of Burpham. Faithful unto death'.*

Walter Wisdom's name was not included on the memorial at the time of the dedication but was added later. The reason for this was said to be that he was not killed in action. But, his sister-in-law, Mary, campaigned to have him included and so his name was added two years later.

Burpham War Memorial at St Luke's Church 2014

On 3rd August 2014 a Commemorative Service was held, when the families of the Great War men who died were invited to join with Burpham residents in remembering the brave young men from Burpham and Jacob's Well who gave their lives. There were hymns, psalms and readings as well as two poems that were read out. The Mesopotamia Poem was written by Tom Durrant, one of the Burpham men, who wrote it on a Christmas card to his family in 1916:

'Christmas greetings from this land
Where the climate ain't too grand,
Buzzing insects beat the band – In Mesopotamia.

Summer's heat and Winter's chill,
Did their best to overfill
India's hostels, we are still – In Mesopotamia.

But cheerio! Here's luck to thee,
Things aren't bad, take that from me,
And it's Christmastime you see – In Mesopotamia.

For the New Year, best of fun,
May the Bosche keep on the run,
And may our work soon be done – In Mesopotamia.'

The second poem was 'For the Fallen' written by Robert Laurence Binyon and published in 1914, which contains the familiar words from Remembrance Services:

'They shall grow not old, as we that are left grow old:
Age shall not weary them, nor the years condemn.
At the going down of the sun and in the morning
We will remember them.'

Inevitably there will always be those who do not wish to go to war, for whatever reason. In 1916 a newspaper reported that Guildford Rural Tribunal considered an application from William Winzer, of New Inn Farm, for farm workers to be exempted from conscription. Conditional exemption was given. The same year

Stanley Martin of Guildford was less lucky. He came up before the Surrey Appeal Tribunal as a conscientious objector. He had obtained work on a farm at Burpham, but the Committee had ruled that farm work must be undertaken at least 20 miles from a man's place of residence. *'You gentlemen don't seem to understand that the committee have no intention to make soft jobs for you, so that you can live at home and have a good time.'*

World War One

War broke out in Europe in late July 1914, triggered by the assassination of Archduke Franz Ferdinand of Austria. Great Britain declared war on 4th August and within weeks Europe was at war. The United States of America joined the Allies in 1917 and an armistice was agreed on 11th November 1918. Almost a million British soldiers died in the Great War, some bodies were identifiable and probably buried close to the front line, but some were unidentifiable and some were simply not found. Many thousands of small burial plots were created on or near the battlefields and those soldiers who were missing and presumed dead are listed on major memorials in the theatres of war, such as the Menim Gate.

There was a Home Guard during this war, known as the Volunteer Force. Their nickname was '*the gorgeous wrecks*' due to the words '*georgeus rex*' on their badges. The force consisted mainly of ex-soldiers who were too old to sign up or men who were unfit. It is likely that any local men who had served in wars such as the Zulu or Boer Wars of the late 19th century would have joined. Unfortunately no records have been found relating to any Burpham men involved in the force.

The Great War changed the role of women in society as it has been estimated that about two million were required to replace men in a wide range of employment. Over 260,000 were working as farm labourers in the Women's Land Army. Mrs Millicent Fawcett, President of the National Union of Women's Suffrage said at the end 1918 '*The war has revolutionised the industrial position of women – it found them serfs and left them free.*'

The German U-boats sank many British ships in an attempt to cut off supplies. Food became scarce and in 1917 panic buying led to shortages and in 1918 rationing was introduced as a measure to ensure supplies rather than as an attempt to reduce consumption. People back home were urged to raise funds to help the war effort and in 1915 donations were sought on behalf of the Queen's Prisoner of War Comforts Fund. Lists of donors were often published in the newspapers, for instance a donation of coffee, milk and chocolate amongst other things were given by Mrs Burbidge of Marlyn's.

The Burpham War Memorial at St Luke's Church records the 18 local soldiers who died. In 2014 the 'Burpham Will Remember Them' project team used various sources of information to create commemoration folders for each one, including The Burpham War Memorial by Jean Shail, the 1901 and 1911 censuses, and the Commonwealth War Graves Commission website. Families and descendants were traced through genealogical research. Varying amounts of information have been found for the men, some have very little and some have lots of detail.

Frederick Adams – Private, 40017, 1ˢᵗ Battalion, Bedfordshire Regiment
Frederick was the eldest of ten children of Henry (Harry) and Eliza Adams, born in 1896 in Liphook. His father worked as a cowman on farms, moving from Petersfield to Burpham where they lived in

Pimm's Row and then Burpham Court Farm Cottages. All his surviving younger siblings attended Burpham School. Frederick joined the 1ˢᵗ Battalion of the Bedfordshire Regiment, having been transferred from the Suffolk Regiment. In 1916 the battalion was involved in several phases of the Battle of the Somme and Frederick was killed in action on 25ᵗʰ September 1916 at the Battle of Morval, on the Somme, aged 19 years. He has no known grave but was remembered on the Thiepval Memorial for the Missing of the Somme. The memorial bears the names of 72,000 officers and men of the United Kingdom and South African forces who died in the Somme sector before 1918 and have no known grave; over 90% of those commemorated died between July and November 1916. Frederick was also remembered on the Leatherhead War Memorial.

Sergeant William Frederick Collis – L/8929, Serjeant, 8ᵗʰ Battalion, The Queen's (Royal West Surrey) Regiment, MM and bar
He was one of only three soldiers on the memorial who was married. He was born in 1888 in Buryfields, Guildford, to William James and Mercy Gertrude Collis, and lived there with his parents and six siblings until the early 1900s. By 1911 he had enlisted and was recorded in the 21ˢᵗ Battalion The Queen's (Royal West Surrey Regiment), serving in Arabia, Cyprus and Gibraltar. In 1915 he married Mary Stone by special licence, then early in 1916 his daughter Dorothy May Irene was born and baptised at St Luke's. William transferred to the 8ᵗʰ Battalion of the same regiment at some point and was awarded the Military Medal for bravery in 1916 after the Battle of the Somme. But, two years later Sergeant Collis was killed in action on 26ᵗʰ March 1918, aged

29 years, having been decorated again for bravery by the award of a Bar to his Military Medal. He was remembered on the Pozieres Memorial on the Somme.

Burpham War Memorial - WW1

The Durrant family has been part of the Burpham community for over 100 years. Thomas, a scaffolder, and Agatha Durrant came from Bellfields to Burpham between 1901 and 1911, and lived at 4/5 Pimm's Row. They lost two sons in the Great War.

Tom Durrant - Private, 200997, 1st/4th Battalion, Hampshire Regiment

Tom was born in 1893 in Bellfields, the oldest son of Thomas and Agatha, but the family, with ten children, moved to Pimm's Row in 1911. Tom worked for about six years as a letter press printer for Frank Lasham, Printer and Stationer, in Guildford. When he

408

applied for a job in Shanghai he had a glowing reference from Mr Fyfe at Stoke Church, who said '...*an honest, reliable young man, always willing to do his best in every work*'. Tom also worked as a printer for the Guildford Times.

He enlisted in 1914 and joined the 1st/4th Battalion of the Hampshire Regiment. He served in India and Balochistan (a province of Pakistan) before going to Mesopotamia with the Expeditionary Force – they fought the Turks in what is now Iraq. In addition to the poem read out at the Commemorative Service Tom also wrote an 11 verse poem called 'The Ever Scratching Army', with the final verse reading:

> '*I appeal to all, go in and win! Aye!*
> *Scratching all the way.*
> *Hang the fleas, the flies and frogs.*
> *So long as we win the day.*'

Tom was wounded in Iraq and taken to Amara (Al 'Amarah) where he died on 12th March 1917. He was 23 years old and was buried in the Amara War Cemetery on the banks of the River Tigris. The cemetery was rediscovered in 2003 by men of the Royal Irish Regiment. It has 4,000 graves and was being cared for by an Iraqi keeper who did so in the face of great personal danger.

Harry Durrant – Private, L/10041, 2nd Battalion Signals, The Queen's (Royal West Surrey) Regiment
Harry, also known as Dick, was born in 1895 in Bellfields, second son to Thomas and Agatha, and was recorded as working as a brewery labourer in the 1911 census. He was chosen to be a

409

bodyguard for King George V during three days of special manoeuvres. He enlisted in 1912 but did not go abroad until 1914, going to France as part of the British Expeditionary Force. He fought at the First Battle of Ypres. He was killed in action on 7th November 1914, aged about 19 years, the first of the Burpham soldiers to lose his life, and has no known grave. He is remembered on the Menim Gate at Ypres In Belgium.

Harry's parents, Thomas and Agatha were distraught at the loss of both sons and after the war they adopted a Canadian soldier from Niagara, Ontario, Jack Laughlin, who had lost his own parents. Jack came to live with the Durrant family and in 1925 he married their daughter Agatha and they had three children. Both Thomas and Agatha were buried in St Luke's.

Private Charles William David Grey (misspelt as Gray on the memorial) was born in 1898 in Puttenham to Charles and Kate Grey. He was known as Charlie within his family. The family moved to Pimm's Row where they were living from 1900 to about 1909. The 1911 census records Charles as living at Jacobs Well Farm (now called Jacob's Well Cottage – a three-bay open hall house with one bay, built about 1500) and he was still at school aged 13 years. He went to Merrow School in 1904. His five younger siblings all attended Burpham School from 1909 onwards, but it is not clear how long they stayed there.

It should be noted that the school records also misspell the family surname and although this was quite common the census enumerators got it right. Charlie was employed on his father's farm before joining the army. He became engaged to Miss Maud Kench but then enlisted in December 1916 with the 16th Batallion of the Middlesex Regiment. He went to the Western Front in May 1917, working as a signaller. In August 1917 he received severe shrapnel wounds in his thigh and abdomen, while fighting in the Ypres area – one of 83 men wounded that day from his battalion.

The Surrey Advertiser reported that he was wounded while fighting on the Western Front and he was transferred to a military hospital in Exeter, where he died on 8th September 1917, aged 19 years. He was only at the front for three months before being wounded. His body was brought back to Guildford and he was buried at Stoughton Cemetery, where the last rites were accorded semi-military honours. Revd. J W Clarke, curate in charge at Burpham, officiated.

The Gunner family has lived in and around the Burpham area for many years and has many branches. In 1901 Frank and Emily Gunner's family were living at Burpham Church Cottages, just past St Luke's on Burpham Lane. In 1908, when four of their younger children were admitted to Burpham School, the family were living in Bower's Cottages; but by 1911 they were living at Gunner's Farm on Stringer's Common with most of their 16 children (10 boys and six girls). Frank had inherited the farm, a 15th century house, from a cousin and eventually he became the farm bailiff. Frank was variously a carter on one of the local farms, a labourer and a chimney sweep.

Percy George Gunner - Lance Corporal, 9199, 8th Battalion, Somerset Light Infantry, DCM

Percy was the third eldest of the boys, born in 1894 in Ash and baptised at St Mark's, Wyke. He attended Perry Hill School Infants' Department and then in 1900 went to Merrow School. He lived with his family in Burpham Church Cottages in 1901, but by 1911 he was already in the army and was found at Taunton Barracks as a Special Reservist. While he was there the soldiers marched past Elm Cottage on their route to the practice range. Living at the cottage was Edna Hughes, who was a silk winder, with her family. Percy and Edna fell in love and got engaged. He became a Lance Corporal in the 8th Battalion of Prince Albert's Somerset Light Infantry.

Percy entered the theatre of war in August 1914 and became the most highly decorated of the soldiers on the War Memorial, gaining the Distinguished Conduct Medal – the second highest award to non-commissioned officers in the British Army. Percy was killed in action on 6th December 1915, shortly after his 21st birthday. He was buried in the New Military Cemetery at Chapelle-D'Armentieres, France. The Taunton Courier reported in May 1916 on the deaths of Edna's two brothers and said '*While the family were mourning the loss of sons and brothers, there came the welcome news that a prospective son-in-law, Lance Corporal P Gunner, 8th Battalion, Somerset Light Infantry, formerly 1st Battalion, had been decorated for conspicuous gallantry, the London Gazette announcing that he had been awarded the DCM and Russian Order (4th Class) and describing his act as follows "for conspicuous gallantry when he carried*

412

important messages under heavy fire. He has been previously recommended for his bravery and ability on an occasion when he took command of his platoon after all the non-commissioned officers had been killed or wounded." Following upon these welcome tidings comes the news of the Lance Corporal's death and since he had willed all his effects to his fiancée Miss E Hughes, she has now received the two medals from the War Office.'

In December 1914 Edna had given birth to a daughter, Doris May Hughes, 'Dulcie'. So Percy went to war knowing that his child was to be born. Edna went on to marry another soldier in 1920, but this marriage broke down. Edna's parents brought up Dulcie as their own child.

Edward Gunner – Private, 160864 103rd Company, Machine Gun Corps Infantry

Older than Percy by almost two years, born in Cobbett's Hill and baptised at St Mary's Church Worplesdon in 1893, was the last of the Burpham soldiers to die in the Great War. He must have joined up somewhat later than his brother as he was still living with the family at Gunner's Farm in 1911, working as a domestic coachman. Edward enlisted in the 103rd Company of the Machine Gun Corps and survived the duration of the war. However, very sadly he succumbed to influenza in 1919, dying of double pneumonia on 26th March, aged 22 years. He was buried in the Communal Cemetery at Valenciennes (St Roch), Nord, France. The Spanish Flu pandemic was rife in 1918-1920, infecting 500 million people across the world, and taking its toll on the already

413

weakened survivors of the Great War. It was one of the deadliest natural disasters in human history, taking the lives of young and old alike.

Two other brothers also served in France. Frank, of the Duke of Cornwall's Light Infantry, had his leg blown off in Étaples in 1915 and, on his return to England, he spent several months in the Warren Road war hospital, later to become St Luke's Hospital. Herbert was the oldest brother and was known as Jack, he served with the 16th Lancers Irish Guards, was reported killed in April 1918 but two months later his joyful family received a card telling them that he was alive, but a prisoner of war.

Meanwhile, another Gunner family lived at Stringer's Common – James Gunner, third cousin of Frank, lived with his wife Elizabeth and their ten children, two of whom appear on the War Memorial.

John Ernest Gunner – Private, G/23498, 2nd Battalion, Middlesex Regiment
John was born in 1879 to James and Elizabeth Gunner and baptised at St Mary's Church Worplesdon. He had nine siblings. In 1900 he married Amelia Burgess and they had six children, three of whom were baptised at St Mary's and the youngest three at St Luke's. *'Amelia was very good at sewing. She had a hand cranked "Superba" sewing machine and made clothes for all the family, including bustles for the ladies' skirts.'* In 1901 they were living at Hurst Cottages and he was working as a carter on the farm, by 1911 they were living at Elm Cottage in Jacobs Well and his occupation was recorded as Removal Contractor Labour.

414

'*Many country dwellings were tied cottages so a change of employer could necessitate a change of address and people moved about quite readily.*' John enlisted in Guildford with the 2nd Battalion of the Duke of Cambridge's Own (Middlesex Regiment) and was killed in action on the Somme on 22nd March 1917, aged 38 years. He was buried in the Peronne Communal Cemetery in the Somme district of France.

Samson Albert Gunner – Private, 6676, 11th (Prince Albert's Own) Hussars

Samson (or Albert Samson according to his baptism record), was born in 1885 and baptised at St Luke's. He went to school at Perry Hill Infants and then St Mary's National School in Worplesdon, but left aged 12 years. He was recorded as working as a stable helper/groom and living at Trinity Church Yard in 1901, but by 1911 he was a soldier in India. It seems that he joined up as a boy soldier and left military service after 13 years when he worked for a builder in Woking. He re-enlisted in 1914 at Aldershot, re-joining his former regiment. This was one of the British Army's more famous regiments, known as 'cherry pickers', a nickname dating from the Peninsular War, when the 11th Light Dragoons (as they were then named) were attacked while raiding an orchard in Spain. In 1854 the regiment charged with the Light Brigade in the Crimean War.

Samson went to France with 26 officers, 523 NCOs and men and 608 horses. They went into action in August 1915 when the Battle of Mons began. Samson died on 11th November 1917, aged

32 years, as a result of a fall whilst on duty and was buried in the Boulogne Eastern Cemetery, Pas de Calais, France.

James Knight – Pioneer, 6th Army Tramway Company, Royal Engineers

James was born in Headley in 1869 to James, a bricklayer, and Emily Knight and had three sisters. After school he worked as a bricklayer with his father. He married Clara and they had six children. James had been a member of the Surrey Police Constabulary for 19 years, in Godstone and other places from 1891, and moved to Burpham sometime between 1901 and 1911. The family lived in Bower's Cottages and he was working at Sutton Place as a green keeper at the golf links in 1911. James's two youngest children attended Burpham School. *'So quiet and peaceful was Burpham in those days that the children at Bower's Cottage could hear when a motor car was coming up the London Road. Such was the novelty that they used to run down Burpham Lane to see it go by.'*

He enlisted in October 1915 in Westminster, Middlesex with the Corps of Royal Engineers, probably working on the narrow gauge railways built to carry ammunition and supplies to the front lines. The Surrey Advertiser said that ten days after joining up he went to the Western Front with a labour battalion of the Royal Engineers and afterwards he transferred to the Army Tramway Company. He was killed in action on 5th June 1917, aged 47 years and was buried in Bard Cottage Cemetery near Ypres in Belgium. It was later said that after James died it was fairly certain that the family would not have been evicted from their home by his employer, the Duke of Sutherland. The Duke's grandson said that if his grandfather had tried to do so, and the Duchess had got to hear of it, she would have dealt with him. James' wife, Clara lived in Trodds Lane after the war and died in 1928 after being knocked down by a motor cycle. She was buried at St Luke's.

Robert Charles Knight – Lance Corporal 19944, 14th Battalion, Machine Gun Corps Infantry

Robert was one of James's six children, born in 1892 in Frimley. In 1911 he was living with his family in Bower's Cottages and was working as a gamekeeper at Sutton Place with his father. The Surrey Advertiser reported that he had been employed as underkeeper to Mr Johnson, Marsh Court, Kings Someborne, Hants, before joining the army. It is possible that he may have been in the Territorial Army with the Queen's before the war. He enlisted in Winchester, aged 23 years, in 1914 and saw service at first with the Rifle Brigade and then with the Machine Gun Corps. He died on 17th June 1918, aged 27 years, in a Prisoner of War Concentration Camp and was buried in Premont British Cemetery, Aisne, France. Robert's youngest brother, Signaller J A Knight, had enlisted in the 1/5th Queen's at the age of 15 years as a drummer boy and his brother in law Pte G F S Clee was serving in France at the end of the war.

Norman Arthur Phillips – 2nd Lieutenant, 54 Squadron, Royal Flying Corps

Born in Basingstoke in 1889, to Thomas Arthur Phillips, who was a coal merchant and JP, and his wife Annie, he had three siblings. In the 1911 census he was recorded as visiting Hugh Lancelot

Robson in Orchard Cottage in Burpham, and Norman's occupation was a fruit grower, as was Lancelot's. In 1916 a newspaper report referred to him as foreman at Guildford Fruit Farm, Burpham, when he identified the body of a victim of a motor accident on London Road. The London Gazette reported that in May 1916 he was appointed 2nd Lieutenant in the Royal Flying Corps, which was the forerunner of the Royal Air Force. He was the only officer amongst the Burpham fallen and also the only one not in the army as a soldier.

He learned his early aviation skills at Oxford on a Maurice Farman biplane, then obtained his flying certificate at Military School in Birmingham. His name was listed in the Surrey Advertiser casualty list, saying that '*he was so stout-hearted and such cheery company*'. The Hants and Berkshire Gazette wrote that his Squadron Commander said '*He is a great loss to the Squadron and also to the R.F.C., as really good scout pilots are very hard to get and must be absolutely fearless and have a lot of flying experience. He had done so well during the short time he had been out, having brought down one German aeroplane by himself...He had been engaged in numerous fights in which hostile machines were driven down.*' He was killed in an aerial combat, flying a Sopwith Pup aircraft, in France on 25th March 1917, aged 28 years. He was buried in Grand-Seraucourt British Cemetery, Aisne, France and also remembered on the Basingstoke War Memorial.

John (Jack) Albert Russell – Private, 242438, 6th Battalion, Queen's (Royal West Kent) Regiment

John was the son of Albert and Sarah Alice Russell, who lived in Winkfield, Berkshire before moving to Burpham, where they lived in Collingbourne Cottages in 1911. Albert was a market gardener and Jack helped his father on the smallholding. Jack was born in 1898 in Winkfield, the eldest of three children, and the younger two both attended Burpham School. He went to Merrow School and attended Sunday School at St Luke's Church. He had two hobbies, collecting birds' eggs and also postcards of soldiers in uniform. At the outbreak of war his family lived in Weyside Cottage, close to the towpath near Bower's Lock. He was training with the 5th Queen's when war broke out and he volunteered for active service in Guildford in 1914, joining The Queen's (Royal West Surrey Regiment) but later transferred to the 6th Battalion Queen's Own (Royal West Kent Regiment).

Jack sent postcards home to his family. One, to his brother, said 'Well Frank, I have been wondering if I shall be home for the birds' nesting season. I am only a kid yet, though I should not like anybody else to say so'. Another, to his father in 1916, said 'Dear Dad, we had a lovely train ride from Cairo to Alex during which I pictured the land of Egypt in my mind's eye in case of never again seeing it, which would not trouble me greatly. If I should again be required for active service, France would suit me best. With love from Jack.' He was wounded in Egypt in 1916 then travelled by hospital ship back to England. Then he went back to France, where he was wounded and died in Rouen on 31st March 1918, aged 20 years. A newspaper report in 1918 recorded that 'The matron of a hospital wrote that he had received a compound fracture of the right arm, was shot in the leg, and was very ill. In

419

a subsequent note it was stated that *Pte Russell never rallied and died.'* He was buried in the St Sever Cemetery Extension, Rouen, Seine-Maritime, France. His name is on the Worplesdon Roll of Honour, which was published that September. Jack had a younger brother who was serving in the Royal Fusiliers.

Shoeing Smith Thomas Searle – 8735, Shoeing Smith, 19th (Queen Alexandra's Own Royal) Hussars

Thomas was born in 1891 and lived with his parents, Frederick, a brickmaker, and Ellen Searle in New Cross Road, Stoke Next Guildford, before moving to Stringer's Common where he was found living in Watt's Cottages in 1911. *'The family were very poor and Watts Cottage was very basic, consisting of two rooms downstairs and two up. There was no electricity and no bathroom. The bathtub hung from a hook inside the shed. There was a cast iron coal-fired range. There was an outside toilet up the garden, under the pear tree. His granddaughter remembered going there one evening to find a big toad sitting on the seat, so she ran off to get someone to remove it.'*

Tom worked as a builder's labourer but enlisted at Aldershot into the Household Cavalry and Cavalry of the Line as a Shoeing Smith. The army relied on horses for transport of supplies and the movement of artillery. *'When he came home on leave from The Front, mother insisted he stripped off and had a bath in the garden to get rid of the lice. He was not allowed into the house until he had done so.'* He was killed in action on 23rd March 1918, aged 27 years, and was buried in the Ham British Cemetery, Muille Vilette, Somme, France.

George Stilwell – Private, G/4228, 1st Battalion, The Queen's (Royal West Surrey) Regiment

George lived with his family in Jacobs Well after moving from Slyfield Green. He was born in 1888 to George and Ellen Stilwell, and was baptised at St Luke's in 1889. He had one brother, Arthur, and one sister, Annie. His father was a self-employed market gardener. His parents were both buried at St Luke's. In 1911 the family were living at Crabtree Cottage, Jacobs Well, and George was recorded as working as a market gardener. He enlisted with the 1st Battalion of The Queen's (Royal West Surrey Regiment) and was killed on the Somme, during the battle for High Wood, on 15th July 1916, aged 28 years. He has no known grave but is remembered on the Thiepval Memorial for the Missing of the Somme.

Private Henry Ernest Williams – G/3148, 2nd Battalion, The Queen's (Royal West Surrey) Regiment

According to the 1911 census he was living with William and Phoebe Ellis, possibly his foster parents but recorded as a lodger, at Yew Tree Cottage, aged 28 years and working as a labourer builder. Jean Shail's history of the War Memorial suggested that he was fostered by the Ellis family but there was no sign of him with them in the 1901 census. He was baptised at St Luke's in 1893 when he was 11 years old, having been born to Mary Ann Williams in 1882. He enlisted at Guildford aged 35 years and it is possible that he was a member of the Territorial Army before the war. He died of wounds on 28th August 1915, aged 33 years. He was buried in Hinges Military Cemetery, Pas de Calais, France. He is also remembered on Alfold's war memorial but the reason for this is not known.

Walter Wisdom – Private, 917, 7th Battalion, The Queen's (Royal West Surrey) Regiment, MM and Bar

Walter was the only ex-pupil of Burpham School to be mentioned on the War Memorial. Born in Ockham, near Ripley, in 1897, the youngest of six children, to John and Eliza Wisdom. His father was a farm worker and carter. Walter joined Burpham School as a pupil in 1909, aged 12 years old, so presumably did not stay very long. He was recorded at that time as living at 5 Pimm's Cottages. Having moved from Tolworth (in 1901), by 1911 he was living at Elm View on London Road and was recorded as being an errand boy.

Walter, along with his four brothers (George, Harry, Albert and William), enlisted at Stoughton Barracks, where Colonel Treeby was Recruiting Officer, in September 1914. Walter was in the 7th Battalion of the Queens (Royal West Surrey Regiment) and fought throughout the war. Towards the end he came home on leave and succumbed to Spanish Flu. He insisted on returning to the Front, but had not fully recovered and died in France on 3rd November 1918, aged 21 years, just eight days before the Armistice. He was awarded the Military Medal and Bar, proving that he was a very brave soldier, but no records survived to say how it was earned. He was buried in the Busigney Communal Cemetery Extension, Nord, France.

Robert Worsfold – Private, 30138, 1st/5th Battalion, East Lancashire Regiment

Although the memorial says Robert the evidence points to this being Walter Charles Worsfold - there seems to be no reason for the different name, apart from the possibility that he did not like his initials, in common with Winston Churchill. He was the son of John and Ann Worsfold; his father was an agricultural carter. He was born in 1898 at Stoke Park Farm Cottages (his grandfather's home) on London Road, baptised at Stoke Next Guildford, and the family lived there at the time of the 1901 and 1911 censuses. He was the youngest of seven children, six sons and one daughter – four of the sons served in the Great War in France and sadly the daughter, Fanny, died of influenza in 1918. William Worsfold (the grandfather) was married to Emma Tickner, who died in 1868. William lived with the family until his death in 1913 and he was buried at St Luke's.

At some point, probably after William's death in 1913, the family moved to Marlyn's Lodge on London Road. By 1918 the family was living at New Inn Farm Cottage, then Merrow, but Walter's brother George was living at Marlyn's Lodge in 1928 with their father, after their mother had died. Walter had enlisted in Guildford in 1916, aged 17 years, first joining the East Surrey Regiment and later transferring to the 1st/5th Battalion of the East Lancashire Regiment. He died of wounds on 20th November 1918, aged 20 years, and was buried in the St Sever Cemetery Extension, Rouen, Seine-Maritime, France.

The Surrey Advertiser reported in November 1918 'A *Double Bereavement.* Mr and Mrs Worsfold, Marlyns Lodge, Burpham, last week received news that their youngest son Pte W C Worsfold, 20, East Lancs. died on Nov 20ᵗʰ of wounds received on Nov 6ᵗʰ. He joined up in January 1916 and had been twice wounded. He was one of four sons who served in France. The death took place from influenza and pneumonia at Castle Cottage, Castle Street, Guildford of Mrs Fannie Ellis, wife of Driver J H Ellis ASC now in France and only daughter of Mr & Mrs Worsfold of Marlyns Lodge. Deceased who was taken ill only a week before her death was 32 years of age. The interment took place at Burpham Cemetery on Thursday of last week.'*

There have been many Worsfolds living in the Guildford area over the years. There was one Worsfold child at Burpham Primary School but not until after the war finished and there is no guarantee that it is the same family, but he could possibly have been Walter's nephew.

World War One was the first time that aerial bombardment was used and in 1915 it was recorded that 12 bombs were dropped by Zeppelin L13 on the St Catherine's area of Guildford. The sole casualty was one swan.

At the end of the Great War the families of all those who had lost their lives in the conflict received a Commemoration Plaque and a Scroll from King George V. The plaque was a circular bronze disc, which came to be known as a Dead Man's Penny or a Death Plaque, showing Britannia holding a trident and standing with a lion. The name of the soldier was cast in a rectangular tablet below an oak wreath. Two dolphins swam around Britannia, symbolising Britain's sea power. Around the picture the legend read 'He died for freedom and honour'. The reverse was blank. The scroll read:

'I join with my grateful people in sending you this memorial of a
brave life given for others in the Great War.
George R.I.'

The only mentions in the Burpham School Log Book to indicate that there had been a war were an extra week's holiday at the end of the summer 1919 *'being in Celebration of Peace'* and on 26th September the school was closed for the afternoon because it was *'hired to entertain demobilised soldiers of the village'*.

World War Two

When war broke out at the beginning of September 1939 a range of emergency plans were put into action, including creating a register of everyone so that ration books and identity cards could be produced and evacuating children from areas deemed to be at risk. This 1939 Register provides modern-day readers with varied information about people living in a community and how they were employed at the time. When this was made available in 2016 there were some gaps, as information about people who might still be alive at the time was not released. However, it gives a fascinating insight into community life just before the war as everyone had to have an entry in the Occupation column. Most married women in 1939 were recorded as 'unpaid domestic duties' because it was still the norm for women to give up their jobs when they married. Single women carried out a wide range of jobs, including shorthand typists, clerks, telephonists, laundress, chambermaid and shop assistants. A few were teachers or nurses but both professions at the time required women to leave work when they married.

Men had mainly moved away from agricultural jobs, though there were a few still recorded. Market gardeners and smallholders, or gardeners, were quite common as were various types of labourer, builder and tradesman. However, it is the growth of 'white collar workers' that stands out. Insurance managers, sales representatives, engineers, architects, surveyors, police officers and teachers appeared in Burpham for almost the first time. There were, inevitably, some errors, such as Reginald Maggs who was recorded as being an expectant mother.

In October 1939 the Burpham Primary School Log Book recorded that *'Mr Swayne visited the school and inspected the trenches.'* These were dug as an early form of air raid shelter, but were soon replaced by a proper shelter that was dug into the slope behind the school building. A few days later the school doubled in size when 26 children were evacuated from two schools in Fulham, bringing with them four teachers. This was part of Operation Pied Piper, which started at the beginning of September 1939 and in the first few days had transported about three million people, mostly schoolchildren, from towns and cities that were deemed to be at risk from enemy attack to places of safety in the countryside. Ron Puttnam was one such evacuee from a London school. He was placed with Harry Cutt and his wife who lived in the bungalow on the corner of Marlyn's Drive and Burpham Lane. Harry had a bakery in Merrow. Ron went back and forth between Burpham and his family but he attended Burpham Primary School for a while.

Miss Chesterfield, Burpham Primary School's Headmistress from 1940 to 1972, recorded life for the children during the war. She complained that at times of air raids the children were taken down to the shelter, but then it was not possible to hear the siren sounding to tell them it was all over. Some children remember her standing at the door of the shelter instead of being in there with them – Barbara Morson wondered what would happen if she was bombed or shot down. Perhaps she stood outside so that she might hear the 'All Clear'. The siren was located at The Kingpost on London Road, a fair distance from the school.

427

Margaret Woods remembered that chocolate powder was sent from Canada for schoolchildren, '...*we were asked to take a tin to school for drinking chocolate powder. Whatever sized tin we took to school was filled with the wonderful sweet tasting powder, which we took home. However, not all of it reached home, as we walked home dipping our fingers into it and licking the delicious powder off our fingers!*'

Children at Burpham Primary School tending their gardens in 1945
(N Hamilton)

During the war the children did their bit in the 'Dig for Victory' campaign, growing vegetables in small allotments, next to the market gardens. Sadly this land was lost to the school when the A3 was built in the 1970s. In 1941 the Surrey Emergency Committee wanted to requisition the iron railings around the boundaries of the school land in order to melt it down for munitions. However, Miss Chesterfield made her disapproval known and to this day most of the railings are still in place around the school. School lunches were provided at the Village Hall for a while until canteen facilities were built on the school site.

According to a Surrey Advertiser report from 1941 *'meat was in short supply as the German U-boat blockade drastically reduced imports to a level at which butchers were often unable to honour the ration. While some foods were rationed by weight, meat was controlled by price. That way you could choose (on occasions when there was a choice) whether to buy it in expensive or cheap cuts or in even cheaper form as sausages or mince.'* Apparently there was plenty of offal, but many people would not use their meat coupons to buy it. The Guildford Food Control Committee proposed that the Government should create two meatless days a week in all restaurants and canteens as it was thought to be unfair that people who could afford to eat in a restaurant could do so without giving up their meat coupons. Most foods were price controlled and some traders were fined for excessive charging.

In 1943 the Surrey Advertiser ran an advert for Air Raid Shelters from a company in East Horsley. These were for indoor or outdoor use, made of reinforced concrete, and priced at £15 each. Perhaps residents of Burpham bought these for their house or garden? Jean Menzies remembered that Anderson shelters were outdoors, half buried in the earth, whilst Morrison shelters were indoors, making a cage to protect people from masonry and other debris if a bomb hit the house.

Guildford Home Guard

The 4th Guildford Battalion of the Surrey Home Guard was raised by Colonel G W Geddes on 18th May 1940 when about 300 people reported to the headquarters of the Surrey Constabulary in order to enrol in the Local Defence Volunteers (LDV). Colonel Geddes, OBE, DSO, had retired to Guildford in 1934 after 34 years of distinguished military service, including the Boer War and World

Home Guard inspection (J Kemp)

War I. Guildford was a reception area and all the barracks were occupied by the army, so owners of private houses responded patriotically by offering up their garages, and sometimes their homes, as headquarters for the platoons. The Battalion motto was '*Invisibility, Inaudibility, Individuality, Initiative*'. The next day 150 Ross rifles were issued and the Guildford LDV was on duty that night for the first time. Over the next year more resources were issued, including more rifles and ammunition, and some preliminary uniform. Training included weapons training at Westcott and Bisley ranges.

Colonel Geddes wrote: '*May 1942. Exercises to test the ability of the Battalion to man action stations were held. On the 16th the enemy was represented by a young soldier battalion of the East Surrey Regiment. The clash of arms had its amusing side. These*

430

young soldiers, overcome with keenness and excitement, were somewhat contemptuous of the old gentlemen of the Home Guard, and thought they could be pushed aside. Their ardour was somewhat damped by the Home Guard exhibiting a considerable knowledge of unarmed combat, in which a good number had been put through.' The District Commander complimented the efficiency of the Battalion and the turnout.

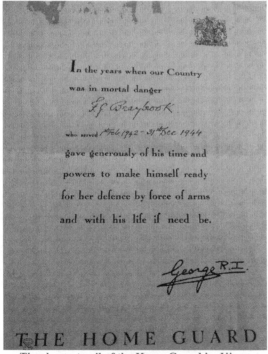

In the years when our Country
was in mortal danger

F G Braybrook

who served *1 Feb 1942 - 31st Dec 1944*
gave generously of his time and
powers to make himself ready
for her defence by force of arms
and with his life if need be.

George R.I.

THE HOME GUARD

Thank you to all of the Home Guard by King George VI (J Kemp)

'B' Company consisted of men from around Burpham, Stoke, Abbotswood, and Merrow. Col. C R Wigan was the Commander of the Company and Platoon No. 5 Commander was Captain R W Black, who lived in Orchard Road. The Headquarters for the platoon was the Green Man and they met upstairs in the Paddock Rooms. Jan Kemp's father, F G Braybrook, served from February 1942 to December 1944 and was awarded a Certificate of Merit in recognition of his service.

A list of Guildford Local Defence Volunteers in 1940 named those from Burpham who served with the Home Guard locally. These included: R W Black of Orchard Rd, A D Coward of Marlyn's Cottage, C Davies of Winterhill Way, J Read of Meadway, J Lever of New Inn Lane, H Round of Glendale Drive, E V Rees of New Inn Lane, G E Lord of Orchard Road, W Daws of Meads Rd, A Manfield of London Rd, G Tasker of Glendale Drive, H J Hayes of London Rd, H C Vickery of Orchard Rd, A E Ratcliffe of The Paddocks, E H Evendon of London Rd, R O Marshall of Paddocks and L Renaud.

Home Guard, Troup 615 (R Keene)

Life in Burpham continued much as usual despite the war going on – the farms had to conduct their normal daily life and those other residents who had not gone to war still had things to do. The Surrey Times in June 1944 reported that *'On Saturday a social and dance at the Village Hall organised by Burpham Women's Institute realised £12 in aid of "Salute the Soldier" Week. The programme was arranged by Mrs Bratt. Mrs Warder was*

432

hostess and Mr Warder M.C. There were games, competitions, music and dancing with songs by Miss Stedman. Prizes were won by Mrs Stock, Mrs Cooke, Miss Mitchell, Miss Lemon and partner, "Ilda" and partner, Mrs Bridgeman, Miss Stedman, Mr Grover and Miss Stotter, Mr P Howard, Mr R Howard and Mr D Marshall, and Mr Murray.'

In 1940 the Surrey Advertiser reported that there was a fundraising Alexandra Rose Day Appeal for the Royal Surrey County Hospital. *'At Burpham nurses in uniform made a charming road barrier'* and using collecting sheets they collected about £20 for the appeal.

Ann Keane remembered that lots of tanks came rumbling down the London Road and the children came out to watch them go by. Also, American soldiers travelled the same route and would throw sweets to the children as they went past. She remembered too that they had a Morrison shelter in the bedroom and when the flying bombs went over it was very frightening.

There was a Prisoner of War camp in Merrow, where many Italian prisoners were kept. Ann remembered that some of them worked on Gosden Hill Farm and some made baskets to sell.

In 1945 the Surrey Advertiser reported that *'Driver R C West, who is serving in Norway, sends the Surrey Advertiser a copy of The Arctic Times, the most northerly English language paper in the world. He has received the Surrey Advertiser regularly from his wife, who resides at Burpham Lane, Guildford. Driver West has*

*been impressed by the beauty of Norway, but finds that the 24
hours of daylight takes some getting used to. Before the war he
was employed by the Stoke Hill and Lee Farm Dairy, and he hopes
to be home again shortly.'*

In 1945 the Surrey Advertiser reported that *'Major Henry E
Donnelly, M.C., who pressed the firing button when the U-boat
pens at Hamburg were blown up on Sunday, is the son of Mr and
Mrs E J Donnelly, of Surrey View, London Road, Burpham. About
60 men of 224 Field Company of the Royal Engineers had been
working to prepare the charges for three weeks. Commanding
Officer of the company, Major Donnelly pressed the firing button
at a point three-quarters of a mile away.'*

**Merrow Lane children having a street party to celebrate the end of the war
(A Keane)**

Ann Keane remembered that there was a street party on Merrow
Lane, where she lived with her family, to celebrate the end of the

434

war. Quite possibly there were others in the community, but this is the only photo that has been found so far.

Someone remembered a story from 1940, when they lived in Burpham and attended Burpham Primary School. Returning to school after lunch at home, in the days before school dinners, walking past the elm trees around St Luke's churchyard, all was quiet and no-one was around. Surrounded by gravestones, a voice was heard shouting '*Hoi*', but no-one was seen. Running for the school playground around the bend, the voice called again. Once safely through the school gates, turning around they caught sight of someone hanging in one of the elm trees on the end of a parachute, wearing dark clothes and waving. Inside the school it was all quiet, but, joining the rest of the children and teachers in the air-raid shelter, safe at last, no word was said about the man in the tree. By the end of the school day the man had disappeared, so must have been found, but it was never known who he was.

Jean Menzies remembered when she attended the old Royal Surrey County Hospital on Farnham Road one day, a German plane flew low over the County School opposite. So low that she could see the pilot's face.

Barbara Stone remembered that her father did his bit in the Home Guard, going out at night in his smart uniform. All the windows in the house had blackout curtains, so that no light shone out. '*We all had gas masks and mine was like a Mickey Mouse one which was red and blue – very smart...we had an air raid shelter dug at the bottom of the garden but I don't remember whether we ever used it. I do remember seeing on the odd night what were known as "dog fights" in the sky with the British planes fighting with the German ones – it was probably rather unpleasant to see at the time although I don't remember being particularly frightened.'*

After the war she remembered that the first time they were able to get bananas she tried to eat the whole thing as she didn't know it had to be peeled first. During the war she remembered that a landmine went off near the railway bridge at the top of New Inn Lane, resulting in the roof of their house being lifted off and coming back down, leaving broken windows and cracks in the walls that had to be repaired after the war.

Her parents took in an evacuee boy, who was very unhappy. He got glandular fever and then ran away. After extensive searching it was assumed that he had tried to return to his family in London. They also had landgirls living with them for a while. There were German prisoners of war cutting the hedges and clearing up the hedgerows in New Inn Lane – *'one seemed very nice and was very good looking to a young impressionable girl!'*

Ron Keene's grandmother was invited by the Duke and Duchess of Sutherland to a garden party at Sutton Place in June 1945, to celebrate the end of the Second World War in Europe.

The Duke & Duchess of Sutherland

request the pleasure of

Mr Saxton   Mrs Thorpe

Company at a Garden Party to be held at

Sutton Place, Guildford

on Saturday, June 2nd, 1945 - 3 to 6 p. m.

R.S.V.P.
  The Secretary,
    Sutton Place,
      Guildford

Invitation to Garden Party 1945 (R Keene)

437

Burpham War Memorial – World War Two

The St Luke's War Memorial names 11 men who lost their lives in the Second World War.

Aubrey Sedley Collins - Sub-Lieutenant (A), Royal Naval Volunteer Reserve

He was the son of Walter George and Vida Beatrice Constance Collins of Hawthorne Way, Burpham. He served on HMS Victorious and died on active service, at sea, on 20th April 1942 aged 20 years. He was buried with his father in St Luke's churchyard. The Surrey Advertiser reported *'Sub-Lieut. Aubrey Sedley Collins, (A)RNVR, a pilot in the Fleet Air Arm, would have been 21 on May 8th, and his mother was buying him a gold watch as a birthday gift. But he lost his life on active service last month, and the sympathy felt with his parents, Mr and Mrs W G Collins, of Ormonde, Hawthorne Way, Burpham, was indicated by the large attendance and numerous wreaths at the funeral service.'* The report went on to say that he had been educated at the Guildford Royal Grammar School, and became a member of the Old Guildfordians' Association. He worked for Barclays Bank, at their West Byfleet branch, before entering the Navy in 1940. His mother was President of the Burpham Women's Institute.

James Alexander Cross - Air Mechanic 2nd Class, 109221, Royal Navy

He was born in Stepney, London, in 1925, the son of Edward and Charlotte Cross, and at the time of his death he was recorded as living at Horse Shoe Cottages, London Road, Burpham. He joined the Royal Navy, Fleet Air Arm, and served at HMS Daedalus, a naval air station and training establishment near Portsmouth. He died on 4th September 1943, aged 18 years, of meningitis at the RAF Hospital at Kirkham. He was buried in St Luke's churchyard. The Surrey Advertiser reported that '*He was aged 19, was 6ft 3in tall, and had been in the Service for eight months, previously having been employed by the Guildford Corporation. His eldest brother, three years his senior, is serving in the Royal Marines in India*'.

Norman William Thomas Drake – Apprentice, Merchant Navy
He was born in Rangoon in 1921. He lived in Orchard Road and had two brothers, the older in the RAF and the younger who fought in the desert campaign in the Army – they both survived the war. He served on MV Silverpalm (London) and died at sea on 9th June 1941, aged 19 years. He is remembered on the Tower Hill Memorial in London.

Jack Dunn - Lance Bombardier, 14265973, 6 Field Regiment, Royal Artillery.
He was born in Staffordshire in 1914 to Harry and Annie Dunn. He lived in Meadow Road. He served in the Palestine and died at a military hospital from his wounds on 12th December 1945, aged 31 years. He was buried in Khayat Beach Cemetery near Haifa, Israel.

Clive Derek Hammond - Sergeant Navigator, 1382637, Royal Air Force (Volunteer Reserve).

He was born in 1921 in Brentford, Middlesex, the son of Aubrey Woolmer and Marie Madeleine Louise Hammond. Both his burial record and his will stated that he lived in Pinner, Middlesex, but by 1944 his parents were living in Jacob's Well. He was killed on active service, when his plane crashed on the Mull of Kintyre, and died on 2nd September 1942, aged 20 years and was buried in St Luke's churchyard.

Burpham War Memorial WW2

Harry Lionel Corbett Hirst – Bombardier, 1616612, 97 (3rd Bn The London Scottish) HAA Regiment of the Royal Artillery.

Harry was born in Manchester in 1920, the son of Harry and Gwendoline Mary Hirst, latterly of Orchard Road. He enlisted with the Royal Artillery in 1940. He was killed by enemy air

440

action on 4th September 1943 in Southern Italy, aged 23 years and was buried in the Salerno War Cemetery in Italy.

Derek Rowland Lord - Flight Sergeant (Pilot), 1169117, in the Royal Air Force (Volunteer Reserve).

Derek was born in 1922 in Wandsworth. He was the son of Gordon Ewart and Flora Marie Lord, who lived in Orchard Road, Burpham from 1927 to 1951. Derek was the only man from the World War Two memorial to have been a pupil at Burpham School. He died on 13th August 1942 aged 20 years, at Hutton Cranswick, Lincolnshire, and was buried in St Luke's churchyard with his father. The Surrey Advertiser reported *'Flight Sergeant Derek Rowland Lord, aged 20, whose death has occurred in the North of England, was the youngest son of Mr G E Lord, manager of the Jewellers' and Silversmiths' Company, High Street, Guildford. He had taken part in more than 30 raids over enemy territory. His parents live at Homewood, Orchard Road, Burpham, and he had been in the Air Force for two years and a month. He was educated at Abbot's School, Guildford and at the Woking County School. Mr and Mrs Lord have two other sons in the Services overseas. The funeral at Burpham on Wednesday was attended by a pilot officer and a flight sergeant of the RAF, and members of the Woking County School and the Home Guard, in which Mr Lord holds a commission.'*

Kenneth Hugh Percival – Corporal, 517975, 802 Squadron Fleet Air Arm, RAF.

He was born in 1916 in Suffolk, the son of Henry Edward and Ellen Eliza Percival, who by 1939 lived in Paddocks Road, Burpham. He died serving on HMS Glorious on 10th June 1940 aged 24 years and was buried in Englefield Green, Surrey and is remembered on the Runnymede Memorial.

Frederick Walter Cecil Ranger – Lieutenant, 145670, 6 (M.) "Z" A.A. Regiment of the Royal Artillery.

He enlisted with the Middlesex Regiment (Duke of Cambridge's Own). He was born in 1902, in Southwark, the son of Frederick and Alice Ranger, and married Daisy Primrose Victoria Fairhall in Staines in 1925. From 1936 to 1938 he and Daisy were living in Winterhill Way and his daughter, Jeanette, was a pupil at Burpham Primary School just before the war. He died on 16th December 1944 aged 42 years, in hospital at Maidenhead, and was buried in St Luke's churchyard. His father had died just two months before him, a double bereavement for his mother.

Samuel Reid – Private, 3645201, Pioneer Corps.

He was born in 1902, the son of Job and Ann Reid. He married Jessie Mabel Reid and they lived at The Mill House, Burpham Lane. He died on 7th August 1945 aged 43 years and was buried in St Luke's churchyard.

Peter Charles Henry Vickery – Captain, 258159, Royal Armoured Corps.

He was born in 1921 in Wandsworth, the elder son of Henry Charles and Ghita Louise Iola Vickery, who lived in Orchard Road from 1930. He was married to Olive Esther Lilian Vickery and they had a daughter, Gillian. He enlisted with the Royal Artillery in 1939, and according to newspaper reports he was a member of the Special Paratroop Forces and was mentioned in dispatches. He served in Burma and was killed in action in the Far East on 1ˢᵗ April 1945 aged 24 years. He was buried at the Chittagong War Cemetery, Bangladesh.

ENTERTAINMENTS AND CELEBRATIONS

Fairs and Markets

As a small community Burpham probably did not have much in the way of celebrations for big events until the 19th and 20th centuries, when the residents would travel to Guildford to watch processions or to join in revelry. The earliest entertainment that seems to have been on offer was St Catherine's Fair, which started in September 1308 when the Rector of St Nicolas obtained a charter from the King, Edward II. The Guildford Borough Council document St Catherine's Conservation Area Appraisal in 2005 explained that '*at first it was a purely commercial fair, dealing mainly in livestock and household goods. When hops began to be grown locally they were also sold to brewers. Increasingly though, recreation became an important element. By the early Victorian period the fair had become rough and disorderly, and official disapproval led to a rapid decline in its popularity. The fair lingered on until 1914, when it was last held.*

Under the terms of the charter all inhabitants "of the manor" were permitted to "sell ale on payment of a small acknowledgment to the Lord" on the Sunday before the fair began. This became known as "Tap-Up" Sunday. Normally a peaceful affair but in 1863 it ended in a riot. It was reported in The Times that "upward of 400 young fellows, many of them being low characters of Guildford, assembled in the village (St Catherine's) lining the road on either side, and when any peaceably inclined passenger approached they closed in and inflicted both insult and injury".' It is more than likely that

Burpham farmers took their livestock to St Catherine's Fairs over the years, but hopefully none of these young men causing trouble came from Burpham.

The last cattle market in North Street 1896 (Ben Darnton)

Guildford was given the ancient right to hold two annual fairs. From 1341 there was a May Fair, mainly for sheep and horses, and a Winter Fair, which was smaller and became more of an entertainment fair. By the 1920s there was little more than an annual funfair on Woodbridge Road.

Guildford had a cattle market on Tuesdays in the High Street in the 19th century until 1865 when it moved to North Street, along with the vegetable market (though this stopped in 1896 and was not revived until after the First World War). Then in 1896 the cattle market moved to Woodbridge Road, where the Law Courts

445

and Police Station are now located. Many people will remember the markets on Woodbridge Road, which ran until 1969, when they moved to Slyfield Industrial Estate, but these eventually stopped completely in about 2000. Markets were essentially for buying and selling, but would often be visited by families as the children found them very entertaining and exciting places to be. In the 21st century these have been replaced by monthly Farmers' Markets held on the High Street, offering a range of produce – but without livestock, along with the weekly market stalls in North Street.

Royal events

Queen Victoria's Diamond Jubilee - procession in North Street 1897
(Guildford Institute – PP/3B.35D)

These included coronations, jubilees and weddings, which were opportunities for celebration away from London as the majority of people were not able to travel there to join in. Guildford must

446

have enjoyed many of these events, but the earliest surviving records show the celebrations of Queen Victoria's Diamond Jubilee in 1897. The flags were put out and there was a procession along North Street, which was watched by thousands of people.

King Edward VII's Coronation Carnival procession on the High Street in 1902 (Guildford Institute – Box 18A - 106)

Then in 1902 Guildford, along with the rest of the country, celebrated the coronation of King Edward VII with a carnival procession on High Street and again the flags and bunting were out. At Ram Corner on Upper High Street a triumphal archway was constructed, with the words Happy and Glorious displayed across the top. How many people from the Burpham community travelled into the town to be part of these events?

King Edward had waited a very long time to become King and sadly he only reigned for nine years. In 1910, George V came to the throne and again the country celebrated his coronation in 1911 with more flags, carnival processions and the lighting of a bonfire on Pewley Down. David Rose, on the Guildford Dragon website, reported that day began with a peal of bells from St Nicolas Church at 3.30am and at 7.00am there was a gun salute from the Castle Keep, followed by a service of thanksgiving at St Saviour's Church. During the day there were promenade concerts and a dinner for 360 elderly people at the County and Borough Halls in North Street.

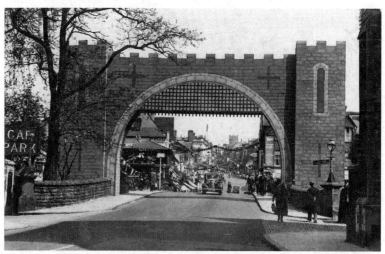

Wooden mock castle erected by the Town Bridge for King George V's Silver Jubilee in 1935 (Guildford Institute – Box 13B - 13)

Then in 1935, when the King celebrated his Silver Jubilee, the flags and bunting came out again, even though the country was in a deep depression. There were a number of events to mark the occasion, including an open-air service of thanksgiving held at the Guildford City Football Club's ground in Joseph's Road, a large carnival procession and buildings were illuminated at night. The day also saw the opening of the rock garden and boating pond in Stoke Park, named the Jubilee Gardens.

The coronation of King George VI in 1937 was not celebrated in the same way as previous monarchs, possibly because it came so soon after the abdication of King Edward VIII and possibly due to the situation in Europe. However, David Rose reported that the town was lit up at night, long narrow banners were hung from buildings and there was a 'Planting of the Coronation Oak near the paddling pool by His Worship the Mayor' in Stoke Park. Also there were 'midnight revels' in the High Street from 11.00pm to 1.00am.

In June 1953 came the coronation of Queen Elizabeth II and the weather was wet and wild. There are lots of photos from newspapers of the time showing people lined up in The Mall, dressed in raincoats and hats, steadfastly waiting to see their new Queen drive by. The highlight of the Guildford celebrations was a pageant in Stoke Park, but this was badly affected by the weather. In the afternoon the carnival procession came through Guildford town in the rain, heading towards the park. A torch-lit procession left the park for The Mount at 11.15pm, where Rover Scouts, the oldest section of Baden Powell's Scout's Association, lit a large beacon. Television sets were relatively rare at this time, but perhaps there were people in Burpham who had one and invited friends and family round to watch the coronation. There may have been other celebrations in the village but the only one found so far was the children on the police estate who had their own party with a fancy dress competition.

Coronation celebrations for the children on the Burpham police estate in 1953 (A Dore)

One of the first BCA newsletters reported that in August 1975 there was a Family Field Event, held on Sutherland Memorial Park, with friendly family games and refreshments. 1977 brought celebrations for the Queen's Silver Jubilee and street parties were held up and down the country. Burpham enjoyed a week of events including a Disco for young teenagers in the Village Hall; a

450

Grand Jubilee Buffet Dance at George Abbot School; the Jubilee Show in Sutherland Memorial Park; a Bangers & Mash Disco in the Green Man car park; and a Children's Tea Party also in the Green Man car park.

Children dressed in Stone Age costume for the Silver Jubilee Pageant at Shalford Park 1977, processing down High Street (Surrey Advertiser)

Jeff Harkman took a cine film of some of the proceedings, which showed a marching band coming down New Inn Lane, stalls set up on Sutherland Memorial Park and also the children's tea party in the Green Man car park. The newsletter reported that the fete and children's party were well attended. Rain held off long enough to make the events memorable occasions. Souvenir mugs were presented to all those who entered the fancy dress parade. However, the Disco and Dance were poorly attended. '*A very enjoyable evening was missed by many!*' Apparently there was also a street party in Paddocks Road.

Children's Tea Party in the Green Man car park 1977 (J Harkman)

In July 1981 Prince Charles married Lady Diana Spencer and the whole country enjoyed the spectacle either on television or by putting on their own street parties. The Surrey Advertiser reported on local events. Burpham organised a street party, which was held in front of the shops at Kingpost Parade. Brian Wheeler remembered that there was a Tug of War between the

Green Man and the Anchor & Horseshoes, which took place on the newly opened A3. Apparently the road was empty, possibly due to the royal wedding, so the contest moved down to use that open space. However, the police came down and reprimanded them.

Queen's Golden Jubilee Tea Party held at Burpham Primary School in 2002 (D Holmes)

A BCA newsletter in 1983 recorded that the 1st Burpham Festival was planned for April/May 1984. This would include a Fun Run, Disco and Spring Fair on Sutherland Memorial Park. Apparently it was a great success. In 2002 the children of Burpham Primary School celebrated the Queen's Golden Jubilee with their own street party, with refreshments and flags, balloons and bunting.

Everyone dressed in red, white or blue and the children made their own crowns or jubilee hats.

The summer of 2012 was busy with both the Diamond Jubilee celebrations as well as the London Olympics. At the primary school, the children and staff were all given a special commemorative mug to remind them of this special occasion – it will be many years before another monarch reaches this milestone.

Merrow Lane children celebrating the end of WW2 (A Keane)

Of course, royal celebrations were not the only opportunities for people to enjoy themselves. At the end of the First World War the Burpham Primary School Log Book recorded that there was an extra week's holiday at the end of the summer 1919 *'being in Celebration of Peace'*. Then in late September the school was closed for an afternoon because it was *'hired to entertain demobilised soldiers of the village'*. Perhaps the church held a

454

service of thanksgiving as well at some point. There were many newspaper reports of people celebrating the end of the Second World War in 1945, but little has been found to show what was happening in Burpham. However, Ann Keane, who lived on Merrow Lane, remembered that a street party was held there to celebrate VE Day. This was during the day for the children and then there was an evening party for the adults, with a bonfire.

In 1984 the Surrey Advertiser reported on the new Burpham Festival, the first of its kind run by the community for the community. The aim was to satisfy the needs of a growing residential area in danger of being split by commercial development and traffic problems, and to regain the village atmosphere before it was too late. There was a three mile fun run for all ages, followed by various events involving the whole community, local schools and a teenage disco. The climax was to be the Spring Fair, held on Sutherland Playing Field. Money raised would go towards future development of the playing field. Ian Lapworth won the fun run with a very good time of 19 minutes.

In 2000, Burpham celebrated the millennium in great style, with a fete held in the park and a car boot sale in the car park. A fun run started the day. The Mayor of Guildford opened the fete, which included stalls around the site, handicraft displays, Punch and Judy, barbecue and a balloon race.

A lasting reminder of the celebrations was The Burpham Tapestry, designed by Pauline Rawlins and Marjory Mingo, made by people aged from 10 to 80 from around the village, depicting most of

455

the important buildings and locations in Burpham. Music and entertainment was provided by the Army Cadet Drums, Guildford Opera Company, and SW Surrey Concert Band, amongst others.

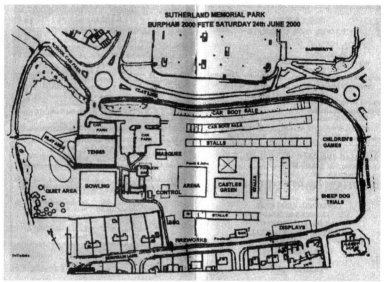

Site plan for Burpham 2000 Grand Fete on Sutherland Memorial Park (Burpham 2000)

Burpham Homes, which were off New Inn Lane, held annual fetes in their gardens. Doreen Marshall remembered manning the sweet trolley at some of these. Joyce Tate remembered that the actress Joyce Grenfell opened the fete one year and the television personality and artist Tony Hart another time. Mrs Hopewell, who lived in Abbotswood, held garden parties, whilst the Mothers' Union and Women's Institute also held events. In 1993 the BCA reported about traffic concerns in New Inn Lane and wondered if Burpham would ever hold a fete again.

Burpham Tapestry in St Luke' Church

The Burpham Church's Free and For Nothing Community Day has been running for several years. It started as three days in August in Sutherland Memorial Park, offering games and activities for young people, as well as refreshments and enjoyment for families in Burpham. The event has reduced to one day annually in the park, but there are still lots of activities on offer. In 2016 there were football and tennis, video games, a treasure hunt, wet obstacle course, pony rides, classic cars, refreshments and lots

457

more. A true community event as it is all free for anyone in the area to join in and enjoy.

Coaching marathon in Burpham 1957 (M Grover)

One of the benefits of being next to Stoke Parish is that Stoke Park is within walking distance. Not only does it provide a lovely environment for walking, but it also has lots of entertainment on offer during the year. Stoke Park was bought by Guildford Corporation in 1925 from H E Budgett, to be used for recreational purposes. It had previously been used for the Royal Counties Show and in 1872 the celebrations for Queen Victoria's 35th anniversary of her coronation were held there. The Lido opened in 1935 and has recently been refurbished and improved. The Wild Wood Adventure in Peacock Wood offers rope bridges, wobbly crossings and zip wires amongst other challenges for those who wish to brave the heights of the tree tops.

Historical pageants have been organised around the country for over 100 years. The first, in 1925, was staged at the Theatre

Royal in North Street; in 1944 one took place at Guildford Technical College; in 1953 there was the Coronation pageant in Stoke Park. In 1957, as part of Guildford's year-long charter celebrations, about 700 people took part in the pageant held in Shalford Park. Many people remembered participating in this event as young children. Vincent Tickner recalled that he was meant to be one of them, but '*I was excluded because I was not prepared to hold hands with the girls. At a later age I would probably have enjoyed it.*' In 1968, for another pageant held in Shalford Park, about 1,000 performers and 100 riders with horses took part.

The Surrey County Show, organised by Surrey County Agricultural Society, has been coming to Stoke Park almost every year since 1961, usually on the late May bank holiday Monday. Many of the Burpham farmers would have shown their livestock there, possibly winning prizes. In recent years the show has offered many other forms of entertainment besides the agricultural show and provides a great day out for the family – as long as the weather is kind. Prince Philip was the first patron of the Surrey County Agricultural Society and the Queen was patron during her Silver Jubilee year, though it doesn't seem that either of them ever attended a show at Stoke Park. Over the years there have been many main ring attractions at the shows, including the Red Devils Free Fall Display, various massed bands, sheep dog displays, Cossacks and hot air balloons as well as seeing all the livestock and retail areas.

Police dog display team at Burpham Carnival c. 1962 (M Grover)

In the 1960s and 1970s there was also the Guildford Town Show, a two day horticultural display with show jumping, on Stoke Park, held annually around the end of August or early September. An artist called Joseph Acheson painted a picture called The Royal Horse Show Guildford 1952, possibly the same as the photo on the next page. The Guildford Carnivals usually ended up at Stoke Park, with lots of floats created by Guildford businesses as well as bands and processions. There have been a number of comments on the Guildford Dragon website suggesting that these should be reinstated.

Stoke Park is the location for the Guildford Lions' Fireworks Night, with bonfire and funfair, each November. There have also been various circus events held next to the Spectrum car park. The use of Stoke Park for events goes back to the 19th century. A newspaper advertisement told of the 13th Surrey Rifle Volunteers holding their Annual Fete in the park in 1864. The event included sports and games, music, refreshments and dancing in the evening. For over 20 years the Guilfest music festivals took place in the park each summer, bringing a wide range of music, theatre and other entertainments to the community. Unfortunately bad weather and the resultant poor ticket sales brought the event to an end, but hopefully there will be more festivals in the future. In recent years, that baton has been taken up by local arts venue, The Boileroom. Its 'Always the Sun' festival is in its second year at the time of writing.

Royal Counties Show c. 1952

In 2012 the Olympic Torch Relay came to Guildford, finishing at the park. One of the torch bearers came from Burpham – Dr Sandra Domizio - who was chosen for her fundraising efforts and her involvement in the Burpham community. She took up doing triathlons earlier in the year and raised £10,000 by completing a Half Ironman event in support of the Haven charity, supporting those with breast cancer. This wasn't the first time that the Olympic Torch had visited Guildford. In 1948 it came

Sandra Domizio carrying the Olympic Torch through Guildford, outside Debenhams, 2012 (S Domizio)

past the driveway of Gosden Hill Farm on its way from the coast to London. Then in 2015 the Armed Forces Day came to Guildford and again Stoke Park was packed with people enjoying a sunny day watching fantastic displays.

The Spectrum Leisure Centre provides a wide range of sports and other leisure activities, again easily accessible from Burpham. There are swimming pools, ice rink, ten pin bowling facilities, as well as an athletics track, squash courts and a gymnasium.

Up in Merrow, the Guildford Races were held from 1701 to 1870, according to Helen Chapman Davies' book Guildford's Hidden History. *'Flat and jump racing took place annually over three days in Whitsun Week, though it was not until 1727 that Guildford's race meeting was officially recognised. Guildford Golf Club's eighteen hole course now covers the site of the horse race course, and the grandstand is believed to have been on the south side of the golf course, at its western end, a few yards from the 12th green.'*

George I stayed at Clandon House while he visited the races. William III had given a King's Plate of 100 guineas as a prize, which was re-named the Queen's Plate during Queen Victoria's reign. The book tells that horse racing at Guildford began to decline from the late 1700s and after the Napoleonic Wars Epsom and Ascot became more accessible and popular. The grandstand was pulled down in 1854 and burned outside Holy Trinity Church during one of the Guildford Guy Riots. Interestingly, Jim Miller referred to a property auction sale of 1877, held at the White Hart in Guildford, which stated that the locality commanded *'most extensive views in all directions'*, including the Grand Stand at Newland's Corner, on the racecourse. Perhaps the auction house was not aware that it had been pulled down over 20 years before. During the Second World War there was a Prisoner of War camp on part of the site. In modern days the area is now Guildford Golf Club, which is probably used by some of the keen Burpham golfers.

Huntsman and hounds starting off from Guildford High Street 1895
(Guildford Institute – Box 21 - 1)

Burpham residents could travel into Guildford to enjoy a wider variety of entertainments, many of which are no longer legal. In medieval times bull-baiting was provided for the amusement of the people of Guildford, sanctioned by the Corporation and this continued at least until the reign of Henry VIII. Cockfighting was also popular, held in the cockpit on the site of the Red Lion Inn in Market Street, which was let for 15 guineas for the week of Guildford Races. Rural Britain Then and Now recorded that hunting had been a popular rural activity since time immemorial, possibly starting in Guildford with the King's Hunting Lodge, providing food, recreation and income for many people. In the

464

16th and 17th centuries deer and hare were hunted, but by the 18th century it was mainly foxes. There is no record of a hunt based out of Burpham, so local supporters would have joined Guildford huntsmen.

In the 20th and 21st centuries Burpham people go into Guildford to enjoy a wide range of entertainments, including theatre, cinema, bars and nightclubs. However, in the late 1800s the Borough and County Halls on North Street became the town's main assembly rooms, according to the Arthur Lloyd Music Hall and Theatre History website. There was a gaslight stage, which allowed theatrical performances, and it was suggested that the first cinematic exhibition in Guildford was there in 1896.

The first purpose-built theatre came to the town in 1912 with the opening of the Theatre Royal on North Street, which offered a broad range of entertainments for the next 20 years, closing in 1932. When the Surrey Assize Courts moved to Kingston upon Thames in the 1920s the Borough Hall was used as a multi purpose hall for stage shows and music, becoming the Guildford (Repertory) Theatre in 1946, but was destroyed by fire in 1963. However, in May 1965 the Yvonne Arnaud Theatre opened in a blaze of glory and continues to this day to bring the joys of theatre to local residents, whilst since 1997 the Electric Theatre has provided a centre for amateur dramatics and music, which will hopefully continue under the new ownership.

The Civic Hall was built in 1962, but is now replaced with G Live, bringing music and more theatre to the town. The first cinema for Guildford was West's Picture Palace, on the site of Constitution

The Skating Rink on Woodbridge Rd, c. 1910 (Guildford Institute – Box 11B - 32)

Hall at the top of the High Street, in 1909. The Plaza Cinema, originally called the Picture Palace, on Onslow Street opened in 1910, but closed in 1956. There were nearly 2,000 seats and ticket prices were 6d or 1s for the balcony, or 3d for adults in the stalls. The Electric Cinema in Woodbridge Road opened in 1911, converted from a skating rink, and later changed its name to the Guildford Cinema and Café in the 1950s, then The Astor in the 1960s, and finally Studio 1 & 2 in the 1970s. From 1922 - 1965 the Tunsgate Picture Playhouse showed films in Guildford, including the first ever 'talkie' – Al Jolsen in 'The Singing Fool' in 1929. The Odeon opened on Upper High Street in 1935 in a building with lovely Art Deco features. There were 1,000 seats and ticket prices for the Grand Opening were 1s 6d each. For 60 years it was a popular cinema, which also provided a venue for the many pop stars whose concerts were attractions for teenagers in Guildford in the 1960s and 1970s, including The Beatles in 1963. It closed in 1996 when the new multiplex opened off Bedford Road.

For many years the only indoor swimming pool in Guildford was the Castle Street Baths. Many people remembered going there with their schools and especially recalled the 'basket room', where people left their clothes in wire baskets, and how cold it was there. It closed in 1972 when the Sports Centre opened in Bedford Road. This closed in 1993 when the Spectrum was built and the old site was converted to become the new cinema multiplex.

However, entertainment for the Burpham Community cannot be complete without mention of the Kingpost Restaurant and Swimming Pool. The first mention of this in Kelly's Directories was in 1934, when the manager was Mr E Yatman. Presumably it was built around then, as there was nothing shown on that site in the OS maps for 1920. Norman Hamilton's booklet said that there had been an 'Astolat garden shop' on the site in the early 1900s, but no evidence has been found to support this - the Astolat garden shops appear to have been in Peasmarsh. Perhaps a tenuous link could be Arthurian? The name Astolat (identified as Guildford, in Sir Thomas Malory's book Le Morte d'Arthur) might link to Hugh <u>Lancelot</u> Robson, who lived in Orchard Cottage and was a fruit grower. Perhaps he sold fruit from his orchard on that site?

In 1936 a newspaper report publicised the grand opening of The Kingpost Country Club, which included music and dancing, as well as a cabaret show and a table d'hote dinner. Apparently under 'entirely new management', the club invited people to join and benefit from the facilities. Members of the Country Club would receive free entry to the swimming pool for that first season, subscriptions were £1 1s for gentlemen, 10s 6d for ladies, and £2 2s for a family. It also mentioned an 18 hole putting course. However, by August 1936 there were problems as the Country Club was struck off the register and disqualified for one year, with the club secretary and manager fined a total of £70 plus costs, for offences under the Licensing Act. Presumably this was the nail in the coffin for the owners as the property was put up for sale in 1937.

Newspaper advertisement for grand opening 1936 (F Phillipson)

The sales particulars gave a detailed description of the site. '*The Kingpost Restaurant and Swimming Pool. This property consists of two acres on a corner site facing the London Road and New Inn Lane. The road frontage to London Road is 270 feet and the frontage to New Inn Lane is 165 feet. The main building and the Restaurant has a sale shop right of the entrance and left is a snack bar, kitchens, and a store room, and adjoining is a large shed previously used as a garage, which has a cement floor and is fitted as a secondary Restaurant for serving teas and refreshments to the Swimming Pool during the time this is open.*

The Swimming Pool is 65 feet by 32 feet; depth 8 feet at one end and 3 feet at the other, enclosed by rails right and left of the pool, which obscure the bathing huts. There are 40 commodious bathing huts and two sets of lavatories – one on each side of the pool. There are two spring boards of the latest pattern, and high diving board. There is underwater lighting and also flood lighting. In a building adjoining the pool is the filter plant, installed by the Turnover Filter Company and it is of the same pattern as at the Lido, Guildford. There is a pay-box and turnstiles and storage for towels and bathing costumes.

There is a well laid out rockery at one end of the pool and sloping grass banks for sunbathing at the other end. The gardens of the Restaurant consist of well laid out flower beds and an 18 hole putting course; a sunk garden surrounded by trellis, and the pool premises are divided from the Restaurant garden by a high ornamental trellis.

The seating accommodation inside the Restaurant is capable of seating 70 people on the ground floor and the gallery, and there is a large paved terrace, access to which is through windows opening to the ground from the Restaurant, and seating accommodation for an extra 80 or 90 people.

There is a large car park sufficient to hold nearly 100 cars. Price £5,000.'

Kingpost Restaurant and Swimming Pool c. late 1930s (D Rose)

An eight foot deep pool doesn't seem very safe for diving off a high diving board – but health & safety clearly wasn't such an issue in those days. Michael Hunt remembered that when the pool had to be emptied the water came out onto New Inn Lane.

Jean Menzies, amongst others, remembered that it cost 2s 6d (half a crown) to get into the Swimming Pool, which seems to have been quite expensive for the time.

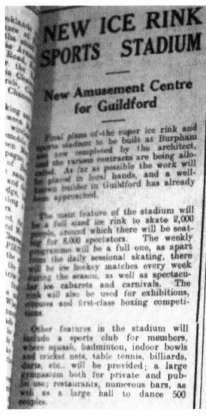

NEW ICE RINK SPORTS STADIUM

New Amusement Centre for Guildford

Final plans of the super ice rink and sports stadium to be built at Burpham are now completed by the architect, and the various contracts are being allotted. As far as possible the work will be placed in local hands, and a well-known builder in Guildford has already been approached.

The main feature of the stadium will be a full sized ice rink to skate 2,000 people, around which there will be seating for 3,000 spectators. The weekly programme will be a full one, as apart from the daily sessional skating, there will be ice hockey matches every week during the season, as well as spectacular ice cabarets and carnivals. The rink will also be used for exhibitions, circuses and first-class boxing competitions.

Other features in the stadium will include a sports club for members, where squash, badminton, indoor bowls and cricket nets, table tennis, billiards, darts, etc., will be provided; a large gymnasium both for private and public use; restaurants, numerous bars, as well as a large hall to dance 500 couples.

Newspaper advertisement for new ice rink and sports stadium 1936 (F Phillipson)

By 1938 Kelly's Directory listed CP & H Fountain as the owners of the Kingpost Restaurant and it seemed that they had big ideas to develop the property. Cyril and his brother Herbert came from Odiham in Hampshire, but in 1935 Cyril had been working for the CID branch of the Guildford Borough Police and, according to the electoral register was living at the Police Offices on Guildford's North Street.

Frank Phillipson's research has unearthed even more details regarding Norman Hamilton's interesting story about the next few years at the Kingpost. In May 1939 two companies were registered – Athenæum (Ice Rinks) Ltd and Guildford Athenæum Ltd. The directors for these were Lord Cecil Charles Douglas, Cyril Percy

471

Fountain and Herbert William Fountain. Lord Cecil Douglas was the younger son of the 10th Marquess of Queensbury and his uncle was Lord Alfred Douglas, a poet and Oscar Wilde's lover. Lord Douglas was a director for a number of companies, as well as getting involved in business ventures including construction, travel and running a laundry.

Shortly after registration, there were newspaper advertisements for The Guildford Ice Rink and Sports Stadium. Facilities included ice skating, ice hockey and ice shows, curling, boxing, badminton, squash, indoor bowls, cricket nets, dancing, table tennis and theatre. There were even plans to run a circus during the season. One newspaper reported '*further, it is intended to incorporate a gas-proof shelter in the stadium, which could be used for local ARP exercises and demonstrations. This can also be used for indoor bowls, skittles, darts, cricket practice nets, etc, when not otherwise required*'. Clearly someone had done some forward planning, just in case the situation in Europe did not improve.

Enquiries were directed to Guildford Athenæum Ltd at The King Post, London Road. With the benefit of hindsight this was clearly not an auspicious time to start up such a venture, as war was declared in September 1939. However, this was a project ahead of its time, planning to provide very similar facilities to those in the Guildford Spectrum 50 years later.

Again there were problems with getting the business off the ground and Athenæum (Ice Rinks) Ltd was struck off the

Companies List in 1940. After re-registering, the accounts filed with Companies House over the next few years showed that nothing happened after the first flurry of activity. Shares in the company were offered at one shilling each, and the directors took 10,000 each. It seems that only seven other shares were sold, so the required money for development was not raised. Lord Cecil Douglas resigned as Chairman in 1950, presumably realising that this was not going to be the successful investment project that had been anticipated. Guildford Athenæum Ltd was struck off the Companies List in 1953, being dissolved in 1954, and that was the end of that project.

However, in 1948 there was a planning application, made by W Gerald Hull and George W Olive to develop the site – perhaps they had bought the site from the Fountain brothers, but no evidence has been found to support this. It is not clear how the two development projects were linked, but the Athenæum company was still in place, with its three directors, at the time of this new application. This proposal was to erect a cinema, shops with maisonettes over, a swimming pool and car park at The Kingpost. The pool was already there and 13 years later the shops with maisonettes and car parking would be built, but the idea of a cinema never saw the light of day. Three months later Guildford Borough Council withheld consent and the project died.

During the war the Kingpost was used for training in Civil Defence and after the war Kelly's Directories just recorded the restaurant until 1953. In the following years the building was variously PSG Coachworks, Wilcox Coachworks, Technical Designs and then

Mid-Surrey Caravans from about 1969. The swimming pool closed around the time of the Second World War, but was not emptied. Apparently it was shut for health and safety reasons after a child drowned there and Dr Parkin was responsible for getting it closed. Many people have remembered sneaking into the site as youngsters and catching newts in the water in the following years. Allen Mead remembered going in to collect tadpoles one day, but someone had complained and the police arrived to tell them off. Others remembered going in for 'skinny-dipping'. Maps up to 1961 seemed to show the swimming pool, but by 1970 it had gone, now in its place is Grosvenor Court.

The Kingpost in 2016

LAW AND ORDER

Guildford Castle Keep, the county gaol for many years

In Medieval times the Guildford Castle Keep was the county gaol for Surrey and Sussex, then the gaol moved to Quarry Street and lastly South Hill, until in 1851 all prisoners were moved to the new gaol at Wandsworth. Although the House of Correction was demolished, the former Governor's House is still there, now called South Hall on Castle Hill. Courts of Assizes heard the most serious cases, which after 1971 became the Crown Court; Quarter Sessions were the local county courts, held four times a year, and became the Crown Court; Petty Sessions were where Justices of the Peace dealt with minor offences and are now known as

Magistrates' Courts. Justices of the Peace had responsibility for licensing alehouses, and would have to be assured of the alehouse keepers' good behaviour, as well as trying offences such as poaching, assaults, vagrancy and theft. The Justices were usually important members of the community, such as clergy, gentry or retired army officers.

Until the late 18th century the ducking stool, according to Russell's History of Guildford, was a punishment for scolds (women who spoke their minds) that took place at Millmead in Guildford. Executions were carried out at Tunsgate and then The Mount, but in 1776 three men were executed, by hanging, on Ganghill Common. James Potter was a highwayman, Christopher Ellis was a burglar and Frederick William Gregg had committed robbery with violence. An alternative to the death penalty was transportation, to America or Australia, and was usually for the more serious crimes, but could include theft if it was a second offence. William Elkins, of the Guildford brewing family that owned the Green Man in Burpham, was Mayor and Chief Magistrate for the town in the early 19th century. He was known as Billy Whip, because it was during his mayoralty in 1830 that the last prisoner was whipped up the High Street, tied to a cart tail.

Prison sentences, to a local House of Correction, could be expected for theft, desertion of a family and non-payment of maintenance for illegitimate children. In 1780 Sarah Otway of Worplesdon robbed the wife of a private soldier in the Jamaica Volunteers of *'two caps, an handkerchief, an apron and sundry pieces of cloth*' and was committed to the Guildford House of Correction. Sarah Wilkins stole various bits of clothing from Hannah Loveland in 1784 and was committed to the Guildford House of Correction where she was to be '*privately whipt and kept to hard labour for two months in Mr Benton's custody*'. Henry Cooke was charged with having '*deserted and left four of his children, whereby they are to become chargeable to the parish of Worplesdon*'. He was sentenced to hard labour for one month in the Newington House of Correction. Whereas William Smith was found guilty of getting Sophia Johnson pregnant, and as the child was likely to be born a bastard it would fall to the Parish to help. William was sent to the Guildford House of Correction until he could come up with the money for maintenance - though if he was in prison it is hard to see how he could raise the money.

Until the mid-1800s the Parish Constable was the main person in charge of law and order for the community. It was an honorary office and in some parishes would have been a time-consuming role. Roger Hunt's Rural Britain Then & Now said that they were '*usually drawn from the ranks of farmers and yeomen, it was the Constable's responsibility to bring lawbreakers to court and to punish miscreants, sometimes with whipping or by administering the ducking stool*'. Legislation in 1405 said that all communities had to have stocks for punishment, but there is no evidence of these in Burpham – perhaps they were in Worplesdon? There were also nightwatchmen who worked for the Parish Constables. From 1837 there was a duty for counties to form their own police forces and the Surrey Constabulary, established in 1851, as well as the Guildford police force, would have been the law enforcement organisations for Surrey.

Many villages had a 'village bobby' – a well-known figure, who usually rode his bike around the community and could be relied upon to give any children who misbehaved a quiet but effective warning. Burpham doesn't seem to have had a village bobby as such, living in a police house, but with the coming of the traffic centre and the police housing on the New Inn Farm estate in the 1950s perhaps there wasn't the same need. John Pidgeon and Allan Mead remembered PC Oliver, Derek Oliver's father, as the bobby on the beat around Burpham in the 1950s/60s. There wasn't a Police Box in the village and no mobile phones in those days, so he would ride his bike from one phone box to the next, waiting at each for a call from the police station to get his instructions.

Drunken and disorderly behaviour was a common occurrence and in 1914 Henry Day, a labourer of Burpham, was fined 10 shillings for having been drunk and disorderly in Waterden Road at midnight on a Saturday night. He disturbed the whole neighbourhood with his filthy language.

In 1916 Joseph Bentley of Burpham was summonsed for having ridden his bicycle on London Road without front or rear lights, but the case was dismissed. In 1944 the Surrey Advertiser reported on a case of drunk driving. A motorist, Arthur Woodhatch, from Rudgwick, hit a stationary bus that was stopped on the London Road, just past the Green Man, and was killed.

478

The inquest decided it was an accidental death after the man had been drinking and then lost control of the car.

By 1953 traffic centres had been set up at Burpham and four other towns around Surrey. There were three cars and a number of motorbikes based at the Coltsfoot Drive centre. By the early 1970s it was felt that improvements were needed, but Guildford Borough Council opposed plans for a two-storey building. Following changed plans and the Chief Constable's undertaking that, except for emergency calls, all traffic would go in and out via Burnet Avenue and New Inn Lane, the Council approved the application. In 1978 the Surrey Advertiser reported that, having demolished the original building, the new and improved Burpham traffic centre was contributing to a boost in staff morale.

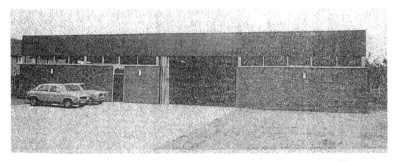

Burpham Traffic Centre new building 1978 (Daily Advertiser)

There were 53 staff based there, highly skilled and highly regarded within the force. By then there were ten patrol cars and 13 BMW motorcycles, out on the road most of each day, clocking up over 1,000 miles each week. The main objective was to improve road safety, assisting with the free flow of traffic and to

479

prevent accidents. However, in 1975 one of the tasks for these officers, in six vehicles, was to accompany the armoured van carrying the men charged in connection with the Guildford pub bombings from holding cells in Godalming to the Magistrates' court in Ward Street every Monday.

In 1975 the Daily Advertiser reported that among the 60 officers working at the Burpham Traffic Centre there were three pairs of brothers. Peter and David Hills, Ian and Tony Parrott, and Derek and Bob Cooper.

Three sets of brothers from Burpham Traffic Centre 1975 (Daily Advertiser)

Traffic has been a problem in Burpham for many years. The by-pass reduced some of the volume, but the increased number of vehicles on the road has resulted in frequent queues (especially near Aldi). In 1976 the Surrey Advertiser reported on traffic counts being carried out along Burpham Lane after parents and staff from Burpham Primary School petitioned for a halt to heavy lorries using the lane as a short cut and thus endangering the children. In later years cars have used the Weylea Farm estate as a short cut through to Burpham Lane and Clay Lane. For a while a Vehicle Activated Sign (VAS) was placed near to the blind bend by Pimm's Row, in order to remind cars of the speed limit. The school employed a 'Lollipop Lady' to safely cross the children from the park to the church.

Burpham seems to have been a fairly law-abiding community and few reports of crimes have been found. In September 1942 the Surrey Advertiser reported that three boys, from an approved school, were in Juvenile Court accused of breaking into Cornfield Cottage, Burpham Lane & stealing a gold ring and home safe containing £2 10s. They admitted this and also breaking into Goose Rye Cottage, on Whitmore Common. The eldest lad, who had absconded eight times, was remanded for transfer to a senior home, one was taken back and the other was remanded for another school to be found. In 1999 an armed robbery took place at Sainsbury's.

In 2004 the BCA archives recorded that there had been ongoing problems of abuse by youngsters against Mr Tony, who had been selling ice creams in Sutherland Memorial Park for 12 years. It seems that there was an altercation and one of the boys told his father, which resulted in Mr Tony being arrested and going to court. However, most of the community were very supportive of the ice cream seller and felt that he was treated very badly.

The BBC reported in 2006 that a brick had been dropped from the bridge on Clay Lane, smashing the sunroof of a car travelling in the middle lane of the A3. In 2010 there was a rape in the wooded area off London Road.

The Church of the Holy Spirit on New Inn Lane was targeted for an arson attack in May 2012. Having broken into the building, through a door at the back, the arsonist made a pile of hymn books and other papers, which was set alight, and various other property was damaged. A teenager was arrested and charged with arson.

Immigration Enforcement has occasionally been an issue and in 2013 the Guildford Dragon reported that police and immigration officers 'swooped on the car wash at Sainsbury's Burpham store... arresting several suspects.' These had either overstayed their visas, were working in breach of their visa conditions or had entered the country illegally.

In 2015 one of the newer houses in Burpham was closed down after evidence showed that it was being used for the unlawful use, supply and production of Class A drugs, together with drugs related anti-social behaviour. In early 2016 vandals smashed the windows of the Tom Thumb Nursery and set it on fire, resulting in the nursery closing for a week while repairs and cleaning up took place. Later in 2016 there was an incident of grievous bodily harm with intent, dangerous driving and damaging property when a young man was hit by a van in Bower's Farm Drive. The driver was sentenced to over five years in prison.

According to the Police.UK website crimes in Burpham and Merrow during 2016 averaged out at about equal instances of all crime types. The website breaks down crime into 14 different types, including burglary, theft, drugs, public order and shoplifting. In November 2016 there were 56 incidents, 25 of which were in Burpham, whereas the previous year there were 38 incidents. Perhaps things are getting better.

IMMIGRATION AND SETTLERS

Great Britain has been a popular destination for people from all over the world for centuries. Before the Romans came in 55 BC, there were the Ancient or Celtic Britons. After the Romans came the Angles, Saxons and Jutes from Germany and Jutland; Vikings from Scandinavia; and the Normans from France. The Picts and the Celts, from Scotland, Wales and Ireland, have always migrated backwards and forwards between their home countries and England. In the 17th century, thousands of Huguenots fled France and came to England. The development of the East India Company brought Indian and Asian immigrants to Britain, then the spread of the British Empire provided opportunities for people from countries such as Australia and New Zealand, Canada, Africa and India to move to this country. However, the greatest change in immigration took place in the 20th century, especially after the second world war.

From the late 1940s onwards there has been an increase in the number of immigrants from Eastern Europe, many of whom were trying to escape from Soviet dominated homelands. Thousands of Asians living in Uganda were expelled by Idi Amin in 1972 and over 27,000 came to Britain. Since then there have been many examples of people fleeing their countries from wars, terrorism and persecution. It is hard to think of anyone being a 'pure blood British' person with such comings and goings over the last 2,000 years. Britain is an ethnic melting pot and in recent years the make-up of Burpham has been a reflection of this.

484

There has been a lot of movement of people both into and out of Burpham over the years. The 1841 census only recorded whether people were born in Surrey or not, and of the 123 people living in the hamlet (not including Jacobs Well) 49 were born in another county. There was movement within the county, especially as agricultural labourers moved from farm to farm, depending where the work could be found. In 1851 all the men working at Bower's Mill had moved into the area, from Sussex, Godalming, Frensham and Cranleigh. Only three Heads of Households were actually born in Worplesdon, but the most distant places of birth were still in the south and south east of England.

In the 1861 census there were signs of more travelling. Joseph Choat, the farmer of New Inn Farm, came from Thurlow in Suffolk, while his wife, Fanny, was born in France. It was interesting to note that the labourers at Winterhill Farm on the night of the census also came from Thurlow, so perhaps Joseph ran both farms or brought his workers with him? At Weylea Farm, Peter Watson, the farmer, came from Scotland. By 1871, there was more evidence of movement around the country with people from Wiltshire, Somerset, Essex, Liverpool and Brighton. William Collis, a miller's carter living in Pimm's Row, was married to Christine, born in Denmark but naturalised as a British Subject. While Catherine Ward, a lady of private means living at Weylea, was American, born in New York, but also naturalised as a British Subject.

In 1891, Charles Gunner, aged 15 years, was a lad working at Burpham Court Farm, seemingly with no family, and he was born aboard a ship in Gibraltar. Possibly his father was working on the ship and had his family with him. Celestia Coldwell, wife of the artist Edmund and living at Marlyn's Cottage, was born in the United States of America. Henry Smith, farmer at New Inn Farm, came from Gloucestershire, but his wife, Margaret, was born in Scotland. Thomas Tigg, a miller living in Pimm's Row, was married to Eliza, who was born in St Petersburg.

In 1901 Burpham had people from all over England, with the occasional representation from Scotland and Wales, along with Sarah Kemp, who was born in the Cape of Good Hope, South Africa. Sarah lived with her husband George, their five children and her father-in-law at Burpham Cottage, probably on London Road but the census does not make the exact location clear.

By 1911, again people were moving around the country and settling in Burpham for a while. There were three people who had been born abroad. Theodore Hudson Smith was living with his uncle and aunt, Harry and Annie Cutt, in The Bungalow on Burpham Lane. Theodore was a civil servant and had been born in China - Tali in the Province of Yunan. He was a British Subject due to his parents being British. At Weylea Adriana Greenhill was working as a Companion for Georgiana Richardson, and she had been born in Bermuda. At The Paddocks, Mary Cristobel Norris was living with her father Arthur Rawson Birks and her daughter Jean. Mary was born in Burma, presumably when her father was working there as a Judge in the Indian Civil Service.

486

Few families seem to have stayed in Burpham for more than two or three generations, though the Heath family are an exception. From George, born just before 1700, seven generations have been recorded living in the village up to the early 1900s. Running the Anchor & Horseshoes and being the village blacksmith made them important figures in community life. However, it is rare to find a family that has consistently lived here for more than 100 years, although there are several families who have lived in and around Burpham, Worplesdon and Stoke parishes, such as Gunner and Christmas - names that keep cropping up. Another family started with Silas Kilby (who came from Bedfordshire), and included the Durrants, the Braybrooks and the Kemps, many of whom attended Burpham Primary School.

No other information is available in the same way as census records (which at present are only available up to 1911) to tell of people's origins, and the 1939 list didn't ask for nationality or place of birth.

One of the migrations to the area was when the Ministry of Agriculture, Food and Fisheries (MAFF), later called DEFRA, moved to Guildford. MAFF had been based in Colwyn Bay, in Wales, but a lot of the staff transferred to Guildford in 1949. Many of these were Welsh speakers and a great number of them lived in Merrow and Burpham. At the time of the 2011 Census the Office of National Statistics (ONS) reported that there were four Welsh speakers in Burpham and several people have remembered knowing more in the community. Apparently it took a long time for the people from Colwyn Bay to integrate into their new homes, and coaches were organised for families to go back for holidays and visits for many years.

The ONS records for 2011 also showed the different languages spoken in Burpham at the time of the census and 13 were recorded in addition to English. These were Arabic, Chinese, German, Hungarian, Italian, Persian/Farsi, Polish, Portuguese, Russian, Spanish, Swedish, Turkish and Welsh. There were 32 people who could not speak English at all. In 2017 the Ofsted report for Burpham Primary School noted that 20% of the pupils had English as an additional language.

The 2011 census statistics show that 4,767 of the total 5,696 people in Burpham were born in Britain; 35 were born in the Irish Republic; 251 were born elsewhere in Europe; and 643 were born in other parts of the world (including 306 in the Middle East and Asia). This spread of ethnic origin also brought diversification of religion, with Buddhist, Hindu, Jewish, Muslim and Sikh representation in the community.

From being a small hamlet in 1882, with a population of 337 people, Burpham had grown to having 5,696 (of all ages) in 2011. That census recorded that Burpham covered 231 hectares with a density of 24.6 people per hectare (one hectare = 10,000 square metres or 2.47 acres). What will the population look like if the proposal to build nearly 2,000 houses on Gosden Hill Farm is agreed?

Why do so many people come to Burpham? Possibly because it is such a convenient place from which to commute to London or the South Coast. But also because of the organisations based in the area, which attract people from far and wide for employment and education, such as the Royal Surrey County Hospital, Surrey University, Surrey Research Park and other businesses. There is an impact on schools as some children arrive without any knowledge of the language in which they will be taught. Equally there is extra demand for housing, healthcare and other services. But on the whole, migrants, in the widest sense of the word, make Burpham a richer place to live.

LANDMARKS

Clearly many of the buildings in Burpham make good landmarks, but some of these are only found with a bit of searching. Driving along the London Road from Guildford there is The Old Chapel, then the Anchor & Horseshoes. The New Inn Surgery is on the right, now the oldest building in modern-day Burpham. At the end of the shops is the Kingpost building, now MJA Car Sales. Opposite the shops there is Aldi, with its Green Man sculpture on the corner wall. Sainsbury's is mostly hidden behind trees and shrubbery, as are Bower's Mill and The Mill House. On Burpham Lane there are the Village Hall, St Luke's Church and, after searching down the cul-de-sac, Burpham Primary School. On New Inn Lane are the Church of the Holy Spirit and the church hall.

Besides the various buildings in the community there are several other landmarks in Burpham, but some are slightly off the beaten track.

Boundary and Mile Stones

London Road

Off Merrow Lane

By Boxgrove Road

490

The boundary stone on London Road, denoted the end of Stoke next Guildford parish and the beginning of Worplesdon parish (nowadays the end of Christchurch Ward and the start of Burpham Ward). There appears to be a similar one in the undergrowth at the junction of London Road with Merrow Lane. The stone next to Dillon Cottages, off Merrow Lane, denoted the boundary of Guildford Borough from 1933, when Burpham was brought into the borough. On the Guildford side of the old AA roundabout is a milestone, showing that it is 26 miles to Hyde Park Corner. Unfortunately the milestone that used to be between Orchard Road and Winterhill Way has disappeared, but it would have looked similar.

The Burpham Oak

On London Road, at the junction with Woodruff Avenue, is the old oak tree. The sign beside the tree asks the question '*is it dead or alive?*'. The tree itself died in 2004, but it provides a habitat for stag beetles and other insects, as well as birds, lichens and fungi. It is maintained by Guildford Borough Council to ensure safety. In 1982 a new

The Burpham Oak

491

roundabout was installed at this junction with a plea to 'Save our Oak Tree'. In late 1987 the BCA reported that the tree had survived the 'hurricane', saying *plainly the Almighty intends that this tree will stand for some time yet.*

The Burpham Oak before it died (P Gardner)

The Burpham Shops Parade Sign

Further along the road into Burpham is the sign for the Burpham Shops, created in 2012. This was designed by Nick Bates of Burrows Lea Forge Ltd in Shere, who won a design competition commissioned by Guildford Borough Council. The sign depicts a stylised meld of Crown (Kingpost) and Cartwheel (London Road). The post has icons pierced in the metal designating the different types of shopping and food outlets in the parade. Nick Bates said

'I didn't want to rely totally on the area's history for a theme nor did I want to create abstract art that may stand against the environment. I consider this area of the Guildford district as a dynamic and changing scene, with plenty of scope for growth. There are many young families and small business in the area, so a simple, instantly recognisable form is respectful to them.'

The London Road and Kingpost Parade signs

The Sutherland Circle

In March 2017 a new landmark was installed in Sutherland Memorial Park. Guildford Borough Council commissioned the project, funded through a Section 106 art contribution, for Burpham Ward. The plaque in the centre recorded that the artwork: '...*celebrates the activities that take place in the park*

*and the natural heritage that can be found here. The nine
standing leaf shapes make reference to the nine men of Burpham,
to whom the Sutherland Memorial Park is dedicated...'* The
artwork is located beside the pavilion in the park. The artist was
Steve Tomlinson, who worked with pupils from Burpham Primary
School to design the nine standing leaf shapes with a plaque in
the middle.

Nine Standing Leaf Sculpture 2017

The plaque also said: *'The artwork contains images of sports,
trees, birds, flowers, animals and insects. See if you can find
them. Table tennis – sycamore/kestrels/sycamore seeds,
ragwort, caterpillar. Tennis – hornbeam, starling, dragon-flies,
'clock' dandelions, slug. Running – wild cherry, song thrush,*

cherries, fleabane, worm. Cricket – silver birch, wren, butterflies, ox-eye daisies, beetle. Football – walnut, magpie, ladybirds, knapweed, hedgehog. Basket ball – field maple, blackbird, bees, dandelions, frog. Swings – horse chestnut, swift, conkers, ice cream/snail. Bowls – lime, goldfinch, bats, dog roses, mouse. Slide – oak, robin, acorns, clover, squirrel.'

It is interesting that there are only nine shapes when the war memorial shows 11 names - so why the anomaly? It seems that the Imperial War Museum's (IWM) UK Inventory of War Memorials has two entries for Burpham. The first, for the memorial at St Luke's, stated quite clearly that there were 11 men remembered for the second world war, but gave no names. The second, for Sutherland Memorial Park, stated that there were nine names on the memorial, but also had a line saying 'Names on Memorial – none recorded', presumably because there is no separate memorial in the park. The original Deed of Conveyance of land by the Duke of Sutherland to the residents of Burpham in 1954 referred to '*providing a Public Recreation Ground and Playing Field as a War Memorial to the residents of Burpham...who were killed on active service during the late War...*', but did not refer to any specific number of men.

On further investigation with the IWM it seems that the Register is '*...only as good as the report made on it, usually by a local volunteer (indeed this one was made by a resident of London Road, Burpham) who reported that there were nine who died and the names are engraved on the St Luke's Church Memorial*'. Quite how this happened is not clear, nor is there any information about who was included and who was not. Unfortunately the IWM doesn't have a record of when this report was submitted, the name of the resident who reported, or when the WW2 engraving of the memorial was done. However, it appeared to exclude two of the men who died but who were remembered on the war memorial in the churchyard. As a result of further contact with the Imperial War Museum, both the UK Inventory entries have been amended, with the St Luke's entry now listing the names of all the Burpham men killed in both wars. Guildford Borough Council agreed to amend the wording on the plaque in the park and the new wording will say *'Sutherland Memorial Park is dedicated to the men of Burpham who lost their lives in the Second World War'.*

Keith Crossman Bench

Keith Crossman Memorial Bench

496

Very near to the leaf sculpture is a bench, dedicated to Keith Crossman, who died in October 2014. Keith had been Chairman of the BCA, founded the Sutherland Memorial Hall Amenities Club, was a founder member of the Burpham Bowling Club and helped to establish the Meadway Neighbourhood Watch. He was also Commodore at the Papercourt Sailing Club. The Guildford Dragon website reported that the Mayor of Guildford, Gordon Jackson, unveiled the bench and plaque in June 2016. Dr Alex Donaldson gave a speech outlining Major Crossman's many achievements, saying *'His selfless voluntary service over more than 40 years made an immense contribution to Burpham and neighbouring communities.'*

Aldi Green Man Sculpture

Green Man sculpture on corner wall of Aldi

When Aldi built their shop on the Green Man site they decided to commission a sculpture on the wall to reflect some of the history

497

of the site. Designed and created by Nick Bates, the Green Man sculpture was manufactured by Burrows Lea Forge in Shere. He described the '*Green Man Public Artwork as elemental, always in the background, ever watchful. The leaves and foliage are larger than life and grow vigorously from his head and body. His body is powerful but indistinct, forever moving and with urgency, elusive but still keen to see what's going on in the space he's vacated.*'

The Village Sign

The Burpham Village Sign

On the roundabout by Sutherland Memorial Park, Sainsbury's and London Road is found the Village Sign. In 1986 the BCA proposed

498

holding a competition to design a village sign. There were four joint winners: Arthur Wren, Will Lawrence, Janice Cooke and John Walker, who all received gift tokens. Pupils at Burpham First School sent in lots of ideas as well. The final design was taken from Don Scott's photo of St Luke's Church. The Mayor of Guildford, Mrs Mary Lloyd-Jones, performed the inauguration ceremony on 4th May 1991, followed by refreshments in the new pavilion. The sign is used by the BCA as their logo.

Boar Sculpture at The Old Chapel

Boris the Boar on London Road

In 2016 a new, albeit apparently temporary, landmark appeared on the London Road. Outside The Old Chapel, now the offices for Emporia Brands Ltd, is the current home for 'Boris the Boar', according to the Get Surrey website. James Rackham, Chairman of Emporia, said that Boris was bought at the Chelsea Flower Show and was destined to become the company's mascot at their new distillery in East Sussex.

Having been kept in his mother's garden in Highclere, off London Road, for a while, it had been moved to The Old Chapel after she died earlier in the year. The company plans to launch a new whiskey named after him. James said that people smile as they see him and even pat him as they go past. A number of people commented on the likeness to the boar in the Harry Potter film, Chamber of Secrets.

The Post Box

Edward VIII Postbox

Just beside the shopping parade signpost is the King Edward VIII postbox. Only 161 of these were made in 1936, of which 10 were in Surrey. Postboxes were introduced in the mid 1800s, following the 1840 postal reforms, and they usually have the insignia of the reigning monarch at the time of being placed. More than 60% carry the Queen Elizabeth II mark, about 15% carry the George V mark (there is one at the entrance to Ganghill) and smaller numbers carry the marks of Victoria, Edward VII and George VI.

500

Presumably the Guildford planners decided to put a new postbox beside the new shopping parade and even though King Edward was never crowned Burpham is the proud possessor of a box with the EᵥₘR insignia.

Burpham Bridge

Burpham Bridge (E Voller)

Before the A3 by-pass was built the original road from Burpham to Jacob's Well wound past the church and the school, then over a little bridge. After Clay Lane was opened, re-routing the main road to Jacob's Well over the new A3 bridge, and the old bridge was left going nowhere. The old road, after the bridge, is now part of the Burpham Court Farm fields and Clay Lane rejoins the road on the way to Jacob's Well. In 1980 the Daily Advertiser reported that '*Residents vote to keep old bridge.*' It seems that the residents of Burpham and Jacob's Well voted to retain the bridge and the National Trust, owner of the River Wey Navigation, undertook to accept future responsibility for the bridge. The bridge is now blocked off by fencing on the field side. Christopher Harris remembered that it was a bit tight going over the bridge, especially if you met a lorry coming the other way. Mrs June Eliott remembered that it was a Bailey Bridge, put in by the army during the Second World War.

Burpham Bridge in 2015

MORE MEMORIES OF BURPHAM

Surrey Advertiser

In February 1952 the Surrey Advertiser ran an article called '*The Hamlet which the Town has Swallowed*', noting the changes to the community over the previous 50 years and talking to some of the residents about their views on the situation.

Mrs Alice Bidwell and Miss Minnie Stevens of Vine Cottages, London Road, 1952 (Surrey Advertiser)

Mrs Alice Bidwell, of Vine Cottages on London Road, had moved to Burpham in 1900 with her husband. In 1952 she was a widow and mother of eight children. She said '*Marlyns, in those days, was to all intents and purposes the manor house, and its owner, Mr William Burbidge, the squire. Many of the villagers sheltered under its wing, among them Fred Bidwell, as the* *coachman. The Green Man, a much smaller and more rural version of the contemporary inn, was the village pub and the Three Horse Shoes, just above Vine Cottages, was merely the stables for the Green Man. There was no village school and the children had to walk down into Charlotteville to school.'* She also thought that *'Burpham was a lovely place in the old days and one can't help regretting the change. The old personalities who kept us together as a community have all gone, but I suppose we must move with the times.'*

Miss Minnie Stevens, who lived at Vine Cottages next door, had lived in Burpham all her life. Her father had been gardener for Mr Burbidge, and to get to her school meant a three-mile walk every day. She said *'Burpham is no longer a homely place to live in.'*

Mr William Winzer farmed the land at New Inn Farm for 42 years. The farm had once embraced over 100 acres, but by 1952 only the farmhouse remained. New council houses had been built behind the house and crowded round the deserted barns and cattle sheds. Mr Winzer said *'They took my livelihood away from me. What chance have I now? This taking of agricultural land for building is a disgrace.'*

Further up the road, **Percy Gatley** had lived in Burpham for all his 54 years, first with his father at Bower's Farm and then with his wife at Winterhill Farm. He remembered that Winterhill had been 65 acres and he could stand in any of his fields, look in any direction, and count the buildings in sight on his fingers. By 1952 he only had 13 acres left to carry on his calf and pig rearing, and he is surrounded by houses. *'I remember when my father and uncle farmed all the land between here and Nightingale Road, Guildford, on the south side of the road, Whitehouse Farm, and Weylea, Burchetts, Stoke and Nightingale farms. I've seen thousands of acres of good land go; I've seen Burpham spoilt and it was sad to watch.'*

Arthur Manfield, originally a Detective Sergeant with the Borough Police, opened his tobacconist cum confectioner cum Post Office business on London Road in 1936. Although he felt that the changes had been good for traders, *'We miss the rustic scene – the cows grazing and the ploughing, mowing and reaping.'*

Mrs Emma Turner, retired from running the village shop, still lived in Burpham Lane. *'We are nice and quiet down here and we want it to stay that way. Why take good agricultural land when there is so much waste land about?'*

Then in January 1960 the newspaper ran another article entitled ' ***...but, they insist Burpham is still a village***'.

Mrs Emma Turner, who moved to Burpham 61 years earlier and ran the village shop, said *'There were a few cottages around the Green Man – the old Green Man, you know, with the horse trough outside – the cottages in Pimm's Row, a cottage on the corner and two down near the church...I liked the old Burpham best, although I have nothing again the new people. It's better to look over a green field than bricks and mortar.'*

505

Mr Harry Cutt moved to Burpham 50 years earlier and recalled that in 1910 he paid £180 for a four acre field in Burpham Lane, where he built his bungalow, then two more houses 20 years later. *'There was no need for planning permission in those days.'*

Harry Cutt 1960 (Surrey Advertiser)

Miss Ruth Durrant, who had lived in Burpham for 48 years said *'We resent the spread of development from Guildford because it makes Burpham a bit too townified.'* Though she appreciated that people had to live somewhere, she preferred the old houses to the new ones. Her house in Pimm's Row was an old one, but it had a number of modern amenities, as well as privacy that she felt would be lacking on the new estates in Burpham.

Mr F Sturgess of Burpham Lane said *'It's one of the finest places to live; I wouldn't live anywhere else'* and he proudly referred to Burpham as 'The Village'. Having lived here for 33 years he had nothing against the new estates, *'The more the merrier'*.

Mr R J Cownden had lived on the New Inn Estate for eight years and felt that speculative building had made the area grow too fast, resulting in a lack of soul. *'We keep apart and don't have time to gossip with our immediate neighbours.'*

Mr F Sturgess 1960 (Surrey Ad)   Mr R J Cownden 1960 (Surrey Ad)

Mrs I D Mills, a Canadian who had moved to Burpham recently, said '*I find the people friendly. My husband says that because I am a Canadian, I find people friendly and kind. Whenever anyone asks where I live I always say Burpham, never Guildford. I regard Burpham as a separate part, although it's no longer a village.*'

Other memories:

Ron Putnam was evacuated to Burpham in 1939 from Beaufort House School in Fulham. He stayed with Mr & Mrs Cutt in The Bungalow on Burpham Lane. He remembered that they had a smallholding with chickens. There were four children originally evacuated to the house, but only two stayed. Mrs Cutt was very strict and naughty behaviour resulted in being made to face the wall. The boys had tricycles and would ride out to Sutton Park.

Philip Hudson attended Burpham Primary School and remembered singing in the St Luke's choir, when Revd

Theodosius was vicar, and the boys flicked paper pellets at each other. When two unexploded bombs were left in Jacob's Well the children had to walk to school via Sutton Place, then to Bower's Lock and walk on the tow path. He remembered swimming in the lock, where the water was very clean. Miss Hartley, one of the teachers at the Primary School, took the children on nature walks to collect dandelions so that she could make wine. He remembered seeing a Charlie Chaplin film at the Village Hall.

Jean, John and Colin Andrews (J Menzies)

Jean Menzies remembered that her family moved to Burpham in 1937 from Hindhead and then lived in Orchard Road. She followed her mother into the Women's Institute and remembered that members cleared the Sutherland Memorial Park of rubble and stones so that they could have proper turf for the new pitches in the 1950s. She and her two brothers all attended Burpham Primary School. There were just 36 pupils there and two classrooms, with outdoor toilets. After passing the 11 plus examination Jean moved on to grammar school – Guildford County School. Jean remembered that Mrs Hopewell in Abbotswood held garden parties.

Linda Oliver remembered the traffic snarl-ups before the A3 was built; caravans on the MJA site; and fields opposite the school, where she saw a foal being born.

Mamie Grover (M Drakeford)

Mamie Grover, born in 1914, lived in Burpham from 1936 to 1963, with her husband Charles. She attended Burpham Primary School for four weeks in 1922, while staying with relations in Collingbourne Cottages on Burpham Lane. She remembered that Mr Cutt had two motorbikes, Mrs Turner running the shop and Post Office from her front room, and the Kingpost shopping parade was just a field. In Marlyn's House there was an old lady who was pushed out and about in a wheelchair, and the nightwatchman lived in Merrow Lane. The Council Cottages on Burpham Lane (now replaced by a gated development) were built in the 1920s. There have been Grovers in Burpham for over 200 years. In Michael Drakeford's book, A History of Abbotswood, she remembered a kissing gate and a sheep walk from Stoke Park Farm to Stoke Church. Her father-in-law, who was a bricklayer, moved to Burpham in 1922 when he became one of the first tenants of a council house. Mamie worked as a maid for Mrs Leighton of Albury House, Abbotswood. Her grandfather worked as a lengthsman, sweeping the road from the boundary stone on the London Road to the Sutton Lodges. He also worked as a caddy for the Duke of Sutherland's sister, Lady Betty, at the Sutton Place golf course.

David Seymour remembered playing football for Burpham Football Club. The original pitch ran in front of the old changing rooms. Cyril West, who was the best referee in Saturday/Sunday League football, went to matches on his bike.

Mel Lewis remembered a Crimewatch film about the armed robbery in Sainsbury's. The BBC staff bought lunch at the Green Man and one of the cameramen choked on his steak. Someone helped by performing the Heimlich manoeuvre and all was well.

Penny Inskip (nee Stephen) lived in the flat above Burpham Motor Company, now Tyre City, on London Road. Her father ran the garage for a number of years, fixing cars and selling Skoda cars, then ran a building company from the same address. She remembered the pig farm opposite, with a very large but run down house. She used to play over there when the Weylea Estate was being built. She also remembered going fishing at Bower's Lock with her father and brother, then losing her shoes in the water, so her mother was not happy.

Ralph Marshall remembered when there were only two classrooms at Burpham Primary School. The dining room was heated by a coal stove, there were outside toilets and an air raid shelter in the playground.

Christine Colby remembered having to drink milk at playtimes – warm with lumps in it in the summer, frozen in the winter with icicles popping out of the top of the bottle. She also remembered going in to have a look at the Kingpost swimming pool and see the newts there. One day when the water was covered with ice she and her friends tried to walk on it, but it cracked. Luckily they were at the shallow end.

Oliver John Mason remembered that Paul Getty had lions at his house, Sutton Place (there is a clip on YouTube showing them), and on a summer's evening they could be heard from Bower's Lane. Nick Maiklem, who farmed Burpham Court Farm, used to leave a small silver urn of freshly milked cow's milk on their doorstep every morning, so fresh it was still warm. Oliver's parents met at the Anchor & Horseshoes, where his mother was a barmaid. His grandfather used to sit in the saloon side with his best friend Percy. The saloon side was separated from the bar with a door; the trades and smokers on one side and the posh people on the other side. His father was gamekeeper at Sutton Place. His mother had attended George Abbot Girls' School.

Christopher Harris remembered that Purkiss the Ironmongers used to have an old Bedford lorry, which went round Burpham selling Esso Blue Paraffin.

Vincent Tickner remembered the walk from home in Glendale Drive to the Primary School in the 1950s. *'The only interesting thing on the route was the ruined "haunted" house just after the Green Man pub. None of us dared to go in it, which is probably just as well, as it looked structurally fairly unsafe. To make the journey more interesting, I liked to go jumping the big ditch that ran along the south side of New Inn Lane for much of the first part of the journey. This was great fun until the day that I slipped, and I fell back into the ditch onto my back, and got my school uniform and myself completely covered in mud. Sometimes I went with a few other boys up to Burpham Woods at the end of New Inn Lane to play there.'*

After moving to New Inn Lane he remembered *'Stanley Hyman lived next door. His Jewish parents kept him in a lot to learn Hebrew, and they were not inclined to mix socially much with us. The school policy was to gender mix the double seating of school desks. Accordingly, I was first with Heather Earl, and later with Anne Crump. The girl who attracted me, however, was Elizabeth Adams, who lived on the Council Estate. I once got into trouble for sending her a postcard from my holiday on the Isle of Wight'.* Vincent also remembered James Grant, son of the butcher in the shopping parade, Brian Seaman, Patricia Quigley, Roger Lemon, Ronald Crofts, Anthony Warsop, David Enticknap and Paul Critchley. *'With James Grant I would often go across the road to the old swimming pool area that was abandoned, and private, we were not meant to be going there, but we tried to catch newts from the swimming pool. One day a chap came in there and chased us off.'*

512

Mary Fry remembered living in one of the first houses on Woodruff Avenue, that '*Life was very different. Only some of the households owned a car, and there were regular deliveries of things like groceries, and coal. (All the houses had coal sheds). A rag and bone lady used to go around with her horse and cart, which was always a welcome diversion...I remember the farm at the bottom of the road, where Weylea now stands. The main farm building stood facing Woodruff Avenue. I think it was a pig farm. Whatever it was, the smell which wafted up our road when the wind was in the wrong direction, was very strong! A stone wall ran along the farm's boundary with the London Road, and there was a driveway leading into the farm a little further along. My mother and I used to go to buy eggs from the house which stood near this entrance.*'

Barbara Stone (née Gow) remembered that her parents moved to New Inn Lane in 1938, where the house cost £750. Her father worked for Cow & Gate, which had offices at the top of North Street. During the war he had to travel to milk factories that had been bombed in order to get them up and running again. Because this was so important he was one of the few people in Burpham to have both a telephone in the house and a car to get around. He invented the first milk bottle washing machine. She remembered neighbours called Quigley, Rees and Gray, also Levers, Duval and Atkinson. Barbara's mother kept hens and chinchilla rabbits for eggs, meat and rabbit skins during the war. People would give her their potato and vegetable peelings, which were cooked up for the hens. Barbara would go gleaning in the

513

wheat fields of New Inn Farm, bringing back wheat heads for the hens. Her mother would use the skins to make slippers and gloves.

Barbara went to dancing classes with Mrs Rees in New Inn Lane and the class would give dancing displays in Burpham Village Hall. Two of them were on the Guildford Festival Queen's float at one of the summer celebrations at the Cricket Ground in town. She remembered Mr Cutt, opposite the Village Hall, had a huge dog, possibly a Bull Mastiff.

Barbara also remembered being on the bus into Guildford when it had to slow right down because a herd of cows was being taken along London Road to the market. One of the cows took it into her head, and the whole herd followed her, to go into a rather grand garden of a big house, where the lady owner stood at her front door trying to shoo the cows back onto the road. These cows probably came from one of the Burpham farms.

Michael Hunt lived with his grandparents on New Inn Lane whilst his father was in the RAF. His great uncle was Chief Coxswain on the R101 airship, and was killed when it crashed in 1930. There was a house on New Inn Lane that was built of wood and covered with plaster render on the outside. He remembered a Tudor barn that was between the Green Man and the Tudor cottages, but it was pulled down by a bulldozer. Miss Draper lived in New Inn Lane and there was a ditch down the side of her garden, which took water from the Merrow stream, but this eventually got piped in. Michael's father was a teacher in Ash Vale, and he travelled to and from the school by public transport. His sister Teresa was a hairdresser in Guildford, who had worked for Mr Teasy Weasy, the famous London hairdresser. Their house in New Inn Lane had a pond in the front garden and looked so pretty that artists would come along to paint the front of the house and garden.

Richard Oliver remembered that one of his brothers was a Mod and the other was a Rocker in the 1960s. One time when they were all going down to the South Coast for the regular fights between the two groups, they met up first at the Green Man. Instead of the expected punch-up the two brothers greeted each other warmly and started chatting, so the planned fight on the beaches did not happen.

Joyce Tate and her son Stephen remembered buying lemon bombs and sherbert from Fentons. Stephen worked in Muellers, stacking shelves; the Co-op delivered milk to the house; and Mario, an Italian Prisoner of War delivered eggs from a van. Joyce took the trolley of sweets round to the residents at Burpham Homes.

Ann Keane remembered all the coaches in the Green Man car park and the restaurant at the back, which was open all day and sold ice cream. The Kingpost swimming pool was freezing cold. She lived with her family on Merrow Lane and there was a brick built post-box outside their house, which the children used as a wicket when playing cricket. She would push neighbours' babies in their prams for a small fee. She also remembered a gypsy man who drove a milk lorry. Her father worked at Gosden Hill Farm, which had a pig club. When a pig was slaughtered half had to go to the Ministry of Agriculture, Fish and Food on Epsom Road, while the other half was cut up and given to farm workers. Ann would write out the list of what everyone received. She remembered that the actor Terry Thomas's parents lived on Merrow Lane and he used to visit them. Coal was still rationed until 1957, so they had electric fires in the bedrooms to take off the chill. Her father had chickens in the garden, which had to be fed a special rationed feed from Fogwill's in Friary Street. Her mother would shop at Kimber's and had to register her ration book with them in order to buy goods. There was a lady in New Inn Lane who gave ballet lessons in her house.

Dorothy Keene, Leo Keene's daughter, remembered going to a 21st birthday party at Bower's Mill in the late 1940s. It was held in the garden with everyone wearing evening dress as very well off people lived there. Instead of signing a card they all wrote on a mirror with a diamond. She also remembered that the actress Florence Desmond lived in Ripley and Gosden Hill Farm supplied the straw for her horses.

Jan & Morriss Kemp remembered Mr & Mrs Stokes, who lived in Bower's Mill Lodge; Margaret Stedman, who married Bob Murray of Biddle's the printers (the company where Morriss was a Director); Mr Carter, in the 1960s, would push bars of chocolate through the letterbox for the children; Marlyn's Drive was a cart track and there was a copse on the corner where the children used to play. Mrs Stock was one of the organisers for events in the community, including the Women's Institute.

516

Keith Powell remembered that there used to be a big barn on the land behind Pimm's Row, but it was knocked down. When Sainsbury's came to Burpham there was some horse-trading of land and a plan to have a community centre. However, the Government took back the Surrey County Council money, so it never happened.

Ron Keene with his grandparents and brother at the back of The Paddocks, late 1940s (R Keene)

Ron Keene remembered that his grandparents and their two daughters were evacuated to the Mill House during the Second World War and that his grandmother worked as a cleaner for the Duke of Sutherland. One of the daughters was Ron's mother, who married after the war and moved to The Paddocks house, behind the Green Man, where Ron lived with his parents and his grandparents. Then, in 1952 they moved to the Upfolds Estate, where his mother lived until 2002.

Ken & Doreen Marshall remembered coming to the village in 1956. Ken made swings and seesaws for the children and Doreen did meals on wheels for the elderly residents in the community.

John & Valerie Boon remembered Edgar Hunt (Michael Hunt's father), who was the Deputy Headteacher at a school in Ash, where he cycled to every day. He had been in Bomber Command during the war. When he shopped in Sainsbury's he would give the girls on the tills maths lessons. He and his wife kept cats and they named a couple of dahlias after their cats. They also remembered that Peter Conisbee had a car business at Falcon House on Burpham Lane.

Tony Mallard came to live in Burpham in 1986 and was Chairman of the BCA for ten years. He remembered that his cousin was the preferred builder for Sainsbury's, who removed the marble tops from stores to turn them into self-service. He also recalled that Roger Marjoribanks was a prime mover for the building of the Spectrum Leisure Centre, but he lost his place on the Council as a consequence. Tony also remembered that Michael, Lord Onslow, used to drive a pony and trap around the area, and would stop for a chat on the way. Tony was Chairman of Governors at Burpham Primary School for ten years. His wife, Rebecca, was President of the Women's Institute for several years.

Ted Mayne remembered that Jennifer Jordan, twice Mayor of Guildford, was a teacher at George Abbot School. James Purnell, Labour politician under Gordon Brown, was the grandson of Jim

Ireland, Deputy Head at George Abbot, who lived next door to the Anchor & Horseshoes.

Liz Critchfield remembered that in 1959, her mother bought eggs from Winterhill Farm, then later from Bower's Farm. She also remembered her mother saying '*you won't get bay leaves in Burpham*' and '*house deeds say that you're not allowed to have a milk round*'.

Anne Marshall, on Burpham Lane, remembered that the next door house was wooden and had gas mantles. Her husband fitted up electricity for the owners.

Allen Mead and John Pigeon remembered that the Duke of Sutherland allowed local children into the Sutton Park estate to go fishing. John was on the committee for Burpham Football Club for a while and remembered that in the 1950s white socks were knitted for the team, but they went all fluffy when washed. There was local rivalry between Burpham and Merrow football teams. The Civic Hall was the place to go to see groups play. At George Abbot the Deputy Head was Peter Cobbett and Mr Laker was caretaker in the 1960s; Malcolm Spalding was Head Boy in 1966; Percy Potts was the French teacher, who lived in New Inn Lane.

Jackie Lamble remembered that her father was caretaker at George Abbot in the 1950s, under Mr Raynham. They lived in the caretaker's cottage, behind the Old Chapel. It was a tied cottage and had an orchard, which backed onto the school grounds. The boys at the school in the late 1950s wore straw boaters. Jackie helped with the animals and harvesting at Weylea Farm, just over the road. John & Mary Heard, the farmers, lived at Weylea Lodge and the farmhouse had a big front garden, which was enclosed. When Jackie was a student at Art School, at the Technical College, around 1960, she worked at the farm to earn money, as well as doing a paper round. She was Akela for Merrow Cubs. She married an American soldier, whom she met in Spain on a painting holiday. Her son, Rodney, sang in the Burpham church choir.

Peter Servian remembered being at George Abbot in the 1960s and especially a school cruise on the SS Nevasa. He also remembered Prince Philip visiting the school around 1963/4 as part of supporting his Duke of Edinburgh Award Scheme. He said that the Anchor & Horseshoes was very popular with the 6th form, as the staff didn't ask too many questions about age.

Pete Gardner remembered cycling down to the river to go fishing. Also that there was a big culvert off London Road, down in the ditch, which was like entering a tunnel, but was big enough to walk through. He remembered the traffic around the Green Man and one day he was nearly knocked off his bike by a coach coming out of the car park exit on Burpham Lane. Great Oaks Park was built where the council houses ended and Pete recalled finding a mask, possibly a gas mask, there.

Jackie Ring remembered coming to Burpham in the 1980s. Her son, Nicholas, went to Burpham First School, so had to move to Bushy Hill Middle School, but her daughter, Stephanie, was at

Burpham Primary School for seven years. Jackie remembered helping Mary Pearce with the '*Toy Swop*' in the late 1980s, as well as being a member of the Women's Institute. At the Primary School she was a key member of the Parents' Support Group (PTA), a parent governor and ran the after school club for a while.

William Lawrence moved into his house in Burpham Lane and while digging in the garden found a lot of old bottles. Could they tell some interesting stories about the village?

Bottles found in Burpham Lane (W Lawrence)

WHAT NEXT FOR BURPHAM?

In 2017 Burpham is no longer a village, but a suburb on the way into or out of Guildford. The farms along the London Road have given way to housing and retail developments, leaving only Burpham Court Farm and Gosden Hill Farm as agricultural land. Hopefully the Burpham Neighbourhood Plan will ensure the protection of green spaces in the area, but will the Guildford Borough Council Local Plan be implemented, bringing development onto the Gosden Hill Farm land? Will the proposed link road between the Slyfield estate and Clay Lane be approved, bringing a much higher volume of traffic into Burpham, on roads intended for a much lighter volume? Will the A3 be developed, possibly with a tunnel to go underneath Guildford? Will a new station be created at Merrow and how will this impact on New Inn Lane?

In April 2016 Martin Grant Homes published their vision for the development of 'Gosden Hill Village' on the site of Gosden Hill Farm. This vision document described: the building of 2,000 new houses (including affordable homes); approximately 4-5 hectares of land for employment, such as offices; a local centre providing a new primary school, retail, GP surgery and a community facility; new access with the A3; a park and ride alongside the A3; facilitating the delivery of a new rail station at Merrow; approximately 38.4 hectares of Suitable Alternative Natural Greenspace; a range of other publically accessible open spaces including informal amenity space, formal sports provision, children's play, and strategic landscaping.

Proposed development of Gosden Hill Farm published by Martin Grant
Homes 2016

Tony Teal, current Chairman of the BCA, said *'Predictions are
notoriously difficult to make. The biggest problem Burpham faces
is complete urbanisation and a loss of identity. We are
exceedingly fortunate to have the Burpham Neighbourhood Plan
in place. This will regulate and control within limits what
happens within the boundary of the ward. However, the biggest
threat comes from factors outside. The development of the A3,*

the building of houses on Gosden Hill, the link road and a lack of support in maintaining a renewal of the infrastructure (roads, sewers, traffic) without linking it to further commercial activity is a real worry. The Local Plan is a sword of Damocles that hangs over us all. With sensible and sustainable planning Burpham has many features that will help it to retain its character. Sutherland Memorial Park and the Riverside Nature Park are two outstanding features and provided the thin swathe of Green Belt is not breached, then the village will be an attractive place for people to live and work in for the foreseeable future. It has also the advantage of being a springboard into the Surrey Hills and surrounding towns and villages. Its close proximity to the airports, university and the capital make it an obvious place to settle and expand, but it behoves all of us to be vigilant to ensure that it is simply not exploited beyond all recognition.'

Jim Allen, current Vice Chairman of the BCA, recalled that '*The station at Merrow was decried by the Council in 1984 as a potential extension to become a London Estate, yet now they wish to consider it, while Network Rail show no inclination to build any new stations in Guildford. The A3 currently – Highways England has no intention of looking at the A3 through Guildford until 2020, yet GBC want to install, at irrational locations, junctions, which are not fit for purpose in their locations and the capacity of the side roads. As for the housing at Gosden Hill – this was rejected in 1984 due to total lack of infrastructure and inadequate site access unless a four-way intersection and link road to the A25 was installed.'*

It has long been the case that effective development requires effective infrastructure. Will the proposals for Burpham achieve this? Over the last ten years there has been greatly increased pressure on primary schools across the country, and secondary schools will be next. There is a national shortage of family doctors and many hospitals are almost at breaking point. The volume of traffic increases all the time, with small problems escalating into gridlock. Community facilities need to support the needs of the people living in the area.

In 1977 Norman Hamilton's view on change was '*Doubtless there will be many regrets. No one relishes change in a familiar scene. There are elderly people living in Burpham today who sigh for the pre-war years when it was a small village; and it is a strange fact that no one opposes further change more fiercely than a new arrival. But some change is inevitable. What we must all hope is that it will be done in a way that preserves, and if possible, enhances, the pleasant character of the place which is home to so many of us.*'

Back in 1997 Roger Marjoribanks concluded that '*The threats that loom over Burpham, however, are two-fold. The first is geographical; at present the village has natural boundaries to the east, north and west – Merrow Lane, the boundary between Guildford and Woking and the River Wey, reinforced fortuitously by the new A3 and, more effectively, by the Metropolitan Green Belt. It therefore sits to the north of Guildford within its natural limits; should these limits be breached by a further sprawl of development into the Green Belt its integrity and inevitably its sense of identity would irrevocably be destroyed.*

The other threat is the sheer dead weight of numbers. With thousands living in Burpham solely because it is a convenient centre for travel to work there is always the possibility that most will not care very much about the village which houses them. It looks as if there may be a period of at least relative freedom from further major development and it will be a test of the vigour of the village institutions to see whether they can use this reprieve to bring such people into the community. To judge by the enthusiasm which many of their members display they may well succeed.'

There will always be change – some good and some bad. People will always have different opinions on what is acceptable and what is not, so there will always be discussion about proposals and challenges to authorities. Burpham has changed enormously over the last 100 years and it is quite possible that over the next 100 years there will be further changes that make it quite unrecognisable. Will Burpham become a soulless sprawl or can we maintain the character of a village, where people can live and work in comfort? Let us hope for the latter.

WEBSITES

www.weyriver.co.uk/the river- Wey Navigation website is a fabulous source of information about the Wey Valley, including photos, maps and memories

www.burphamneighbourhoodforum.com - the full details about the Burpham Neighbourhood Plan can be found here

www.burphamca.weebly.com – the website for the Burpham Community Association

https://www.british-history.ac.uk - British History Online

https://a-blacksmith.co.uk– Kingpost Parade sign specification

www.discovery.nationalarchives.gov.uk – National Archives

www.fsmitha.com - World History Timeline

www.jwra.org – Jacobs Well Residents' Association website

www.attfield-tree.com – the website for the Attfield family of Worplesdon

www.turnpikes.org.uk – website about turnpike trusts

www.thewi.org.uk – website for the Women's Institute

www.ancestry.co.uk – website for family historians

www.findmypast.co.uk – website for family historians

www.thegenealogist.co.uk – website for family historians, including the Tithe Maps of 1838

www.britishnewspaperarchive.co.uk – website for searching through old newspapers

www.educationengland.org.uk/history - Derek Gillard's history of changes in education

www.cwgc.org - website for the Commonwealth War Graves Commission, for finding information about members of the British armed forces during WW1 and WW2

www.britishlistedbuildings.co.uk - information about listed buildings in Guildford and Worplesdon

www.wikipedia.com - a vast resource of information about just about everything, but some of the details do need to be checked and I have endeavoured to cross-reference wherever possible

workhouses.org.uk – Peter Higginbotham's fantastic website giving information about workhouses

www.lnr.naturalengland.org.uk - information about Riverside Park www.iwm.org.uk/memorials - details of the Burpham War Memorial at St Luke's Church and Sutherland Memorial Park

www.surreyarchives.org.uk - the website for the Surrey History Centre

www.getsurrey.co.uk - news and information about Surrey

www.guildford-dragon.com - news about Guildford

www.burpham.surrey.sch.uk - website for Burpham Primary School

www.georgeabbot.surrey.sch.uk - website for George Abbot School

www.ukcensusdata.com/burpham - website giving demographic information about Burpham, from the 2011 Census, Office of National Statistics

www.guildfordu3a.org.uk - website for the Guildford U3A

www.facebook.com - social media with the Guildford Town Past and Present Group

www.google.co.uk/maps - website for looking at modern maps of Burpham and Guildford

BIBLIOGRAPHY

Victoria County History, published by University of London, Institute of Historical Research

A Topographical History of Surrey – E W Brayley, 1801

Burpham, Norman Manor to Suburban Village - Roger Marjoribanks – 1997

The History of Burpham - Norman Hamilton – 1977, updated by Linda Flynn 1984

History of Abbotswood - Michael Drakeford

Guildford and Villages: Then and Now - David Rose – 2003, Breedon Books Publishing Co Ltd

Guildford History Tour – David Rose and Bernard Parke – 2015, Amberley Publishing

Guildford Life: Past and Present - Stanley Newman – 2014, DB Publishing

Guildford as it was by Matthew Alexander - 1978

The Agricultural Labourer in 19th Century England, Kay Handford – 2011, GHP Ltd

1934 - ? - Living the Changes in Agriculture - Dorothy S Keene

Old Cottages and Farmhouses in Surrey by W Curtis Green and W Galsworthy Davie - 1908, B T Batsford

Using Manorial Records, by Mary Ellis, PRO publications

The Breweries and Public Houses of Guildford - Mark Sturley 1990

A History of Surrey by Peter Brandon

Rural Britain, Then and Now by Roger Hunt

Surrey Roads from Turnpike to Motorway by Gordon Knowles - 2015, SIHG

Watermills of Surrey by D Stidder - 1990, Barracuda Books

SCC Centenary 1889-1989 - Transportation Planning Unit

A History of Burpham Primary School 1908 - 2014 - Moira MacQuaide Hall - 2014

A Brief History of St Luke's Church, Burpham - Burpham Churches

The Burpham War Memorial by Jean Shail - 2003

A History of Woking by Alan Crosby

531

ACKNOWLEDGEMENTS

I am very grateful to everyone who has helped me in any way to write this book and especially the following:

Surrey History Centre – the staff there have answered questions, found documents and generally been very tolerant with me over the last two years while I researched this book. Photographs and other images marked Surrey History Centre have been reproduced by permission of the Surrey History Centre and are the copyright of Surrey History Centre.

Burpham Community Association – who allowed me access to their archives, where I found lots of fascinating information

Guildford Museum – especially **Andrew Longworth**, who brought out artefacts that had been found in Burpham and helped me to take a photograph of the Samian Bowl.

Surrey Archaeological Society – who allowed me to use the photo of the Samian Bowl.

Guildford Institute – for allowing me to use photos from their collection and **Philip Wilkinson** for checking through to find anything relating to Burpham for me.

West Surrey Family History Society – who have indexed parish records and wills, making it a lot easier for me to check through and find people from Burpham.

Burpham will Remember Them – who shared their research into the stories behind the War Memorial for the Great War.

Frank Phillipson – who kindly shared his research findings about Burpham and allowed me to use them.

David Rose – who let me use images of some of the postcards of Burpham that he had collected.

Guildford Dragon – where I've found lots of news stories about Burpham.

Andre Langlois of the Surrey Advertiser – for allowing me to go through old news stories about Burpham and to use their photos.

Ben Darnton and his Facebook group Guildford Town Past & Present – for allowing me to ask questions, seek memories and photos about people's life in Burpham.

Burpham Pages – for allowing me to request memories and photos from the residents of Burpham.

Norman Hamilton – whose history of Burpham in 1977, updated by Linda Flynn in 1984, provided a great springboard from which to start my research.

Roger Marjoribanks – whose history of Burpham in 1997 provided me with lots of information and photos.

Michael Drakeford – whose history of Abbotswood provided me with information and memories.

Jim Miller – who shared his research with me and whose history of Jacob's Well gave me information about that end of the Manor of Burpham.

Richard Cant – Stoke Lengthsman for the Wey Navigation, National Trust, who shared old photos of the waterways and the history of the Navigation.

Vincent Tickner – who shared his research about the Heath family of Burpham and their connections.

Cathy Greaves – who kindly proofread the final version of this book.

Karen Robinson – whose research on Burpham Primary School unearthed documents that were very interesting about the wider village history.

Teresa Bass – who helped me to bring better quality to some of the old photos.

Martin Hall – who helped me with numerous technical issues, as well as final proofreading, and designing the cover.

And finally, everyone – who has shared photos, memories and stories about life in Burpham over the years. Sometimes there will be conflicts, possibly due to rose tinted glasses as we all get older, but all shared with the best intentions. I hope that you have all been as enthralled by the history of Burpham as I have.